KING LEAR

HARCOURT SHAKESPEARE

KING LEAR
SECOND EDITION

Series Editor: Ken Roy

edited by
Ken Roy

Harcourt Canada

Toronto Orlando San Diego London Sydney

National Library of Canada Cataloguing in Publication Data

Shakespeare, William, 1564-1616
    King Lear

2nd ed.
(Harcourt Shakespeare)
ISBN 0-7747-1486-7

I. Roy, Ken   II. Title.   III. Series.

PR2819.A2R69 2002   822.3'3   C2001-903166-1

Harcourt Shakespeare: Series Editor, Ken Roy

Project Manager: Deborah Davidson
Developmental Editor: Jane Clark
Editor: Sasha Patton
Senior Production Editor: Karin Fediw
Production Coordinator: Cheri Westra
Page Composition: Carolyn Sebestyen
Cover and Text Illustrations: Marika and Laszlo Gal

∞ Printed in Canada on acid-free paper.
1 2 3 4 5   05 04 03 02 01

To the Reader

The story of King Lear and his three daughters is a very old one that was related by many writers before Shakespeare used it as the basis for his play. Shakespeare's version of the story, however, is a very complex one. It communicates on many levels, appealing both to feelings and to intellect. As you read the play, you will probably notice that you relate in many different ways to the situations and the characters, and to the tensions created by the interplay of the two. You may want to examine parts of the play again to discover what Shakespeare has done with a relatively simple plot.

King Lear is the only Shakespearean tragedy to contain a fully developed subplot that runs parallel to, and frequently merges with, the main plot. The subplot highlights the play's major themes and underscores a violence and ruthlessness that rivals anything contemporary. As you read, you will encounter motivations of fear, guilt, pride, revenge, greed, and ambition that will bring to mind situations current in television soap operas and the more sensational newspapers. And you will probably find that the issues and questions that the play raises are as relevant to you as they were to Shakespeare's audiences.

Before reading each scene, you will have the opportunity to explore ideas and themes. Your personal experiences may also contribute to your understanding of the play's characters and events. You will be encouraged to discuss and share your opinions co-operatively in small groups. As well, you will have the opportunity to write personal responses in a journal.

Each scene is followed by activities related specifically to that scene. You may choose to pause after each individual scene, a group of scenes, or the end of each act before responding to them. Most of the activities, like the questions before each scene, invite both group and personal responses.

1

Now that you have some idea about how the play is presented, and about the many ways you might experience it, the overview of major themes of the play that follows will help you get started.

Getting Started

Everyone is familiar with stories in which a situation that initially seems uneventful quickly turns sour: things simply don't turn out the way they are supposed to. Suddenly wrong answers are given to straightforward questions, unreasonable demands are made, loyalties are misinterpreted, actions are directed by greed, and people are falsely accused. In short, the world is turned upside down and the lives of the people caught in these situations are changed forever.

The following activities will help you explore what causes the upheaval of the world in *King Lear*. Discuss some of them in groups before you start reading the play. Use your journal to respond to any activities you find particularly interesting, thought provoking, or personal. You may wish to refer to these entries and to alter or expand them once you begin reading and discussing the play.

1. You are all probably familiar with the story of Cinderella. Briefly summarize the main points of this story in your journal or notebook. Discuss your version with your group. Revise it if necessary, and keep for future reference.

2. We have all seen, on television news and documentaries, examples of ways in which countries have suffered after political upheaval. With a partner or in a group, discuss some of the details and opinions that you have found in the media. Make a list of your observations and share them with the class. Keep this list for future reference.

3. What do you believe is the state of the traditional family today? What factors do you think caused this condition?

Note your observations in your journal and share some of your less personal ideas with a group. Complete your journal notes by explaining what you think creates a strong family unit.

4. In Shakespeare's time, women did not have the same rights as they do today. With a partner (of the opposite sex) discuss what rights you think women *do* have as opposed to what rights they *ought* to have. Share some of these ideas with the class.

5. When you think you have been unfairly treated, how do you usually respond? Record your thoughts in a journal entry.

6. When you see an adult behave in what you believe to be an unreasonable manner, what course of action do you usually take? What course of action do you think you *should* take in such a situation? In your opinion, if you did take action, would you make any difference in the person's behaviour?

7. Describe a man and a woman who best fulfill your idea of "manliness" and "womanliness." Are the two in any way similar? Discuss your views with a partner.

8. Write a note explaining the difference between taking action to support a decision you have made and seeking revenge on a person who doesn't do what you expect of him or her.

9. When two people are competing for a job or a position and one is chosen out of favouritism, what is your reaction to a) the person chosen, and b) the person who does the choosing? How often do you think this situation happens in real life? When it happens, how do you deal with it?

10. Have you ever tried to persuade a person you know that he or she has made a wrong decision? What were the results? Would you do the same thing again?

11. We tend to assume, rightly or wrongly, that adults always make rational decisions. Recall a situation, either real or from a story, in which this was not the case. What were the results? What advice would you have given the adult(s)?

If a similar circumstance occurred in your experience, how would you respond?

12. What is your definition of an egomaniac? What person do you know, either real or from a movie or television, who fits this description? What might you say to this person to help correct her or his behaviour?

13. Have you ever been insulted, or been present when someone was insulted in front of friends? How did you (or the insulted person) feel? What might you say to people who insult others?

14. Do people always get what they deserve? Relate a situation in which someone got more, or less, than he or she deserved. How did you feel about the outcome? Could you have done anything to change it?

Dramatis Personae
(Characters in the Play)

Lear, King of Britain
Goneril
Regan } Lear's daughters
Cordelia
Earl of Gloucester
Edgar, Gloucester's son
Edmund, Gloucester's illegitimate son
Earl of Kent
Duke of Albany, Goneril's husband
Duke of Cornwall, Regan's husband
King of France, Cordelia's suitor
Oswald, Goneril's steward
The Fool
Duke of Burgundy, Cordelia's suitor
Curan, a courtier
Doctor
A Captain in Edmund's employ
An old man, Gloucester's tenant
Gentlemen, a Herald, Servants of Cornwall
Knights in Lear's service, Officers, Messengers, Soldiers,
    Attendants
Scene: Britain

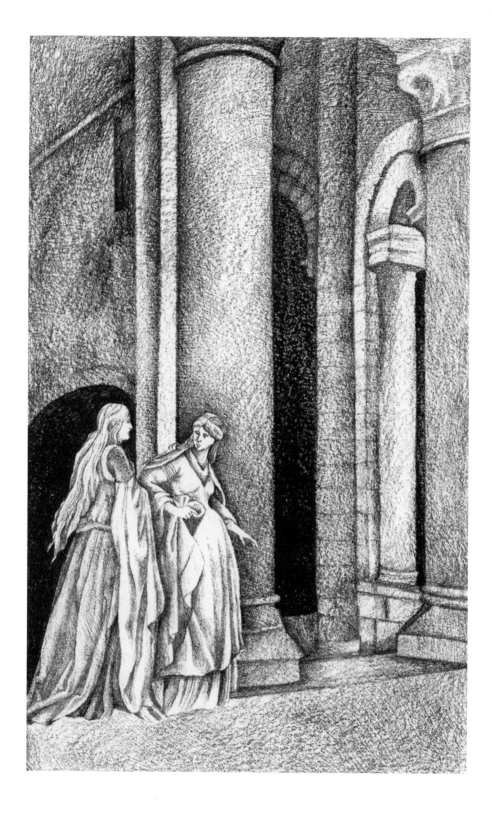

Act 1, Scene 1

In this scene ...

The scene begins with Gloucester and Kent discussing King Lear's decision to divide his kingdom. Gloucester introduces his illegitimate son, Edmund, who has been out of the country for nine years.

King Lear, Cornwall, Albany, Goneril, Regan, and Cordelia enter and the division process begins. Lear asks each of his daughters how much they love him. It is on the basis of their answers that he will apportion his lands. The elder daughters, Goneril and Regan, flatter Lear, professing to love him more than anything else in the world. When Cordelia is asked what she can say to receive the largest share of Lear's kingdom, she replies, "Nothing." Her response enrages Lear who immediately disowns and disinherits her. When Kent attempts to intervene on Cordelia's behalf, he is banished.

At this point, the Duke of Burgundy and the King of France enter. Both have been seeking Cordelia's hand in marriage. Once the Duke of Burgundy discovers that Cordelia will not have a dowry, he withdraws his offer of marriage. The King of France, however, accepts her as she is and prepares to take her to his kingdom. In a parting speech, Cordelia condemns her sisters for their hypocrisy.

Left alone, Goneril and Regan discuss what has happened. They say they will agree to take turns in accommodating their father and his one hundred knights. Now they are afraid that Lear is mentally unstable and worry that they may suffer from his irrationality as Cordelia has. In order to protect themselves from their father's whims, they agree to work together.

1	*affected:* favoured, preferred, i.e., showed more affection for
2	*Albany:* a part of Scotland that, according to Holinshed's *Chronicles*, extended from "the river Humber to the point of Caithness"
5	*qualities ... weighed:* The portions are equally balanced.
6-7	*curiosity ... moiety:* Careful analysis by neither one can make that person prefer the other's half (moiety).
9	*His breeding ... charge:* I am responsible for his birth.
10	*acknowledge him:* recognize him as my son
11	*brazed:* hardened, accustomed, unashamed (literally, plated with brass, as in the word "brazen")
12	*conceive:* understand; pun on the word "conception"
16	*smell a fault:* smell (sense) a sin or wrongdoing with an intended allusion to the female genitals
17	*issue:* outcome, offspring or children
18	*proper:* handsome, excellent
19-20	*by order of law:* legitimate; *some year elder:* about a year older (than Edmund)
21	*knave:* boy. Here, the word is used in an affectionate sense rather than a derogatory one.
22	*fair:* beautiful
23	*whoreson:* literally, son of a whore. Here, it is likely used in a good-natured manner.

Act 1, Scene 1

Inside Lear's palace.
Enter Kent, Gloucester, and
Edmund, in rear.

Kent: I thought the King had more affected the Duke of
   Albany than Cornwall.
Gloucester: It did always seem so to us; but now, in the
   division of the kingdom, it appears not which of the
   Dukes he values most, for qualities are so weighed   5
   that curiosity in neither can make choice of either's
   moiety.
Kent: Is not this your son, my lord?
Gloucester: His breeding, sir, hath been at my charge. I have
   so often blushed to acknowledge him that now I am   10
   brazed to it.
Kent: I cannot conceive you.
Gloucester: Sir, this young fellow's mother could, whereupon
   she grew round-wombed, and had indeed, sir, a son
   for her cradle ere she had a husband for her bed. Do   15
   you smell a fault?
Kent: I cannot wish the fault undone, the issue of it being
   so proper.
Gloucester: But I have a son, sir, by order of law, some year
   elder than this, who yet is no dearer in my account.   20
   Though this knave came something saucily to the
   world before he was sent for, yet was his mother fair,
   there was good sport at his making, and the whoreson
   must be acknowledged.—Do you know this noble
   gentleman, Edmund?   25
Edmund: [*Advancing.*] No, my lord.
Gloucester: My Lord of Kent: remember him hereafter as
   my honourable friend.

29	*My services to your lordship:* I am at your service, sir. A polite way of acknowledging an introduction.
30	*sue:* beg, would like
31	*study deserving:* try to be deserving
32	*out:* away, out of the country

Stage Direction – *sennet:* a trumpet call; *coronet:* a small crown

| 35 | *Attend:* here, a royal command: wait upon; be of assistance to |

37	*we:* the "royal" plural. As king, Lear embodies, or represents, the kingdom as a whole. He stands for "king and country"; therefore, he refers to himself in the plural.
38	*Know:* be informed that
39	*fast intent:* firm intention

| 42 | *crawl:* move slowly |

44	*constant will:* fixed purpose or unwavering intention; *publish:* make public, make known to everyone
45	*several dowers:* separate gifts; separate portions of Lear's kingdom
46	*prevented:* stopped (before any strife starts)
47	*rivals:* contestants
48	*amorous sojourn:* amorous visit; time spent at Lear's court for the purpose of wooing Cordelia
50	*divest:* give away
51	*Interest:* legal ownership

53	*largest bounty:* biggest share, greatest reward
54	*Where nature ... challenge:* to the daughter whose worth will match my natural affection as a father, and will entitle her to the largest portion of my kingdom
56	*than word ... matter:* than words can ever express
57	*space:* freedom to go where I choose; *liberty:* freedom to think and speak as I please
58	*what:* whatever
59	*grace:* popularity, favour
60	*found:* i.e., in a child
61	*A love ... unable:* a love that is beyond speech or expression
62	*Beyond all ... much:* more than all of these comparisons

Edmund: My services to your lordship.
Kent: I must love you, and sue to know you better.   30
Edmund: Sir, I shall study deserving.
Gloucester: He hath been out nine years, and away he shall
    again.   [*Sound a sennet.*]
    The King is coming.
    [*Enter one bearing a coronet, King Lear, Cornwall, Albany,*
    Goneril, Regan, Cordelia, and Attendants.]
Lear: Attend the lords of France and Burgundy, Gloucester.   35
Gloucester: I shall, my lord.
               [*Exeunt Gloucester and Edmund.*]
Lear: Meantime we shall express our darker purpose.
    Give me the map there. Know that we have divided
    In three our kingdom, and 'tis our fast intent
    To shake all cares and business from our age,   40
    Conferring them on younger strengths while we
    Unburdened crawl toward death. Our son of Cornwall,
    And you, our no less loving son of Albany,
    We have this hour a constant will to publish
    Our daughters' several dowers, that future strife   45
    May be prevented now. The princes, France and
        Burgundy,
    Great rivals in our youngest daughter's love,
    Long in our court have made their amorous sojourn,
    And here are to be answered. Tell me, my daughters
    (Since now we will divest us both of rule,   50
    Interest of territory, cares of state),
    Which of you shall we say doth love us most?
    That we our largest bounty may extend
    Where nature doth with merit challenge. Goneril,
    Our eldest-born, speak first.   55
Goneril: Sir, I love you more than word can wield the matter;
    Dearer than eyesight, space, and liberty;
    Beyond what can be valued, rich or rare;
    No less than life, with grace, health, beauty, honour;
    As much as child e'er loved, or father found;   60
    A love that makes breath poor, and speech unable.
    Beyond all manner of so much I love you.
Cordelia: [*Aside.*] What shall Cordelia speak? Love, and be
    silent.

64	*Of all ... this:* Lear points to areas on a map. Evidently, he has decided on these areas beforehand, and his actions are mere ceremony.
65	*champaigns riched:* fertile fields
66	*wide-skirted meads:* abundant pastures
67	*issues:* children
68	*perpetual:* in absolute possession forever
71	*self metal:* same material or substance
72	*And prize ... worth:* value myself the same as my sister
73	*my very deed of love:* my love exactly; my love is exactly the same as hers.
74-76	*Only she ... possesses:* She falls short of expressing my love; the joys that I experience with the most sensitive part of my nature cannot compare with the joy of loving you.
77	*felicitate:* made happy
78	*In your dear Highness' love:* in the love I have for you
80	*More ponderous than my tongue:* My love is heavier than my words.
81	*hereditary:* descendants
83	*validity:* value, worth; *pleasure:* ability to give pleasure
85	*least:* smallest
86	*vines ... milk:* references to the main industries of the two regions
87	*interessed:* interested, closely concerned with
88	*more opulent:* richer, more valuable
92	*Nothing will come of nothing:* a Latin proverb *Ex nihilo nihil fit* – Out of nothing comes nothing
93-94	*I cannot ... mouth:* I cannot pretend to love you more than I do.
95	*According to my bond:* according to the duty of a child to a father and a subject to a king
97	*mar:* impair or ruin
99	*right fit:* as they properly should be

Lear: Of all these bounds, even from this line to this,
With shadowy forests and with champaigns riched, 65
With plenteous rivers and wide-skirted meads,
We make thee lady. To thine and Albany's issues
Be this perpetual.—What says our second daughter,
Our dearest Regan, wife of Cornwall? Speak.
Regan: I am made 70
Of that self metal as my sister,
And prize me at her worth. In my true heart
I find she names my very deed of love,
Only she comes too short, that I profess
Myself an enemy to all other joys 75
Which the most precious square of sense possesses,
And find I am alone felicitate
In your dear Highness' love.
Cordelia: [*Aside.*]   Then poor Cordelia!
And yet not so, since I am sure my love's
More ponderous than my tongue. 80
Lear: To thee and thine hereditary ever
Remain this ample third of our fair kingdom,
No less in space, validity, and pleasure
Than that conferred on Goneril.—Now, our joy,
Although our last and least; to whose young love 85
The vines of France and milk of Burgundy
Strive to be interested; what can you say to draw
A third more opulent than your sisters? Speak.
Cordelia: Nothing, my lord.
Lear: Nothing? 90
Cordelia: Nothing.
Lear: Nothing will come of nothing. Speak again.
Cordelia: Unhappy that I am, I cannot heave
My heart into my mouth. I love your Majesty
According to my bond, no more nor less. 95
Lear: How, how, Cordelia? Mend your speech a little,
Lest you may mar your fortunes.
Cordelia: Good my lord,
You have begot me, bred me, loved me; I
Return those duties back as are right fit,
Obey you, love you, and most honour you. 100
Why have my sisters husbands, if they say

103   *plight:* promise of marriage

106   *To love my father all:* to love my father only

110   *dower:* dowry, the property you take with you when you marry
112   *Hecate:* queen of witches and goddess of darkness
113   *operation of the orbs:* the influence of the planets and stars
         on the lives of humans
115   *disclaim:* give up, renounce
116   *Propinquity:* closeness of relationship, filial ties – here,
         father to daughter
118   *this:* my heart; *Scythian:* an ancient tribe of southern
         Russia, supposed to be particularly brutal
119   *makes his generation messes:* eats his children
122   *Good my liege:* My good lord. Said, likely, in astonishment.
124   *Come not ... wrath:* Do not step between the fiercest beast
         and its anger. The dragon was probably Lear's own
         heraldic symbol.
125-126 *to set ... nursery:* to risk everything on the strength of
         receiving nursing care from Cordelia. "Rest" means
         "remainder"; *Hence and ... sight:* It is not clear to whom
         Lear directs this command.
128   *Who stirs?:* probably directed at someone who makes a
         noise and distracts Lear when he is demanding the court's
         attention
130   *digest:* combine, absorb
131   *Let pride ... her:* Let her own pride, which she calls frank-
         ness or plain speech, be her dowry to attract a husband.
132   *invest you jointly with:* bestow upon both of you
133   *Pre-eminence:* authority
133-134 *effects that troop with majesty:* all the things that go along
         with kingship
134   *by monthly course:* every other month
135   *reservation:* a right to; a group of knights especially
         reserved for Lear
137   *by due turn:* The two daughters, in turn, will have Lear as a
         guest.
138   *additions:* honours, titles; *sway:* power
139   *Revenue:* income; *execution of the rest:* the carrying out of
         the remaining royal duties and responsibilities

They love you all? Happily, when I shall wed,
That lord whose hand must take my plight shall carry
Half my love with him, half my care and duty.
Sure I shall never marry like my sisters,   105
To love my father all.
Lear: But goes thy heart with this?
Cordelia: Ay, good my lord.
Lear: So young, and so untender?
Cordelia: So young, my lord, and true.
Lear: Let it be so! Thy truth then be thy dower!   110
For, by the sacred radiance of the sun,
The mysteries of Hecate and the night;
By all the operation of the orbs
From whom we do exist and cease to be;
Here I disclaim all my paternal care,   115
Propinquity and property of blood,
And as a stranger to my heart and me
Hold thee from this for ever. The barbarous Scythian,
Or he that makes his generation messes
To gorge his appetite, shall to my bosom   120
Be as well neighboured, pitied, and relieved,
As thou my sometime daughter.
Kent: Good my liege—
Lear: Peace, Kent!
Come not between the dragon and his wrath.
I loved her most, and thought to set my rest   125
On her kind nursery.—Hence and avoid my sight!—
So be my grave my peace as here I give
Her father's heart from her! Call France! Who stirs?
Call Burgundy! Cornwall and Albany,
With my two daughters' dowers digest the third;   130
Let pride, which she calls plainness, marry her.
I do invest you jointly with my power,
Pre-eminence, and all the large effects
That troop with majesty. Ourself, by monthly course,
With reservation of an hundred knights   135
By you to be sustained, shall our abode
Make with you by due turn. Only we shall retain
The name, and all th' additions to a king. The sway,
Revenue, execution of the rest,

141   *part:* share

145   *make from the shaft:* avoid the arrow; i.e., do not try to
     stand in the way of my decision
146   *fork:* double-pointed arrow head which inflicted a more
     painful wound than a single point
147-148 *Be Kent ... mad:* Kent may be unmannerly when you
     behave like a madman; *old man?:* Kent is obviously upset
     and speaks exceptionally bluntly.
149-151 *Thinkest thou ... folly:* Do you think that my sense of loyalty
     to you will make me afraid to speak out when you give up
     your royal power to those who flatter you? My honour forces
     me to speak plainly when a king begins to act foolishly.
     These lines contain six examples of metonymy: *duty, power,*
     flattery, plainness, honour, majesty. Metonymy is the use of
     a characteristic or attribute to denote a particular subject.
     For example, "duty" could be used as a metonym for "loyal
     subject."
151   *Reserve:* keep
153   *Answer my life my judgement:* I stake my life on my judge-
     ment.
156   *Reverb:* reverberate, echo; *hollowness:* both insincerity and
     loudness
157   *pawn:* in chess, the least important piece. The pawn can be
     used to protect the most important piece, the king. Here, it
     is an expression of Kent's total loyalty to Lear.
161   *blank:* white spot in the centre of the target. Kent implies
     that Lear should listen to his wisest advisor.
162   *Apollo:* Greek god of the sun and the god of order
163   *vassal:* the lowest of servants; *miscreant:* literally, unbeliever,
     i.e., in the god Apollo because Kent uses the reference "thy
     gods"
164   *forbear:* be merciful, or understanding
165-166 *Kill thy ... disease:* Kill your doctor and pay the disease
     instead. The implication is that Lear's rash judgement is a
     symptom of a sickness.
168   *recreant:* traitor

170   *That:* since
171   *durst:* dared; *strained:* excessive

Beloved sons, be yours; which to confirm,   140
  This coronet part between you.
Kent: Royal Lear,
  Whom I have ever honoured as my king,
  Loved as my father, as my master followed,
  As my great patron thought on in my prayers—
Lear: The bow is bent and drawn, make from the shaft.   145
Kent: Let it fall rather, though the fork invade
  The region of my heart! Be Kent unmannerly
  When Lear is mad. What wouldst thou do, old man?
  Thinkest thou that duty shall have dread to speak
  When power to flattery bows? To plainness honour's
    bound   150
  When majesty falls to folly. Reserve thy state
  And in thy best consideration check
  This hideous rashness. Answer my life my judgement,
  Thy youngest daughter does not love thee least,
  Nor are those empty-hearted whose low sounds   155
  Reverb no hollowness.
Lear: Kent, on thy life, no more!
Kent: My life I never held but as a pawn
  To wage against thine enemies, nor fear to lose it,
  Thy safety being motive.
Lear: Out of my sight!
Kent: See better, Lear, and let me still remain   160
  The true blank of thine eye.
Lear: Now by Apollo—
Kent: Now by Apollo, King,
  Thou swearest thy gods in vain.
Lear: O vassal! Miscreant!
  [*Reaches for his sword.*]
Albany, Cornwall: Dear sir, forbear!
Kent: Kill thy physician and thy fee bestow   165
  Upon the foul disease. Revoke thy gift,
  Or, whilst I can vent clamour from my throat,
  I'll tell thee thou dost evil.
Lear: Hear me, recreant!
  On thine allegiance, hear me!
  That thou hast sought to make us break our vows,   170
  Which we durst never yet, and with strained pride

172   *sentence:* decree, decision
173   *nor ... nor:* neither ... nor; *nature:* temperament; *place:* status as king
174   *potency made good:* royal power asserted; *reward:* punishment
176   *disasters:* accidents or misfortunes

179   *trunk:* body
180   *Jupiter:* used here as one of the gods of wrath

182   *Since thus:* in this manner
183   *Freedom lives ... here:* To keep my freedom, I must leave Britain. Since banishment means the loss of my freedom, my true banishment is here in Britain where there is no freedom.

186   *large:* noble-sounding; *approve:* confirm, demonstrate, i.e., may your actions be as noble as your promises sound
187   *effects:* results

189   *shape his old course:* carry his old ways of speaking plainly; also, direct his life or find his way

Stage Direction – *Flourish:* a fanfare of trumpets to mark the entry of important people – in this case, an earl, a duke, and a king. The fanfare is sounded by Lear's musicians.

193   *rivalled:* competed for Cordelia's hand in marriage
194   *require:* ask; *present:* immediate; *dower:* dowry

196   *crave:* desire

198   *dear:* both beloved and valuable; *hold:* consider, regard

200   *aught:* anything; *that little seeming substance:* that little creature who seems so genuine but is so false
201   *pieced:* added
202   *fitly like:* be to your complete liking

To come betwixt our sentence and our power,
Which nor our nature nor our place can bear,
Our potency made good, take thy reward.
Five days we do allot thee for provision   175
To shield thee from disasters of the world,
And on the sixth to turn thy hated back
Upon our kingdom. If, on the tenth day following,
Thy banished trunk be found in our dominions,
The moment is thy death. Away! By Jupiter,   180
This shall not be revoked.
Kent: Fare thee well, King. Since thus thou wilt appear,
Freedom lives hence, and banishment is here.
[*To Cordelia.*] The gods to their dear shelter take thee,
maid,
That justly thinkest and hast most rightly said!   185
[*To Regan and Goneril.*] And your large speeches may
your deeds approve,
That good effects may spring from words of love.
Thus Kent, O princes, bids you all adieu;
He'll shape his old course in a country new.   [*Exit.*]
[*Flourish. Enter Gloucester, with France and Burgundy;
Attendants.*]
Gloucester: Here's France and Burgundy, my noble lord.   190
Lear: My Lord of Burgundy,
We first address toward you, who with this king
Hath rivalled for our daughter. What in the least
Will you require in present dower with her,
Or cease your quest of love?
Burgundy: Most royal Majesty,   195
I crave no more than hath your Highness offered,
Nor will you tender less.
Lear: Right noble Burgundy,
When she was dear to us, we did hold her so,
But now her price is fallen. Sir, there she stands.
If aught within that little seeming substance,   200
Or all of it, with our displeasure pieced,
And nothing more, may fitly like your Grace,
She's there, and she is yours.
Burgundy: I know no answer.

204	*infirmities:* weaknesses, defects; *owes:* has, suffers from
205	*Unfriended:* without a friend; *adopted to our hate:* accepted only as an object of my hatred
206	*Dowered with our curse:* with only my curse on her as her dowry; *strangered with our oath:* made a stranger, or disowned, by my oath
208	*Election makes ... conditions:* No one can choose under such conditions. Burgundy is withdrawing his offer of marriage.
209	*by the ... me:* I swear by whatever god made me
210	*For:* as for; *King:* the King of France
211	*I would ... stray:* I would not stray so far from your friendship.
212	*To:* as to; *match you where I hate:* to have you married to one I hate; *beseech:* beg
213	*To avert ... way:* to turn your affection to a more worthy woman
214	*wretch:* an outcast; *nature:* the conditions into which all humans are born, as in Mother Nature
216	*best object:* favourite
217	*argument:* theme, constant subject; *balm:* comfort
218	*trice:* amount, instant
219-220	*dismantle/So ... favour:* strip away so many layers of affection; *Sure:* certainly
221	*unnatural:* contrary to what is natural in human behaviour
222	*monsters it:* makes it a monster, or something ugly and abnormal; *fore-vouched:* previously stated
223	*Fall into taint:* becomes bad, corrupted, spoiled, or questionable
223-225	*which to ... me:* which goes so much against reason that only a miracle could make me believe it
226	*glib and oily art:* the art of using words easily and smoothly
227	*and purpose not:* intend not to do what I say
228-235	*that you ... liking:* I beg you to make it clear that you have not deprived me of your affection because of some crime, but because I lack the cleverness to beg favours constantly and I do not have a flattering tongue, though not to have it has cost me your affection.
237	*a tardiness in nature:* natural reluctance or slowness
238	*unspoke:* unspoken

Lear: Will you, with those infirmities she owes,
  Unfriended, new adopted to our hate,   205
  Dowered with our curse, and strangered with our oath,
  Take her, or leave her?
Burgundy: Pardon me, royal sir.
  Election makes not up in such conditions.
Lear: Then leave her, sir; for by the power that made me,
  I tell you all her wealth. [*To France.*] For you, great
    King,   210
  I would not from your love make such a stray
  To match you where I hate; therefore beseech you
  To avert your liking a more worthier way
  Than on a wretch whom nature is ashamed
  Almost to acknowledge hers.
France: This is most strange,   215
  That she whom even but now was your best object,
  The argument of your praise, balm of your age,
  The best, the dearest, should in this trice of time
  Commit a thing so monstrous to dismantle
  So many folds of favour. Sure her offence   220
  Must be of such unnatural degree
  That monsters it, or your fore-vouched affection
  Fall into taint; which to believe of her
  Must be a faith that reason without miracle
  Should never plant in me.
Cordelia: I yet beseech your Majesty   225
  (If for I want that glib and oily art
  To speak and purpose not, since what I well intend,
  I'll do it before I speak), that you make known
  It is no vicious blot, murder, or foulness,
  No unchaste action or dishonoured step,   230
  That hath deprived me of your grace and favour;
  But even for want of that for which I am richer,
  A still-soliciting eye, and such a tongue
  As I am glad I have not, though not to have it
  Hath lost me in your liking.
Lear: Better thou   235
  Hadst not been born than not to have pleased me better.
France: Is it but this—a tardiness in nature
  Which often leaves the history unspoke

240	*What say you to:* i.e., will you have
241-242	*mingled with ... point:* mixed with other motives (the dowry), not connected with the main object (love)
243	*dowry:* gift (of nature or fortune)
244	*but:* just, only; *that portion which yourself proposed:* the original share to be given to Cordelia
249	*Peace be with Burgundy:* a formal dismissal or farewell
250	*respect and fortunes:* the honour due to his rank and the calculating desire for wealth
252	*most rich, being poor:* i.e., having nothing but yet possessing everything
254	*seize upon:* take possession of
255	*Be:* if it is
257	*inflamed:* passionate; *respect:* a word used in a different sense by Cordelia in the previous speech; here, it means affection
258	*dowerless:* another reference to Cordelia's inheritance, now lost
260	*waterish:* both having many rivers (waters) and weak (morally diluted)
261	*unprized precious:* unappreciated by Lear and Burgundy, but precious to me; *of:* from
262	*though unkind:* though Lear and Burgundy are unkind
263	*here, a better where:* These words are used as nouns. "Where" means a better place or a better station in life (than "here").
267	*benison:* blessing
270	*jewels:* an ironic reference to Goneril and Regan as Lear's precious possessions; *washed:* both tearful and clear-sighted, in the sense of "washed clear of illusion"
272	*loath:* unwilling, hesitant
274	*professed bosoms:* the love you have claimed to be true

That it intends to do? My Lord of Burgundy,
What say you to the lady? Love's not love   240
When it is mingled with regards that stand
Aloof from th' entire point. Will you have her?
She is herself a dowry.
Burgundy: Royal King,
Give but that portion which yourself proposed,
And here I take Cordelia by the hand,   245
Duchess of Burgundy.
Lear: Nothing! I have sworn; I am firm.
Burgundy: I am sorry then you have so lost a father
That you must lose a husband.
Cordelia: Peace be with Burgundy!
Since that respect and fortunes are his love,   250
I shall not be his wife.
France: Fairest Cordelia, that art most rich, being poor;
Most choice, forsaken; and most loved, despised!
Thee and thy virtues here I seize upon.
Be it lawful I take up what's cast away.   255
Gods, gods! 'tis strange that from their coldest neglect
My love should kindle to inflamed respect.
Thy dowerless daughter, King, thrown to my chance,
Is queen of us, of ours, and our fair France.
Not all the dukes of waterish Burgundy   260
Can buy this unprized precious maid of me.
Bid them farewell, Cordelia, though unkind.
Thou losest here, a better where to find.
Lear: Thou hast her, France; let her be thine; for we
Have no such daughter, nor shall ever see   265
That face of hers again. Therefore be gone
Without our grace, our love, our benison.
Come, noble Burgundy.
[*Flourish. Exeunt Lear, Burgundy, Cornwall, Albany,*
   Gloucester, and Attendants.]
France: Bid farewell to your sisters.
Cordelia: The jewels of our father, with washed eyes   270
Cordelia leaves you. I know you what you are;
And, like a sister, am most loath to call
Your faults as they are named. Love well our father.
To your professed bosoms I commit him;

275   *stood I:* if I stood; *grace:* favour, blessing
276   *prefer:* recommend, i.e., promote him to a better position

278   *Prescribe not us:* Do not dictate to us; *study:* purpose, intention, endeavour

280   *At fortune's alms:* as an act of charity; *You have obedience scanted:* You have neglected obedience (to your father)
281   *And well ... wanted:* deserve the loss of what you have both desired: a dowry and parental love
282   *unfold:* reveal; *plighted cunning:* cunning that has been concealed by pledges of love
283   *derides:* laughs at or mocks with contempt

286-287 *appertains to:* concerns; *will/hence:* will leave this place

290   *changes:* whims, quirks

293   *grossly:* too obviously, plainly
294-295 *he hath ... himself:* He has always been impulsive; i.e., he has seldom known his own mind. Goneril expands on this observation in her reply to Regan.
296   *of his time:* period of his past life

298   *imperfections of long-engraffed condition:* faults arising from long habit; *engraffed:* chronic, habitual, longstanding
299   *therewithal:* together with the imperfections; *infirm:* senile
300   *choleric:* irritable
301   *unconstant starts:* sudden impulses

303   *compliment of:* formality or ceremony
304   *hit together:* agree, act together
305   *carry authority:* wields power; *disposition:* attitude of mind
306   *last surrender:* giving up of the throne; *offend:* is simply a nuisance

308   *i' the heat:* immediately. Similar to our expression "strike while the iron is hot."

But yet, alas, stood I within his grace, 275
I would prefer him to a better place!
So farewell to you both.
Goneril: Prescribe not us our duty.
Regan: Let your study
Be to content your lord, who hath received you
At fortune's alms. You have obedience scanted, 280
And well are worth the want that you have wanted.
Cordelia: Time shall unfold what plighted cunning hides,
Who covers faults, at last with shame derides,
Well may you prosper!
France: Come, my fair Cordelia.
                    [*Exeunt France and Cordelia.*]
Goneril: Sister, it is not little I have to say of what most 285
nearly appertains to us both. I think our father will
hence tonight.
Regan: That's most certain, and with you; next month with
us.
Goneril: You see how full of changes his age is. The obser- 290
vation we have made of it hath not been little. He
always loved our sister most, and with what poor
judgement he hath now cast her off appears too grossly.
Regan: 'Tis the infirmity of his age; yet he hath ever but
slenderly known himself. 295
Goneril: The best and soundest of his time hath been but
rash; then must we look from his age to receive, not
alone the imperfections of long-engraffed condition,
but therewithal the unruly waywardness that infirm and
choleric years bring with them. 300
Regan: Such unconstant starts are we like to have from him
as this of Kent's banishment.
Goneril: There is further compliment of leave-taking between
France and him. Pray you let's hit together. If our
father carry authority with such disposition as he bears, 305
this last surrender of his will but offend us.
Regan: We shall further think of it.
Goneril: We must do something, and i' the heat.   [*Exeunt.*]

Act 1, Scene 1: Activities

1. You are a reporter covering the events at King Lear's court. You are anticipating a fairly routine appearance of the King despite the rumours of a proclamation. When the announcement is made you now have to record the shock that ripples through the court and report the chaotic events that follow. Write your story.

2. This scene should give you some sense of what the characters are all about.

   a) Choose a character and write five thoughts that the character could have had that are not actually made clear at the time that person initiates a decision. Be able to justify each thought using the text and your understanding of what might be going on in that character's mind at the time.

   b) You have discovered the diary of the person you wrote about in question 2 (a). What are some of the entries that you have read?

3. If you could have written or spoken to King Lear before he considered the division of his kingdom (lines 37–122), what might you have said to prevent him from making the decisions he did?

4. King Lear states that he has decided to "set" his "rest" on Cordelia's "kind nursery" (lines 125–126). With a partner, discuss what it is, exactly, that Lear means. Decide whether or not it is particularly wise to "set" your "rest" on anyone. If you were Kent, would you, too, have interceded in the proceedings at this point? How could you have done it differently? Is Kent's interjection particularly significant?

5. With your group, discuss how a person might be able to tell a flatterer from a friend. How does flattery operate in this scene—who wants it and who gives it? What seems to be the result when this form of deception is employed? Include your findings as a brief chapter in *The Book of Great Flatterers* that you are in the process of writing.

6. In your group, role-play an interview with Goneril and Regan. The interviewer should try to get the sisters to reveal their true feelings toward their father, their youngest sister, and each other. A list of ten carefully prepared questions should achieve the desired results.

   Write a newspaper or magazine gossip column, using the information you have gleaned from your interview, or present the rehearsed interview to the class.

7. Soliloquies are speeches in which actors talk to the audience about themselves and their intentions. The other characters in the play are either not present or do not hear what is said. Write a soliloquy for Kent in which he reveals his feelings about his banishment. You may wish to write it in modern English. The speech should fit logically into the play and develop from actual events in it. Perform a brief dramatic reading of your soliloquy for your group or for the rest of the class.

8. Create a "map" or web of Act 1, Scene 1. To do this, first select a quote that you think is particularly significant to the action of the scene, to the setting, or to the revelation of a character or a theme. Now brainstorm with your group for important words, phrases, or impressions that are linked to the quote. Write your responses in clusters or groups that help to show the connections and relationships that are important to the topic you have chosen.

   Post your maps for the rest of the class to see and discuss with the whole class the insights that the maps have given you into the aspect of the play you chose to explore.

9. A playbill is a poster advertising a play. It should contain the title of the play, the names of the better known members of the cast, the name of the director, dates of performance, the theatre, some pertinent critical quotes, and perhaps an illustration. As a group, create a playbill for a performance of *King Lear* as it might appear in the early 1600s. Remember, the object is to entice people to see the play.

10. Cordelia seems to be the sincere daughter that every father would hope for. In your journal, give an account of your impressions of Cordelia and the special characteristics that she possesses. As Cordelia, write a letter of explanation to Kent outlining why you behaved as you did in the division scene, lines 37–122.

11. List all the characters you have met in this scene, and note in your journal your impressions of them. You may wish to add to your list as the play progresses. So far, with which character(s) do you most identify and with which do you least identify?

12. The first scene of a play is important for many reasons. Brainstorm, in groups, to decide what you think an effective opening scene should accomplish. Has Shakespeare lived up to your expectations in *King Lear*? What has he done that you didn't expect? What did you expect him to do that he didn't?

13. In his division speech (lines 37–55), King Lear insists on making choices based on favouritism and flattery. In groups, make a list of the possible reasons why Lear would use this method to arrive at such a major decision as the division of his kingdom. Test the items on your list as the play progresses, eliminating those that do not hold up and adding any new ideas that may occur.

14. This scene would make an ideal tableau in which the main characters are frozen in mid-action at a point that you and your group think appropriate. Create your tableau, write your rationale for your choice, and compare your version to those of the other groups in the class. In your journal, account for the differences in approach and make a note about how interpretations of a scene can differ.

For the next scene ...

We have all at one time or another felt deprived of certain rights. In your journal, list the rights you believe you should be able to take for granted. Of which rights, if any, have you been deprived?

Act 1, Scene 2

In this scene ...

Edmund, Gloucester's illegitimate son, reveals in a soliloquy that he is intent on removing everything that stands in the way of possessing his father's earldom. Edmund determines that he must win his father's affections and cast suspicion on the character of his half-brother, Edgar. By means of a forged letter, he convinces his father that Edgar is plotting Gloucester's death so that he can claim his inheritance. Gloucester rashly believes Edmund's story, feeling that the world is turning upside down. Gloucester then leaves to await Edgar, who arrives at his father's castle moments later. Edmund convinces Edgar that Gloucester is angry with him and that Edgar should flee the household.

3	*Stand in ... custom:* be dependent on hateful conventions, put up with conventional laws
4	*curiosity:* nice distinctions (in the sense of false delicacy), squeamishness; *deprive me:* Keep me from my rights.
5	*For that:* because; *moonshines:* months
6	*Lag of:* short of, behind, as in younger than; *Why bastard? Wherefore base?:* Why is the term "bastard" attached to me?
7	*dimensions:* proportions; *compact:* put together
8	*generous:* noble; *my shape as true:* my figure as true a resemblance to my father
9	*honest:* virtuous; presumably, with the secondary sense of married; *madam's:* woman's; *issue:* child
10	*base? ... Bastardy?:* Edmund protests against the assumption that because he is illegitimate, he is low and disgusting.
11	*lusty stealth of nature:* the enjoyment of a natural and vigorous sexual life
12	*composition:* completeness, stronger constitution; *fierce:* energetic
13	*within a ... bed:* a reference to the marriage bed and what goes on there
14	*fops:* fools
15	*got:* begot, conceived
15-16	*Well then, ... land:* Edmund feels that he has justified a claim to what Edgar, Gloucester's legitimate son, will inherit.
17-18	*Our father's ... legitimate:* Our father loves me as much as he loves Edgar; *Fine word:* but, after all, only a word
19	*speed:* should succeed, bring about the expected results
20	*invention thrive:* plan should prove successful
22	*stand up for bastards:* take the side of, but also a sexual pun
23	*choler:* anger
24	*Prescribed:* limited, restricted
25	*Confined to exhibition?:* limited to an allowance of money (from Goneril and Regan)
26	*Upon the gad?:* on the spur of the moment

Scene 2

Inside Gloucester's castle.
Enter Edmund the Bastard, a letter
in his hand.

Edmund: Thou, Nature, art my goddess; to thy law
  My services are bound. Wherefore should I
  Stand in the plague of custom and permit
  The curiosity of nations to deprive me,
  For that I am some twelve or fourteen moonshines   5
  Lag of a brother? Why bastard? Wherefore base?
  When my dimensions are as well compact,
  My mind as generous, and my shape as true,
  As honest madam's issue? Why brand they us
  With base? With baseness? Bastardy? Base, base?   10
  Who, in the lusty stealth of nature, take
  More composition and fierce quality
  Than doth, within a dull, stale, tired bed,
  Go to the creating a whole tribe of fops
  Got 'tween asleep and wake? Well then,   15
  Legitimate Edgar, I must have your land.
  Our father's love is to the bastard Edmund
  As to the legitimate. Fine word, "legitimate"!
  Well, my legitimate, if this letter speed
  And my invention thrive, Edmund the base   20
  Shall top the legitimate; I grow; I prosper.
  Now, gods, stand up for bastards!
  [*Enter Gloucester.*]
Gloucester: Kent banished thus? And France in choler parted?
  And the King gone tonight? Prescribed his power?
  Confined to exhibition? All this done   25
  Upon the gad? Edmund, how now? What news?
Edmund: So please your lordship, none.
  [*Puts away the letter.*]

32	*terrible dispatch:* desperate putting away
34	*Come:* Gloucester expects to be given the letter.
35	*spectacles:* Elizabethan gentlemen, but not those of Lear's time, wore spectacles.
37	*o'er-read:* read over
39	*o'erlooking:* looking over
41	*detain:* keep
42	*blame:* blameworthy
45	*essay or taste:* test
46-48	*This policy ... them:* This custom of revering and respecting the elderly makes life miserable for us when we should be enjoying it most; it denies us our fortune (what we are entitled to; inheritance) until we are too old to appreciate it.
49	*idle and fond:* useless and foolish; *bondage:* oppression, slavery
50-51	*aged tyranny:* tyranny of an older person (Gloucester); *sways:* rules; *not as ... suffered:* not because he has power so much as because we allow him to
52-53	*If our ... him:* a thinly veiled suggestion of murder
53	*revenue:* estate, wealth
56-57	*Had he ... this?:* Could he possibly have written this?
60	*casement:* a French window (a window that opens like a door)
61	*closet:* room
62	*character:* handwriting
63	*matter:* content of the letter; *durst:* would dare
64	*fain:* gladly, willingly

Gloucester: Why so earnestly seek you to put up that letter?
Edmund: I know no news, my lord.
Gloucester: What paper were you reading? 30
Edmund: Nothing, my lord.
Gloucester: No? What needed then that terrible dispatch of
  it into your pocket? The quality of nothing hath not
  such need to hide itself. Let's see. Come, if it be
  nothing, I shall not need spectacles. 35
Edmund: I beseech you, sir, pardon me. It is a letter from
  my brother that I have not all o'er-read; and for so
  much as I have perused, I find it not fit for your
  o'erlooking.
Gloucester: Give me the letter, sir. 40
Edmund: I shall offend, either to detain or give it. The
  contents, as in part I understand them, are to blame.
Gloucester: Let's see, let's see!
Edmund: I hope, for my brother's justification, he wrote
  this but as an essay or taste of my virtue. 45
Gloucester: [*Reads.*] "This policy and reverence of age makes
  the world bitter to the best of our times; keeps our
  fortunes from us till our oldness cannot relish them. I
  begin to find an idle and fond bondage in the oppression of aged tyranny, who sways, not as it hath 50
  power, but as it is suffered. Come to me, that of this
  I may speak more. If our father would sleep till I waked
  him, you should enjoy half his revenue for ever, and
  live the beloved of your brother."
EDGAR.
  Hum! Conspiracy? "Sleep till I waked him, you should 55
  enjoy half his revenue." My son Edgar! Had he a
  hand to write this? a heart and brain to breed it in?
  When came you to this? Who brought it?
Edmund: It was not brought me, my lord; there's the cunning of it. I found it thrown in at the casement of my 60
  closet.
Gloucester: You know the character to be your brother's?
Edmund: If the matter were good, my lord, I durst swear it
  were his; but in respect of that, I would fain think it
  were not. 65
Gloucester: It is his.

69   *sounded:* sounded you out, tested your feelings

72-73   *at perfect age:* when fully mature; *declined:* past their best
            years; *ward:* a person under the care of a guardian

76   *brutish:* animal-like
77-78   *sirrah:* an old term for "fellow" or "sir" which expresses
            annoyance or impatience, usually addressed to a servant;
            apprehend: arrest
78   *Abominable:* hated, unnatural
80   *suspend your indignation:* Control your anger.

82   *you should ... course:* You would be following a well-
            designed and safe plan of action; *where:* whereas
84   *make a great gap:* create a breach, undermine
85   *shake in pieces ... obedience:* destroy the spirit of his duty
            as a son; *pawn:* stake, bet
86   *writ:* written; *feel:* test
87-88   *to no other pretence of danger:* with no dangerous intention

90   *judge it meet:* think it fit
91-92   *auricular assurance:* assurance of your own hearing

97-100   *wind me into him:* Worm your way into his confidence for me;
            frame the ... wisdom: Carry out the plan according to your
            own common sense; *I would unstate ... resolution:* disinherit,
            give up my estate to be sure whether he is innocent or guilty
102   *withal:* soon or immediately after that
103   *late:* recent; *eclipses in the sun and moon:* An eclipse of
            the sun occurred in October 1605, and an eclipse of the
            moon in September. Scholars use this information in dating
            the play; *portend:* give warning of
104   *wisdom of nature:* our reasoning powers
105   *reason:* explain; *nature:* our world; *scourged:* punished,
            afflicted
106   *sequent effects:* results that follow
106-109   *Love cools ... father:* these are some of the "sequent
            effects"

Edmund: It is his hand, my lord, but I hope his heart is
    not in the contents.
Gloucester: Hath he never before sounded you in this
    business?   70
Edmund: Never, my lord. But I have heard him oft maintain
    it to be fit that, sons at perfect age, and fathers
    declined, the father should be as ward to the son, and
    the son manage his revenue.
Gloucester: O villain, villain! His very opinion in the letter!   75
    Abhorred villain! Unnatural, detested, brutish villain!
    Worse than brutish! Go, sirrah, seek him. I'll appre-
    hend him. Abominable villain! Where is he?
Edmund: I do not well know, my lord. If it shall please you
    to suspend your indignation against my brother till   80
    you can derive from him better testimony of his intent,
    you should run a certain course; where, if you
    violently proceed against him, mistaking his purpose,
    it would make a great gap in your own honour and
    shake in pieces the heart of his obedience. I dare pawn   85
    down my life for him that he hath writ this to feel
    my affection to your honour, and to no other pretence
    of danger.
Gloucester: Think you so?
Edmund: If your honour judge it meet, I will place you where   90
    you shall hear us confer of this and by an auricular
    assurance have your satisfaction, and that without any
    further delay than this very evening.
Gloucester: He cannot be such a monster.
Edmund: Nor is not, sure.   95
Gloucester: To his father, that so tenderly and entirely loves
    him. Heaven and earth! Edmund, seek him out; wind
    me into him, I pray you; frame the business after
    your own wisdom. I would unstate myself to be in a
    due resolution.   100
Edmund: I will seek him, sir, presently, convey the business
    as I shall find means, and acquaint you withal.
Gloucester: These late eclipses in the sun and moon portend
    no good to us. Though the wisdom of nature can
    reason it thus and thus, yet nature finds itself scourged   105
    by the sequent effects. Love cools, friendship falls off,

108   *bond:* obligation of son to father and father to son
109-110   *This villain ... prediction:* Edgar's actions are consistent with
           the portent or omen of the eclipse
110-111   *the King ... nature:* The King (Lear) departs from his own
           natural tendencies – the love of his child; *bias* refers to the
           natural curve followed by a bowling ball.
112-113   *best of our time:* best example of our times; *hollowness:*
           deceit
115   *it shall lose thee nothing:* You have nothing to lose.

118   *foppery:* foolishness, stupidity
119   *surfeits:* results of excesses
120-121   *make guilty ... stars:* make the sun, moon, and stars guilty
           of our blame or misfortunes
121-122   *villains on necessity:* as if we had no choice but to be
           villains
123   *spherical predominance:* power of the planets

126   *divine thrusting on:* supernatural influence
127   *whoremaster:* a term of contempt suggesting the coarse-
           ness of human sexual nature; *goatish:* lustful, lecherous
128   *charge:* responsibility, liability
128-129   *compounded with my mother:* coupled with my mother (to
           produce me)
129   *under the Dragon's Tail:* a reference to the position of the
           moon and the constellation Draco, the Dragon
131   *that:* what
132   *maidenliest:* most innocent; *firmament:* starry heavens
133   *bastardizing:* conception
134   *Pat:* on the dot, exactly as needed; *catastrophe:* contrived
           incident completing the plot of a play
135-136   *Tom o' Bedlam:* name given to those who had been in
           Bedlam Hospital, the insane asylum of St. Mary of
           Bethlehem, in London; *divisions:* between brothers

143   *he:* Edmund is thinking of the author of the predictions he
           mentions.
144   *unnaturalness:* an end of the natural affection between
           parent and child
145-146   *dearth:* shortage, famine; *dissolutions of ancient amities:*
           breaking up of old friendships

brothers divide. In cities, mutinies; in countries, dis-
cord; in palaces, treason; and the bond cracked 'twixt
son and father. This villain of mine comes under the
prediction; there's son against father: the King falls   110
from bias of nature; there's father against child. We
have seen the best of our time. Machinations, hollowness, treachery, and all ruinous disorders follow us
disquietly to our graves. Find out this villain,
Edmund; it shall lose thee nothing; do it carefully.   115
And the noble and true-hearted Kent banished! His
offence, honesty! 'Tis strange.   [*Exit.*]
Edmund: This is the excellent foppery of the world, that,
when we are sick in fortune, often the surfeits of our
own behaviour, we make guilty of our disasters the   120
sun, the moon, and stars; as if we were villains on
necessity: fools by heavenly compulsion; knaves,
thieves, and treachers by spherical predominance;
drunkards, liars, and adulterers by an enforced obedience of planetary influence; and all that we are evil   125
in, by a divine thrusting on. An admirable evasion of
whoremaster man, to lay his goatish disposition to the
charge of a star! My father compounded with my
mother under the Dragon's Tail, and my nativity was
under Ursa Major, so that it follows I am rough and   130
lecherous. Fut! I should have been that I am, had the
maidenliest star in the firmament twinkled on my
bastardizing.
[*Enter Edgar.*]
Pat! he comes, like the catastrophe of the old comedy.
My cue is villainous melancholy, with a sigh like Tom   135
o' Bedlam. O, these eclipses do portend these divisions!
Fa, sol, la, mi.
Edgar: How now, brother Edmund? What serious contemplation are you in?
Edmund: I am thinking, brother, of a prediction I read this   140
other day, what should follow these eclipses.
Edgar: Do you busy yourself with that?
Edmund: I promise you, the effects he writes of succeed
unhappily: as of unnaturalness between the child and
the parent; death, dearth, dissolutions of ancient ami-   145

146	*divisions in state:* differences of opinion within the country; *maledictions:* curses, false rumours
147-148	*diffidences:* instances of mistrust; *banishment of friends:* probably a reference to Kent
148	*dissipation of cohorts:* disbanding of soldiers; *nuptial breaches:* breaking up of marriages
150	*a sectary astronomical?:* a follower of astrology
151	*When saw ... last?:* Edmund answers Edgar's question, but not in a way that Edgar can understand.
158	*Bethink yourself:* think carefully, consider
159	*at my entreaty:* with my strong urging; *forbear his presence:* give up seeing him
160-161	*qualified the ... displeasure:* has softened his anger
161-162	*with the ... allay:* that his anger would scarcely be satisfied, even if you were physically harmed
164-165	*That's my fear:* the quick, insincere reply of an easy liar; *continent forbearance:* controlled restraint
167	*fitly:* at a suitable time
170	*to the best:* to the best of my ability and knowledge
171	*meaning:* intention
172	*faintly:* only partly, inadequately
173	*the image and horror:* the horrible reality. This is an example of a device called hendiadys, which is the use of two words joined by a conjunction. The phrase ordinarily would be "the horrible image" or "the image of horror."
174	*anon?:* soon, in due time
176	*credulous:* believing, trusting; *noble:* honourable
179	*practices:* intrigues; *ride easy:* go easily (as the experienced rider fits the horse's back and rides smoothly and comfortably); *I see the business:* I see the way I must go (to achieve my objectives).
181	*All with ... fit:* To me everything is fitting and justifiable if I can use it to achieve my purposes.

ties; divisions in state, menaces and maledictions against
king and nobles; needless diffidences, banishment of
friends, dissipation of cohorts, nuptial breaches, and I
know not what.
Edgar: How long have you been a sectary astronomical?   150
Edmund: When saw you my father last?
Edgar: The night gone by.
Edmund: Spake you with him?
Edgar: Ay, two hours together.
Edmund: Parted you in good terms? Found you no displea-   155
sure in him by word nor countenance?
Edgar: None at all.
Edmund: Bethink yourself wherein you may have offended
him; and at my entreaty forbear his presence until
some little time hath qualified the heat of his displea-   160
sure, which at this instant so rageth in him that with
the mischief of your person it would scarcely allay.
Edgar: Some villain hath done me wrong.
Edmund: That's my fear. I pray you have a continent for-
bearance till the speed of his rage goes slower; and, as   165
I say, retire with me to my lodging, from whence I
will fitly bring you to hear my lord speak. Pray ye, go!
There's my key. If you do stir abroad, go armed.
Edgar: Armed, brother?
Edmund: Brother, I advise you to the best. I am no honest   170
man if there be any good meaning toward you. I have
told you what I have seen and heard; but faintly,
nothing like the image and horror of it. Pray you, away!
Edgar: Shall I hear from you anon?
Edmund: I do serve you in this business.   [*Exit Edgar.*]   175
A credulous father! And a brother noble,
Whose nature is so far from doing harms
That he suspects none; on whose foolish honesty
My practices ride easy! I see the business.
Let me, if not by birth, have lands by wit;   180
All with me's meet that I can fashion fit.   [*Exit.*]

Act 1, Scene 2: Activities

1. In your journal, paraphrase Edmund's theory of nature (lines 1–22). Respond to this soliloquy and discuss your ideas with a group. Decide what the consequences would be if everyone had the same theory. Predict and write down what you think might happen when Edmund puts his theory into action.

2. Gloucester says "Love cools, friendship falls off, brothers divide ... and the bond cracked 'twixt son and father" (106-109). With your group, discuss how these comments about mutual mistrust are reflected in this scene, and suggest what they might imply for the action to come. If Gloucester recognizes these things are happening, why doesn't he do something about the situation rather than accepting it? How do the other characters in the play react in terms of Gloucester's observation? What do you think might remedy the situation? Share your suggestions with the class.

3. Visualize the structure of this scene by diagramming it so that it becomes a visual model. You may choose a central character conflict, a major structural pattern, or the relationship of the scene to the setting as your focus around which to arrange the rest of the events of the scene. Post your diagram for the rest of the class to comment on. In your journal, note how this activity helped you to better understand how the scene would work on the stage.

For the next scene ...

In your journal, recount a situation in which one or more of your acquaintances wished to make someone else in your group of friends feel truly unwanted and outcast. What was done to accomplish this? How effective was it? How did you feel about the tactics used and the outcome? What advice might you give people who employ such measures?

Act 1, Scene 3

In this scene ...

Goneril is discussing with Oswald, her steward, the difficulties she is having as she plays host to her father and his knights. Because she wants to be rid of Lear as soon as possible, she instructs Oswald to provoke Lear so that his actions will give her a reason to evict him.

1   *chiding:* scolding; finding fault with
4   *By day and night:* constantly; (possibly an oath)
5   *flashes into ... other:* has outbreaks of impulsive behaviour, involving large, significant offences
7   *riotous:* boisterous and unrestrained. Probably a lie Goneril will use for her own purposes; *upbraids:* complains about, finds fault with
8   *trifle:* matter of slight importance
10   *If you ... services:* if you serve (Lear) with less attention than before
11   *the fault ... answer:* I will take the responsibility for your actions.

Stage Direction – *Horns:* The calls sounded on hunting horns were important in keeping the hunt properly organized. Here, the horns are used by Lear to announce his return. He evidently expects to be received royally.

13   *Put on what weary negligence:* pretend whatever neglect (of Lear) because of fatigue
14   *fellows:* fellow servants; *I'd have ... question:* I want it (this neglect) to be discussed.
15   *distaste:* dislikes; *to:* go to
16   *Whose mind ... one:* whose views are the same as mine in this matter
17   *Not to be overruled:* not to be changed by any authority that Lear may attempt to use; *Idle:* foolish
20-21   *Old fools ... flatteries:* Goneril suggests that Lear is in his second childhood and, like a child, must be treated with restrictions and rebukes as well as flatteries in order to make him behave.
24   *grows:* comes as a result
25   *I would ... occasions:* I wish to create opportunities (for complaint against Lear) from these contrived grievances.
27   *To hold my very course:* to use (or keep to) the same course of action that I am taking

Scene 3

Inside the Duke of Albany's palace.
Enter Goneril and Oswald,
her Steward.

Goneril: Did my father strike my gentleman for chiding of
   his fool?
Oswald: Ay, madam.
Goneril: By day and night, he wrongs me! Every hour
   He flashes into one gross crime or other   5
   That sets us all at odds. I'll not endure it.
   His knights grow riotous, and himself upbraids us
   On every trifle. When he returns from hunting,
   I will not speak with him. Say I am sick.
   If you come slack of former services,   10
   You shall do well; the fault of it I'll answer.
                              [Horns within.]
Oswald: He's coming, madam; I hear him.
Goneril: Put on what weary negligence you please,
   You and your fellows. I'd have it come to question.
   If he distaste it, let him to my sister,   15
   Whose mind and mine I know in that are one,
   Not to be overruled. Idle old man,
   That still would manage those authorities
   That he hath given away! Now, by my life,
   Old fools are babes again, and must be used   20
   With checks as flatteries, when they are seen abused.
   Remember what I have said.
Oswald: Very well, madam.
Goneril: And let his knights have colder looks among you.
   What grows of it, no matter. Advise your fellows so.
   I would breed from hence occasions, and I shall,   25
   That I may speak. I'll write straight to my sister
   To hold my very course. Prepare for dinner.   *[Exeunt.]*

Act 1, Scene 3: Activities

1. You are a set designer. Design or describe the set you would create for this scene, or as a costume designer, how would you dress Goneril and Oswald?

2. One really effective way to capture the mood of a scene is to turn it into a contemporary photograph. Select a scene that you think you could illustrate using one effective photograph you have taken with that scene in mind. Write a rationale for your choice based on your understanding of what mood the scene is attempting to create.

3. As an actor, you have been given the part of Oswald. Decide how you would play this character, based on the information provided in this scene. With a partner as Goneril, role-play the scene for your group or for the class.

4. As Goneril, write the letter that you send to Regan. With a partner, role-play Regan's response to the contents of the letter.

5. Goneril says at the end of the scene, "I would breed from hence occasions." What do you think she is "breeding"? Why is she determined to do this and what does her comment reveal about her character? As Oswald, what is your impression of her? Discuss these questions with your group.

For the next scene ...

What do you think a medieval court fool or jester might look like? What sort of costume might the character wear? What role would the person play in a royal court?

Who might be a contemporary version of the court fool? Name as many people as you like, describe what you think their chief function is, and try to identify the source of their popularity.

If you were the fool in Lear's court, and knowing all that has transpired, what kinds of things might you say to him? How do you think he would respond? Write a note in your journal, as a fool, on the nature of your job.

Act 1 Scene 4

In this scene ...

We discover that Kent has not left England as Lear ordered, but has decided to disguise himself in order to serve the old king. Lear meets Kent, decides that he would make a good servant, and instructs Kent to follow him.

A knight enters and tells Lear about the poor treatment he is receiving at the Duke of Albany's palace. Lear decides to discuss the matter with Goneril. Before he is able to do so, he engages in an angry exchange with Oswald. Kent takes Lear's side by threatening to beat Oswald. At this point, the Fool enters and proceeds to point out to Lear the stupidity of his previous decision to divide his kingdom.

Goneril comes in search of Lear and informs him that, if he is to remain in her household, he must reduce the number of his knights. This enrages Lear who then determines to go with his retinue to Regan. Albany, who seems unaware of what has been going on, enters and hears his wife instruct Oswald to inform Regan of Lear's intended arrival. Although Albany does not approve of Goneril's actions, he does nothing to prevent them.

1	*but as well:* in addition to
2	*diffuse:* disguise, cause to be indistinct
2-4	*my good ... likeness:* I may be able to perform the good purpose for which I disguised myself in the first place.
4	*razed my likeness:* destroyed my appearance. Literally, "razed" means shaved, and is likely a pun on "razor," as Kent may, in fact, have shaved off his beard.
6	*So may it come:* it may happen that
7	*full of labours:* ready to do any work that needs to be done

Stage Direction – *Horns within:* hunting horns announcing Lear's return

8	*stay a jot:* wait an instant, moment; *Let me ... ready:* Lear wants instant service and commands as he has always done.

15	*judgement:* the eternal judgement of the soul
16	*to eat no fish:* a phrase with several possible meanings. Kent will ignore fast days. This would indicate that he is not a Roman Catholic but a loyal Protestant (a reference to Elizabethan politics). Kent may also be pointing out that he is not a weakling because he is a meat eater. He may also be making a bawdy, sexual pun. It may be all of the above.

25	*countenance:* bearing, appearance
26	*fain:* willingly, gladly

28	*Authority:* the attitude of a true ruler. This is not flattery on Kent's part.

Scene 4

Inside the Duke of Albany's palace.
Enter Kent, disguised.

Kent: If but as well I other accents borrow,
That can my speech diffuse, my good intent
May carry through itself to that full issue
For which I razed my likeness. Now, banished Kent,
If thou canst serve where thou dost stand condemned,   5
So may it come, thy master, whom thou lovest,
Shall find thee full of labours.
            [*Horns within. Enter Lear, Knights, and Attendants.*]
Lear: Let me not stay a jot for dinner; go get it ready. [*Exit*
    an Attendant.] How now? What art thou?
Kent: A man, sir.   10
Lear: What dost thou profess? What wouldst thou with us?
Kent: I do profess to be no less than I seem, to serve him
    truly that will put me in trust, to love him that is
    honest, to converse with him that is wise and says little,
    to fear judgement, to fight when I cannot choose, and   15
    to eat no fish.
Lear: What art thou?
Kent: A very honest-hearted fellow, and as poor as the King.
Lear: If thou be'st as poor for a subject as he is for a king,
    thou art poor enough. What wouldst thou?   20
Kent: Service.
Lear: Who wouldst thou serve?
Kent: You.
Lear: Dost thou know me, fellow?
Kent: No, sir, but you have that in your countenance which   25
    I would fain call master.
Lear: What's that?
Kent: Authority.

30	*keep honest counsel:* hold my tongue when necessary
30-31	*mar a ... it:* botch an elaborate story in telling it (by not using fancy words); that is, I'm a blunt sort of fellow.
35-36	*Not so ... anything:* Kent answers indirectly and indelicately that since he is young enough to be interested in sex, he is not old enough to be foolishly affectionate for other reasons. His answer evidently pleases Lear, who engages him on the spot.
43	*So please you:* i.e., excuse me, I am busy. Oswald, following Goneril's instructions, ignores Lear's question.
44	*clotpoll:* blockhead, stupid person
45-46	*Where's my ... asleep:* Lear is impatient. This is the second time he has called for his fool, and there is no response (probably one of Goneril's tactics).
47	*mongrel?:* Oswald
51	*roundest:* bluntest, surliest
55	*entertained:* treated
56	*as you were wont:* as you used to be or deserved to be
57	*abatement:* lessening, decrease
57-58	*general dependants:* most of the servants
62-63	*for my duty ... wronged:* Because of my loyalty, I cannot be silent in the face of the wrong done to you.
64	*rememberest:* remind or recall; *conception:* perception
65	*faint neglect:* hardly noticeable neglect, or the weary negligence suggested by Goneril

Lear: What services canst thou do?
Kent: I can keep honest counsel, ride, run, mar a curious   30
    tale in telling it, and deliver a plain message bluntly.
    That which ordinary men are fit for, I am qualified
    in, and the best of me is diligence.
Lear: How old art thou?
Kent: Not so young, sir, to love a woman for singing, nor   35
    so old to dote on her for anything. I have years on
    my back forty-eight.
Lear: Follow me; thou shalt serve me. If I like thee no worse
    after dinner, I will not part from thee yet. Dinner,
    ho, dinner! Where's my knave? My fool? Go you and   40
    call my fool hither.   [*Exit an Attendant.*]
    [*Enter Oswald the Steward.*]
    You, you, sirrah, where's my daughter?
Oswald: So please you—   [*Exit.*]
Lear: What says the fellow there? Call the clotpoll back.
    [*Exit a Knight.*] Where's my fool, ho? I think the   45
    world's asleep.
    [*Enter Knight.*]
    How now? Where's that mongrel?
Knight: He says, my lord, your daughter is not well.
Lear: Why came not the slave back to me when I called
    him?   50
Knight: Sir, he answered me in the roundest manner, he
    would not.
Lear: He would not?
Knight: My lord, I know not what the matter is, but to my
    judgement your Highness is not entertained with that   55
    ceremonious affection as you were wont. There's a great
    abatement of kindness appears as well in the general
    dependants as in the Duke himself also and your
    daughter.
Lear: Ha! sayest thou so?   60
Knight: I beseech you pardon me, my lord, if I be mistaken,
    for my duty cannot be silent when I think your High-
    ness wronged.
Lear: Thou but rememberest me of mine own conception.
    I have perceived a most faint neglect of late, which   65

66-67   *mine own jealous curiosity:* my own watchful suspicion;
         pretence: deliberate showing

75   *Who am I, sir?:* Lear expects the reply "The King."

77   *My lord's knave:* Albany's boy or villain. Lear does not refer
         to Goneril again until she enters (line 184); *whoreson:* This
         word was used frequently in the rather generalized sense of
         base or low.
81   *Do you ... rascal?:* Do you dare to look me in the eye as an
         equal?
83   *football player?:* Football, an early form of soccer, played by
         boys in the street in Elizabeth's day, was regarded as a low
         game and the players were looked on as nuisances.
         Tripping was perhaps acceptable, as well as tackling, in
         this rough sport.
86   *differences:* in rank (between king and servant)
87-88   *If you ... tarry:* If you want to be knocked flat again, stay;
         lubber: a clumsy person
88   *Go to:* exclamation of impatience
88-89   *Have you wisdom?:* Have you sense enough to go (before
         you are flattened again)?
89   *So:* You have the sense to go (likely said as Oswald
         retreats).
91   *earnest:* sum paid in advance to make a bargain binding
92   *coxcomb:* the hat worn by professional jesters, red in colour
         and designed in the general shape of a cock's comb
94   *you were best:* It would be best for you (to take my hat).
96   *For ... favour:* because you are a fool to support someone
         who is out of favour
97-98   *Nay, an ... shortly:* If you cannot go along with prevailing
         opinion, you are sure to be in difficulty soon.
99   *banished:* Lear has made Goneril and Regan independent
         by dividing his kingdom and has therefore "banished" them
         from his former realm; *on's:* of his
100   *a blessing:* Cordelia is Queen of France, though Lear meant
         to punish her by banishment.

I have rather blamed as mine own jealous curiosity than
as a very pretence and purpose of unkindness. I will
look further into it. But where's my fool? I have not
seen him this two days.

Knight: Since my young lady's going into France, sir, the   70
fool hath much pined away.

Lear: No more of that; I have noted it well. Go you and
tell my daughter I would speak with her. [*Exit Knight.*]
Go you, call hither my fool.   [*Exit an Attendant.*]
[*Re-enter Steward.*]
O, you, sir, you! Come you hither, sir. Who am I, sir?   75

Oswald: My lady's father.

Lear: "My lady's father"? My lord's knave! You whoreson
dog! You slave! You cur!

Oswald: I am none of these, my lord! I beseech your
pardon.   80

Lear: Do you bandy looks with me, you rascal?
                                        [*Strikes him.*]

Oswald: I'll not be strucken, my lord.

Kent: Nor tripped neither, you base football player?
                                        [*Trips him.*]

Lear: I thank thee, fellow. Thou servest me, and I'll love
thee.   85

Kent: Come, sir, arise, away! I'll teach you differences.
Away, away! If you will measure your lubber's
length again, tarry; but away! Go to! Have you
wisdom? So.   [*Exit Oswald.*]

Lear: Now, my friendly knave, I thank thee.   90
[*Enter Fool.*]
There's earnest of thy service.   [*Gives Kent money.*]

Fool: Let me hire him too. Here's my coxcomb.
[*Offers Kent his cap.*]

Lear: How now, my pretty knave? How dost thou?

Fool: Sirrah, you were best take my coxcomb.

Kent: Why, fool?   95

Fool: Why? For taking one's part that's out of favour.
Nay, an thou canst not smile as the wind sits, thou'lt
catch cold shortly. There, take my coxcomb! Why,
this fellow has banished two on's daughters, and
did the third a blessing against his will. If thou follow   100

101	*thou must needs:* you absolutely must. "Needs" is emphatic.
102	*nuncle:* a contraction of mine uncle, or my uncle – perhaps as a child would say it or perhaps a familiar term used by a fool to his master
105-106	*If I ... myself:* If I gave my daughters all I owned, I'd be a fool (like you); *mine:* my coxcomb; *Beg:* Lear is now in the position of a beggar, totally dependent upon his daughters.
107	*the whip:* The Fool has gone far enough.
108	*must to kennel:* must go outside to the dog-house
109-110	*Lady Brach may ... stink:* "Lady" was a common name for a hound bitch; "Brach" was a polite term for all hound bitches. Here Lady Brach seems to symbolize flattery or lies. In other words, truth (what the Fool has said) is rejected but flattery and lies are welcomed.
111	*A pestilent gall:* literally, a bothersome or irritating sore (caused by rubbing). However, gall also refers to the secretion of the liver (bile) which is extremely bitter. The comment is likely a reference to Oswald's insolence as well as to the Fool's comments and, perhaps, even to Lear's own deeds.
117	*owest:* ownest (own)
115-124	*Have more ... score:* a string of wise sayings stressing the importance of common sense over impulsiveness
126-127	*Then 'tis ... it:* You get no advice from a lawyer without paying him a proper fee. You got nothing because you gave me nothing.
131-132	*so much ... to:* Since Lear has given away all his land, he can no longer expect to collect rent on it.
140	*for him stand:* stand in his place
137-144	*That lord ... there:* The Fool suggests that Lear is responsible for his own foolish action. He indicates that he is the "sweet" fool and that Lear is the "bitter" fool.

him, thou must needs wear my coxcomb.—How
now, nuncle? Would I had two coxcombs and two
daughters!
Lear: Why, my boy?
Fool: If I gave them all my living, I'd keep my coxcombs   105
myself. There's mine! Beg another of thy daughters.
Lear: Take heed, sirrah—the whip.
Fool: Truth's a dog must to kennel; he must be whipped
out, when the Lady Brach may stand by the fire and
stink.   110
Lear: A pestilent gall to me!
Fool: Sirrah, I'll teach thee a speech.
Lear: Do.
Fool: Mark it, nuncle.
      Have more than thou showest,   115
      Speak less than thou knowest,
      Lend less than thou owest,
      Ride more than thou goest,
      Learn more than thou trowest,
      Set less than thou throwest;   120
      Leave thy drink and thy whore,
      And keep in-a-door,
      And thou shalt have more
      Than two tens to a score.
Kent: This is nothing, fool.   125
Fool: Then 'tis like the breath of an unfeed lawyer—you
gave me nothing for it. Can you make no use of noth-
ing, nuncle?
Lear: Why, no, boy. Nothing can be made out of
nothing.   130
Fool: [*To Kent.*] Prithee tell him, so much the rent of his
land comes to. He will not believe a fool.
Lear: A bitter fool!
Fool: Dost thou know the difference, my boy, between a
bitter fool and a sweet one?   135
Lear: No, lad; teach me.
Fool: That lord that counselled thee
      To give away thy land,
    Come place him here by me—
      Do thou for him stand.   140

146	*that:* the title of fool; i.e., you are a born fool, in the sense of being innocent or naive
148	*fool:* foolish, meaningless
149	*will not let me:* will not let me keep all my foolishness for myself
150	*monopoly out ... part on't:* If I had the sole right to deal in foolishness, the lords and great men would share in it.
152	*snatching:* demanding their share. A common court corruption in Elizabethan times was the granting of monopolies in commodities of any kind, or with particular countries as a way of rewarding courtiers.
152-153	*Nuncle, give ... crowns:* a riddle
157	*clovest:* split
158	*thou borest ... dirt:* You acted like a man who carries his donkey instead of riding it.
159	*crown:* top of the head
160-161	*If ... so:* If I speak truth like a fool in saying this, let him be whipped who first finds it foolish.
162-165	*Fools had ... apish:* Fools are never in more disfavour than now, when even wise men have become foolish (foppish); and fools do not know how to behave, since the wise men have so closely imitated them; *apish:* imitative; like apes, which imitate
167	*sirrah:* used when speaking to servants or social inferiors, or as a term of insult to an equal
168-169	*madest thy daughters thy mother:* when you put yourself into the charge of your daughters, expecting them to care for you
169-170	*when thou ... breeches:* when you gave them the stick with which to punish you and took down your own trousers to be whipped
173	*play bo-peep:* play hide-and-seek. The implication is that Lear has covered his eyes as if playing the childhood game, and has put himself among the fools because of his foolish abdication.
176	*fain:* gladly, willingly
177	*An:* if

    The sweet and bitter fool
      Will presently appear;
    The one in motley here,
      The other found out there.
Lear: Dost thou call me fool, boy?   145
Fool: All thy other titles thou hast given away; that thou
    was born with.
Kent: This is not altogether fool, my lord.
Fool: No, faith; lords and great men will not let me. If I
    had a monopoly out, they would have part on't. And   150
    ladies too, they will not let me have all the fool to
    myself; they'll be snatching. Nuncle, give me an egg,
    and I'll give thee two crowns.
Lear: What two crowns shall they be?
Fool: Why, after I have cut the egg i' the middle and eat   155
    up the meat, the two crowns of the egg. When thou
    clovest thy crown i' the middle and gavest away both
    parts, thou borest thine ass on thy back o'er the dirt.
    Thou hadst little wit in thy bald crown when thou
    gavest thy golden one away. If I speak like myself in   160
    this, let him be whipped that first finds it so.
    [*Sings.*]   *Fools had ne'er less grace in a year,*
        For wise men are grown foppish;
      And know not how their wits to wear,
        Their manners are so apish.   165
Lear: When were you wont to be so full of songs,
    sirrah?
Fool: I have used it, nuncle, ever since thou madest thy
    daughters thy mother; for when thou gavest them the
    rod, and puttest down thine own breeches,   170
    [*Sings.*]*Then they for sudden joy did weep,*
        And I for sorrow sung,
      That such a king should play bo-peep
        And go the fools among.
    Prithee, nuncle, keep a schoolmaster that can teach   175
    thy fool to lie. I would fain learn to lie.
Lear: An you lie, sirrah, we'll have you whipped.
Fool: I marvel what kin thou and thy daughters are. They'll
    have me whipped for speaking true; thou'lt have me
    whipped for lying; and sometimes I am whipped for   180

181	*holding my peace:* keeping quiet
183	*pared:* cut away, peeled
184	*parings:* cuttings, peelings. The Fool refers to Goneril as one of the "cuttings" of Lear's mind; Regan is the other. Nothing remains of his mind according to the Fool.
185	*frontlet:* frown (a "frontlet" was a band worn around the head)
188-189	*an O without a figure:* the mathematical symbol (O) that denotes zero or nothing
194	*nor ... nor:* neither ... nor; *crum:* crumb. The couplet applies, as usual, to Lear.
196	*a shealed peascod:* a shelled or empty peapod – a quite useless thing, emptied of all value
197	*all-licensed:* allowed to do and say what he pleases
199	*carp:* complain
200	*rank:* gross, excessive, brutal; *riots:* fights
202	*redress:* correction, satisfaction
204-205	*protect ... allowance:* Permit this action and encourage it by your permission.
206	*scape censure:* escape sharp criticism; *nor the redresses sleep:* nor would the remedies fail to be applied
207	*tender:* desire (for); *wholesome weal:* healthy state
208	*working:* working out, outcome
209	*else:* otherwise; *were:* would be
205-210	*which if ... proceeding:* Goneril implies if you permit riotousness among your knights, I will place the blame squarely on you. My measures to control your men stem from my desire for a healthy state.
211-213	*For you ... young:* The cuckoo lays its eggs in other birds' nests. Once hatched, the cuckoo outgrows the other young birds by taking most of the food brought by its foster parents.
213	*it:* its
216-219	*I would ... are:* Goneril suggests that Lear's moods are more violent than usual.
217	*Whereof I ... fraught:* which I know you possess
218	*dispositions:* moods

holding my peace. I had rather be any kind o' thing
than a fool! And yet I would not be thee, nuncle.
Thou hast pared thy wit o' both sides and left nothing
i' the middle. Here comes one o' the parings.
[*Enter Goneril.*]
Lear: How now, daughter? What makes that frontlet on?   185
You are too much o' late i' the frown.
Fool: Thou wast a pretty fellow when thou hadst no need
to care for her frowning. Now thou art an O without
a figure. I am better than thou art now: I am a fool,
thou art nothing. [*To Goneril.*] Yes, forsooth, I will   190
hold my tongue. So your face bids me, though you say
nothing.
    Mum, mum!
    He that keeps nor crust nor crum,
    Weary of all, shall want some.—   195
[*Pointing at Lear.*] That's a shealed peascod.
Goneril: Not only, sir, this your all-licensed fool,
But other of your insolent retinue
Do hourly carp and quarrel, breaking forth
In rank and not-to-be-endured riots. Sir,   200
I had thought, by making this well known unto you,
To have found a safe redress; but now grow fearful,
By what yourself too late have spoke and done,
That you protect this course, and put it on
By your allowance: which if you should, the fault   205
Would not scape censure, nor the redresses sleep,
Which, in the tender of a wholesome weal,
Might in their working do you that offence
Which else were shame, that then necessity
Must call discreet proceeding.   210
Fool: For you know, nuncle,
    The hedge-sparrow fed the cuckoo so long
    That it had it head bit off by it young.
So out went the candle, and we were left darkling.
Lear: Are you our daughter?   215
Goneril: I would you would make use of your good wisdom,
Whereof I know you are fraught, and put away
These dispositions which of late transport you
From what you rightly are.

220	*May not ... horse?:* Even a fool may see that things are not right when a daughter instructs her father, a king
221	*Whoop, Jug, I love thee:* possibly an allusion to an old song. Jug, in this context, could mean "whore." In some Elizabethan poems, "Jug" is used to denote the sexual act.
224	*notion:* intellect, understanding; *discernings:* perception
225	*lethargied:* without life or energy, paralyzed; *Sleeping or waking?:* Am I asleep or awake?
228	*marks of sovereignty:* signs by which I know I am a king
229	*false:* falsely
231	*Which:* whom
233-234	*admiration:* pretence of amazement (pretence that he does not know who Goneril is); *the savour of:* the same as
240	*Shows like:* looks like; *riotous:* immoral; *Epicurism:* self-indulgence; *lust:* sexual desire
242	*graced:* honourable, gracious, noble
243	*Be then desired:* be requested
244	*else will ... begs:* otherwise will take into her own hands what she is now requesting
245	*A little ... train:* to reduce your following of knights some-what
246	*remainders:* those that remain; *depend:* stay on as dependants
247	*besort:* be fitting for, suit
248	*Darkness and devils:* an explosion of rage
249	*train:* followers
250	*Degenerate bastard:* Lear means that Goneril has not only become base, but cannot be his lawful daughter.
252	*strike:* hit; *people:* household servants; *disordered rabble:* disorderly knights
253	*betters:* those who are better than they themselves are. The reference is to Goneril's servants.
254	*Woe that too late repents:* woe to whoever repents (of his action) too late

Fool: May not an ass know when the cart draws the horse?　220
　　Whoop, Jug, I love thee!
Lear: Does any here know me? This is not Lear.
　　Does Lear walk thus? Speak thus? Where are his eyes?
　　Either his notion weakens, or his discernings
　　Are lethargied—Sleeping or waking? Ha! Sure 'tis not
　　　　so!　225
　　Who is it that can tell me who I am?
Fool: Lear's shadow.
Lear: I would learn that; for, by the marks of sovereignty,
　　Knowledge, and reason, I should be false persuaded
　　I had daughters.　230
Fool: Which they will make an obedient father.
Lear: Your name, fair gentlewoman?
Goneril: This admiration, sir, is much o' the savour
　　Of other your new pranks. I do beseech you
　　To understand my purposes aright.　235
　　As you are old and reverend, you should be wise.
　　Here do you keep a hundred knights and squires;
　　Men so disordered, so debauched, and bold
　　That this our court, infected with their manners,
　　Shows like a riotous inn. Epicurism and lust　240
　　Make it more like a tavern or a brothel
　　Than a graced palace. The shame itself doth speak
　　For instant remedy. Be then desired
　　By her that else will take the thing she begs
　　A little to disquantity your train,　245
　　And the remainders that shall still depend
　　To be such men as may besort your age,
　　Which know themselves and you.
Lear:　　　　　　　　　　　Darkness and devils!
　　Saddle my horses! Call my train together!
　　Degenerate bastard, I'll not trouble thee;　250
　　Yet have I left a daughter.
Goneril: You strike my people, and your disordered rabble
　　Make servants of their betters.
　　[*Enter Albany.*]
Lear: Woe that too late repents!—O, sir, are you come?
　　Is it your will? Speak, sir!—Prepare my horses.　255
　　Ingratitude, thou marble-hearted fiend,

258	*sea-monster:* probably a reference to the various fearsome monsters that appear in Greek mythology
259	*kite:* bird of prey of the hawk family. Some species are scavengers, hence, the reference to Goneril.
260	*of choice and rarest parts:* of the best and most unusual accomplishments
261	*particulars:* details
262-263	*in the ... name:* are most conscientious in living up to the reputation that they have established
263	*most small fault:* What Lear had considered Cordelia's fault now seems petty and unimportant.
265	*an engine:* a crowbar or lever; *wrenched my frame of nature:* twisted or tore my real nature
267	*gall:* bitterness
272	*Nature:* in this context, goddess of fruitfulness—nature as a creative force
276	*increase:* birth
277	*derogate:* debased, corrupt
278	*teem:* become pregnant
279	*spleen:* malice
280	*thwart disnatured torment:* perverse unnatural ordeal
282	*cadent:* falling; *fret channels:* wear marks
283	*pains and benefits:* cares for her child
286	*Away, away:* addressed to all who are near
288	*afflict:* trouble
289	*disposition:* mood; *scope:* freedom
290	*dotage:* senility, second childhood
291	*at a clap?:* all at once, at one blow

More hideous when thou showest thee in a child
Than the sea-monster!
Albany: Pray, sir, be patient.
Lear: [*To Goneril*] Detested kite, thou liest!
My train are men of choice and rarest parts,   260
That all particulars of duty know
And in the most exact regard support
The worships of their name.—O most small fault,
How ugly didst thou in Cordelia show!
Which, like an engine, wrenched my frame of nature   265
From the fixed place; drew from my heart all love
And added to the gall. O Lear, Lear, Lear!
Beat at this gate that let thy folly in
                    [*Beats his forehead with his fist.*]
And thy dear judgement out! Go, go, my people.
Albany: My lord, I am guiltless, as I am ignorant   270
Of what hath moved you.
Lear: It may be so, my lord.
Hear, Nature, hear! Dear goddess, hear!
Suspend thy purpose, if thou didst intend
To make this creature fruitful.
Into her womb convey sterility;   275
Dry up in her the organs of increase;
And from her derogate body never spring
A babe to honour her! If she must teem,
Create her child of spleen, that it may live
And be a thwart disnatured torment to her.   280
Let it stamp wrinkles in her brow of youth,
With cadent tears fret channels in her cheeks,
Turn all her mother's pains and benefits
To laughter and contempt, that she may feel
How sharper than a serpent's tooth it is   285
To have a thankless child! Away, away!   [*Exit.*]
Albany: Now, gods that we adore, whereof comes this?
Goneril: Never afflict yourself to know more of it,
But let his disposition have that scope
As dotage gives it.   290
[*Re-enter Lear.*]
Lear: What, fifty of my followers at a clap?
Within a fortnight?

294	*shake my manhood thus:* so disturb my manly dignity
295	*perforce:* forcibly, whether I will them or not
293-296	*I am ... them:* Lear is anguished at the thought that Goneril can make him weep.
296	*Blasts and fogs:* Wind and fog, apart from their discomfort, were thought to carry illness with them; hence, the curse.
297	*Th' untented woundings:* raw, open wounds. If a wound were "untented," foreign matter would be left in the flesh, and the wound would fester.
298	*fond:* foolish
299	*Beweep this cause:* if you (the eyes) should weep again because of Goneril's treatment
300	*cast:* throw away; *waters that you loose:* tears that you release
301	*temper:* moisten for mixing
303	*comfortable:* willing to give me comfort
305	*flay:* tear away the skin
306	*the shape:* the former stature or rank
309-310	*I cannot ... you:* Albany feels he must protest, despite his love for Goneril.
311	*content:* be quiet
314-315	*Take the fool with thee:* Take the Fool and your folly or foolishness.
316-320	*A fox ... after:* Even a fool would buy a rope to hang a fox, or a daughter like Goneril, if she were caught. Thus the Fool follows the old master rather than remaining where such creatures are; *halter:* hangman's noose
321	*This man ... counsel:* Lear has been well-advised.
322	*politic:* good policy
322-326	*'Tis politic ... mercy:* Goneril's ironical words seem to be directed towards the more tolerant attitude of her husband.
323-324	*At point:* fully armed and ready for action; *buzz:* whisper; *that on ... dislike:* that on any possible pretext Lear may use their strength to permit him to do as he pleases
325	*enguard:* protect; *dotage:* senility
327	*Well, you ... far:* Albany protests mildly against Goneril's anger.

Albany: What's the matter, sir?
Lear: I'll tell thee. [*To Goneril.*] Life and death! I am
     ashamed
  That thou hast power to shake my manhood thus;
  That these hot tears, which break from me perforce,   295
  Should make thee worth them. Blasts and fogs upon thee!
  Th' untented woundings of a father's curse
  Pierce every sense about thee!—Old fond eyes,
  Beweep this cause again, I'll pluck ye out,
  And cast you, with the waters that you loose,   300
  To temper clay. Yea, is it come to this?
  Ha! Let it be so. I have another daughter,
  Who I am sure is kind and comfortable.
  When she shall hear this of thee, with her nails
  She'll flay thy wolvish visage. Thou shalt find   305
  That I'll resume the shape which thou dost think
  I have cast off for ever.
                    [*Exeunt Lear, Kent, and Attendants.*]
Goneril: Do you mark that, my lord?
Albany: I cannot be so partial, Goneril,
  To the great love I bear you—   310
Goneril: Pray you, content.—What, Oswald, ho!
  [*To the Fool.*] You, sir, more knave than fool, after your
     master!
Fool: Nuncle Lear, nuncle Lear, tarry! Take the fool with
     thee.   315
          A fox, when one has caught her,
          And such a daughter,
          Should sure to the slaughter,
          If my cap would buy a halter.
          So the fool follows after.   [*Exit.*]   320
Goneril: This man hath had good counsel! A hundred
     knights?
  'Tis politic and safe to let him keep
  At point a hundred knights; yes, that on every dream,
  Each buzz, each fancy, each complaint, dislike,
  He may enguard his dotage with their powers   325
  And hold our lives in mercy.—Oswald, I say!
Albany: Well, you may fear too far.

328   *still:* always; *harms:* dangers

331   *sustain him:* keeps him as a guest
332   *unfitness:* unsuitability (of doing so) or unfitness of Lear as
        a house guest; *How now:* a common salutation or greeting.

336   *full:* fully

338   *compact:* complete or make (it) more convincing; add to its
        substance
340   *This milky gentleness and course:* this mild and gentle
        approach
341   *under pardon:* pardon me for saying so
342   *more at task for:* more likely to be taken to task for; *want:* lack
343   *Than praised for harmful mildness:* than you are likely to be
        praised for dangerous mildness.
344   *How far ... tell:* What particular insight you may have, I do
        not know.
345   *Striving to ... well:* better to leave well enough alone
347   *event:* outcome, in the sense of "we shall see what will
        happen"

Goneril: Safer than trust too far.
  Let me still take away the harms I fear,
  Not fear still to be taken. I know his heart.
  What he hath uttered I have writ my sister.   330
  If she sustain him and his hundred knights,
  When I have showed the unfitness—
  [*Enter Steward.*]   How now, Oswald?
  What, have you writ that letter to my sister?
Oswald: Yes, madam.
Goneril: Take you some company, and away to horse!   335
  Inform her full of my particular fear,
  And thereto add such reasons of your own
  As may compact it more. Get you gone,
  And hasten your return. [*Exit Oswald.*] No, no, my lord!
  This milky gentleness and course of yours,   340
  Though I condemn not, yet, under pardon,
  You are much more at task for want of wisdom
  Than praised for harmful mildness.
Albany: How far your eyes may pierce I cannot tell.
  Striving to better, oft we mar what's well.   345
Goneril: Nay then—
Albany: Well, well; the event.   [*Exeunt.*]

Act 1, Scene 4: Activities

1. You are King Lear. Write a letter to your daughter Regan explaining why you think it is time for you to move to her castle. Explain the ways in which you are being mistreated by Goneril and her husband, and what your feelings are about this situation. State clearly why you believe that Regan's behaviour towards you will be much better than Goneril's. You may find it helpful to refer to Act 1, Scene 1.

2. You are Goneril. Suddenly your father and one hundred of his knights arrive at your palace. How do you entertain them? How do you house them and feed them? What concerns do you have? What anxieties do you experience? Create a conversation with your household steward, Oswald, incorporating the questions above. Insert the conversation at a logical place in the act to this point.

3. As Goneril you have been entertaining your father and his knights for some time. Although your father is dependent on your hospitality, he treats your household as his own. Write a letter to your sister Regan providing her with information about recent occurrences at your house. Give her some specific advice for dealing with your father who, you warn her, is on his way to reside at her household.

4. In this scene, the Fool sings several fragments of songs (or perhaps fragments of the same song), the origins of which are obscure, but the sense of them is clear. Complete this song, or one fragment of a song, or create one of your own that accomplishes the Fool's intent. In your journal, note what effect the songs have in the context of the dialogue and why songs are important to the scene as a whole.

5. As Kent, prepare a speech that would explain to a friend why you would want to serve a man who just banished you from his kingdom. Outline the risks you are taking, should you be discovered.

6. In a group, prepare a dramatic presentation of the scene segment in which Lear questions Kent about his allegiance (lines 11–34). The object is to make the action underscore the themes you want to emphasize, as well as to reveal the differences in character.

7. In this scene, we are given no indication of what the Duke of Albany's castle is like, or even where it is. With a partner or in a group, discuss what the setting might look like for a stage production of this scene. Remember to use whatever details you can from the scene. Consider how the castle and the surroundings might appear. What would the weather be like? How would you convey this through the use of lighting? The illustration on page 48 may give you some ideas. Create a sketch of your set and display it for others in the class to comment upon.

8. Select one character from this scene and follow him or her throughout the play. As you read, make a note of key words, phrases, or lines that reveal key information about your character. Make sure that you include the act, scene, and line so that you can easily trace character development. Use many strategies such as the following to help you organize: columns, a map, a character sunburst, or a chart. At the end of the play, prepare a two-minute monologue that reveals the important aspects of your character and present it to a group or to the class.

For the next scene ...

In your journal, write about a time when friends were unjust to you but you realized that, perhaps, the injustice was brought about by something you had done to one of them. How did you feel? What did you do?

Act 1, Scene 5

In this scene ...

Lear's retinue has been reduced to only his most loyal
followers. The old king instructs Kent to deliver a letter
he has written to his daughter Regan in the town of
Gloucester, informing her of Lear's imminent arrival.
He cautions Kent to tell Regan no more than what is
contained in the letter. The Fool continues to remind
Lear of his mistakes, and, as he realizes what has
happened to him, Lear begins to feel the approach of
madness. At the end of the scene, Lear departs for
Regan's household.

1	*before:* ahead; *Gloucester:* the town; *these letters:* this letter
2-3	*Acquaint my ... letter:* Tell my daughter no more than she asks (her demand) as a result of my letter
3-5	*If your ... you:* If you do not hurry, I shall be there before you.
8	*in's:* in his
9	*kibes:* sores caused by rubbing, or chilblains (inflammations of the hands and feet caused by exposure to cold and moisture)
11	*I prithee:* I beg you (literally, I pray you)
12	*slipshod:* wearing slippers or slip shoes. The Fool probably means: You will never have to wear slippers because of chilblains since you have no intelligence, even in your heels, as your journey to Regan shows.
14	*kindly:* a pun, both in an affectionate way and after her kind (according to her nature)
15	*she's as ... apple:* She's as much like her sister as a crabapple is like an apple. (Both are apples but the crabapple is sour and wild.)
16	*I can ... tell:* I know a thing or two about what will happen.
18	*She'll taste ... crab:* She (Regan) will treat you in the same way as Goneril did.

Scene 5

*A courtyard of the Duke of
Albany's palace.*

Enter Lear, Kent, and Fool.

Lear: Go you before to Gloucester with these letters.
Acquaint my daughter no further with anything you
know than comes from her demand out of the letter. If
your diligence be not speedy, I shall be there
afore you.   5
Kent: I will not sleep, my lord, till I have delivered your
letter.   [*Exit.*]
Fool: If a man's brains were in's heels, were it not in danger
of kibes?
Lear: Ay, boy.   10
Fool: Then I prithee be merry. Thy wit shall not go
slipshod.
Lear: Ha, ha, ha!
Fool: Shalt see thy other daughter will use thee kindly; for
though she's as like this as a crab's like an apple,   15
yet I can tell what I can tell.
Lear: What canst tell, boy?
Fool: She'll taste as like this as a crab does to a crab. Thou
canst tell why one's nose stands i' the middle on's
face?   20
Lear: No.
Fool: Why, to keep one's eyes of either side's nose, that
what a man cannot smell out, he may spy into.
Lear: I did her wrong.
Fool: Canst tell how an oyster makes his shell?   25
Lear: No.
Fool: Nor I neither; but I can tell why a snail has a
house.
Lear: Why?

31	*horns:* sign of a cuckolded husband (a husband deceived by his wife) – a favourite Elizabethan butt of humour. Here, the horns seem to suggest the condition of men in general, in that they are made fools of or tricked by women.
32	*forget my nature:* cease to be a kind father
35	*seven stars:* the Pleiades, a cluster of stars in the constellation Taurus; *mo:* more; *pretty:* apt, appropriate

38	*To take it again perforce:* Lear may be thinking about resuming his royalty with the help of Cornwall and Regan. Alternatively, he is thinking about Goneril's ingratitude for taking away the privileges she had earlier agreed to give him.
42-43	*Though shouldst ... wise:* Lear is old enough to be wise but is, instead, a great fool.
44-45	*O, let ... mad:* the first sense of the onset of madness; *in temper:* sane

| 49-50 | *She that's ... shorter:* The Fool, turning to the audience, and perhaps imitating Lear, says in effect: Any young girl who cannot see that the King's departure is a sad one, and merely laughs at his unhappy state, is too stupid to retain her virginity for long, unless men are incapable of seduction. |

Fool: Why, to put's head in; not to give it away to his   30
    daughters, and leave, his horns without a case.
Lear: I will forget my nature. So kind a father!—Be my
    horses ready?
Fool: Thy asses are gone about 'em. The reason why the
    seven stars are no mo than seven is a pretty reason.   35
Lear: Because they are not eight?
Fool: Yes indeed. Thou wouldst make a good fool.
Lear: To take it again perforce! Monster ingratitude!
Fool: If thou wert my fool, nuncle, I'd have thee beaten
    for being old before thy time.   40
Lear: How's that?
Fool: Thou shouldst not have been old till thou hadst been
    wise.
Lear: O, let me not be mad, not mad, sweet heaven! Keep
    me in temper; I would not be mad!   45
    [*Enter a Gentleman.*]
    How now? Are the horses ready?
Gentleman: Ready, my lord.
Lear: Come, boy.
Fool: She that's a maid now, and laughs at my departure,
    Shall not be a maid long, unless things be cut shorter.   50
                              [*Exeunt.*]

Act 1, Scene 5: Activities

1. Brainstorm with your group and write the letter that Lear has Kent deliver to Regan. Share your letter with other groups. How do the letters differ in content?

2. Extract the Fool's speeches from this scene and, with a partner, summarize what he says. Does the Fool make any sense to you? In your opinion, does he make any sense to Lear?

3. As the host of a talk show, role-play an interview with the Fool. Prepare a list of questions to ask him, the answers to which should reveal his true feelings about Lear and his own role in the play. Does he offer any straightforward answers?

4. Suppose you are a reporter for a major newspaper. Write the report you would send back to your newspaper based on the events that occur in Act 1. Remember, you will probably be limited by space so you may have to be selective. Remember too that a good reporter attempts to be objective, relating facts without personal comment. Before you write, gather and select your facts. Share your article with others in the class.

5. If, as a character, you could intervene in this scene, what might you say to Lear? With a partner, role-play the conversations you might have, alternating the roles of Lear and the intervener.

6. Create an alternative rhyming couplet of your own to end this scene. Remember to keep the context of the scene. Share your couplet with the rest of the class.

7. In groups, discuss whether or not it would be possible to cut this scene from the play. Prepare as strong an argument as possible and share it with the rest of the class.

Act 1: Consider the Whole Act

1. You are a servant in Goneril's household. You have decided to apply for a job at another castle. Prepare your résumé, and think about the answers to the following questions that you may be asked in an interview:
   - How long have you been working for Goneril?
   - Why is your job important to this household?
   - Do you need any special training to do your job?
   - Do you get along with others in the household?
   - What have your duties been recently? Describe a typical day.
   - What has led to your decision to seek alternative employment?

   You have asked your supervisor for a reference; what might he or she say? If you returned to Goneril with a new offer of employment, how do you think she would react? If you get this job, what will you tell your new co-workers about the way Goneril treats her father?

   Share your résumé with a partner, or, with a partner, role-play an interview, taking turns as interviewer and servant.

2. The Fool often speaks in riddles, many of which are very puzzling. Make a list of some of your favourite riddles in this act and explain how they fit into the segments of the play in which they appear.

   Create a riddle of your own and place it in an appropriate place in one of the scenes from this act. Have a partner attempt to answer your riddle, and be prepared to explain why you think your riddle is appropriate for the play and for the place you have chosen to insert it.

   Share some of your riddles with the rest of the class.

3. When Lear feels he has been wronged by his daughters, he flies into uncontrollable rages and curses them vehemently. As Lear, write a letter to an advice column explaining your anger with your daughters and why you feel you are justified in feeling this way. Give your letter to a partner who, acting as the columnist, will reply to your letter.

4. It is obvious that the characters in this play have some basic family problems. Imagine you are a social worker or counsellor who might offer advice to Lear or to Gloucester about ways to keep families together. Select one of these two characters and, in your journal, consider what you think went wrong in his family life and what some possible solutions might be.

5. Some of the Fool's responses are in the form of songs – pop songs of his own time. Select two or three of the Fool's songs and substitute some modern lyrics that would be appropriate. Would music enhance or detract from the mood of the play?

   Prepare a narrative version or reading of a segment of the play in which you insert one of your pop songs in place of one used by the Fool. You may wish to present or make a video of the segment and have the class comment on the success of your production.

6. Some directors have argued that the character of the Fool adds nothing to the essence of the play and could easily be cut without damaging the overall impact. From what you have experienced so far, to what extent could you justify such an argument? If you agree, how would you make the transitions in order to exclude the Fool? If you disagree, what would be your argument for leaving the play as it is? Share these observations with your group or with the rest of the class.

7. You have been transported into Lear's world and have been given the opportunity to interview one character from this act. You are permitted to ask only ten questions of that character in order to find out whatever information you wish to know. Remember, the more carefully worded the questions, the more revealing the response.

8. The first act of this play is fairly static. With your group or with a partner, prepare a written sketch or story board in which you show what you would do to maintain audience interest and keep the play moving.

9. Create a landscape in a painting or a collage that conveys the mood of Act 1 of *King Lear*, and give it a title. What will you choose as the focus of your landscape or collage to convey your sense of the atmosphere? Remember that the landscape need not be realistic.

10. There are many references to mythological gods in this act. Find out as much as you can about these figures. What significance do they have to Lear in this act? To which ones does he refer? Why do you think he invokes them on a fairly regular basis? Do these figures mean anything at all to us today? Explain your response.

11. Have each member of your group select one of the major characters in this scene and create a mask for that character. As a group, create a mime in which you act out a portion of the scene in which your characters appear. Your aim is to convey the action and theme of the sequence to the audience.

For the next scene ...

How do you respond to the idea that the end justifies the means – that is, any action is justifiable as long as it achieves the desired goal? What do you think of deception as a means of achieving an end?

Act 2, Scene 1

In this scene ...

This scene takes place at Gloucester's castle. Edmund proceeds with his plan to trick Gloucester into believing that Edgar is seeking his life. He first convinces Edgar to flee for his safety since the arrival of Regan and Cornwall is imminent. While he is alone Edmund stabs himself, planning to say that Edgar attacked him when Edmund refused to help in Gloucester's murder. When Gloucester enters and hears Edmund's accusations, he promises to give Edmund an inheritance which should have been Edgar's.

Regan and the Duke of Cornwall arrive, seeking Gloucester's support in a dispute that has arisen between Albany and Cornwall over their rights to the kingdom. In addition, Regan claims to have left her palace as a means of avoiding Lear.

Regan suggests that Edgar's actions can be blamed on the influence of Lear's "riotous knights." Edmund supports her suggestion and then wins Cornwall's favour when Gloucester describes his apparent loyalty. Regan tells Gloucester that she needs his advice to deal with the conflict that has occurred between Goneril and King Lear.

Scene Description — *severally:* separately, i.e., they meet as if coming from different parts of Gloucester's castle

1   *Save thee:* God save you—a common greeting; *Curan:* his only appearance in this scene. He seems to be a member of Gloucester's household, but in an unspecified capacity.

7   *abroad:* the current news of the world
8   *ear-bussing:* literally, ear kissing, as in "whispered"; *arguments?:* subjects of conversation, here likely in the sense of opinions
10   *toward:* imminent, about to occur; *'twixt:* betwixt, between

15   *weaves itself perforce:* joins in naturally and inevitably; *business:* plot
17   *of a queasy question:* that needs to be handled delicately. Queasy means nauseous and is intended to suggest the delicacy with which such a condition must be treated.
18   *act:* accomplish; *Briefness:* speed or quick action; *Briefness and fortune, work:* May swift action and good luck help to bring me success.
19   *Brother, a ... say:* Edmund calls out to his brother.
20   *watches:* keeps watch; *fly:* escape from
21   *Intelligence:* information (the military sense of "intelligence")
24   *i' the haste:* in a great hurry

26   *Upon his party:* criticizing his dispute
27   *Advise yourself:* consider, try to recall; *on't:* of it

Act 2, Scene 1

A courtyard inside
Gloucester's castle.
Enter Edmund the Bastard and
Curan, severally.

Edmund: Save thee, Curan.
Curan: And you, sir. I have been with your father, and given
   him notice that the Duke of Cornwall and Regan his
   Duchess will be here with him this night.
Edmund: How comes that?   5
Curan: Nay, I know not. You have heard of the news
   abroad—I mean the whispered ones, for they are yet
   but ear-bussing arguments?
Edmund: Not I. Pray you, what are they?
Curan: Have you heard of no likely wars toward 'twixt the   10
   Dukes of Cornwall and Albany?
Edmund: Not a word.
Curan: You may do, then, in time. Fare you well, sir.
                                                                      [*Exit.*]
Edmund: The Duke be here tonight? The better! Best!
   This weaves itself perforce into my business.   15
   My father hath set guard to take my brother;
   And I have one thing, of a queasy question,
   Which I must act. Briefness and fortune, work!
   Brother, a word! Descend! Brother, I say!
   [*Enter Edgar.*]
   My father watches. O sir, fly this place!   20
   Intelligence is given where you are hid.
   You have now the good advantage of the night.
   Have you not spoken 'gainst the Duke of Cornwall?
   He's coming hither; now, i' the night, i' the haste,
   And Regan with him. Have you nothing said   25
   Upon his party 'gainst the Duke of Albany?
   Advise yourself.

29	*In cunning:* as a clever trick, so that we don't appear to be working together; thus, a trick to fool Gloucester
31	*Yield:* surrender; *before:* in front of
32	*So farewell:* likely an expression of satisfaction
33-34	*would beget ... endeavour:* would make people believe that I have had a terrible fight
34-35	*I have ... sport:* Young men under the influence of alcohol, in order to prove their worthiness and commitment, would frequently wound themselves and then drink to the health of their mistresses in a mixture of their own blood and whatever it was they were drinking.
39-40	*Mumbling of ... mistress:* The crescent moon was associated with the horned goddess (*auspicious*, favourable) of witchcraft. Edmund is playing on Gloucester's superstitious beliefs.
41	*Look, sir, I bleed:* a ploy to get Gloucester's attention and to allow Edgar to escape
42	*Fled this way, sir:* Edmund points in the wrong direction.
45	*that:* when
46	*parricides:* the actual murders of fathers by their sons; *bend:* direct
47	*manifold and strong:* Both words have the same meaning.
48	*in fine:* finally
49	*loathly opposite:* hatefully opposed
50	*unnatural:* It is not natural for son to murder father; *in fell motion:* with a deadly thrust (a fencing term)
51-52	*prepared:* already drawn; *charges home my unprovided body:* thrust his sword straight at my defenceless body; *launched:* lanced, pierced
53	*best alarumed spirits:* my spirit, aroused to its highest pitch
54	*Bold in the quarrel's right:* made bold by the justice of my cause
55	*gasted:* terrified, panic-stricken
56	*Full:* quite
58	*And found—dispatch:* And when he's found, kill him.
59	*arch and patron:* chief protector

Edgar: I am sure on't, not a word.
Edmund: I hear my father coming. Pardon me!
  In cunning I must draw my sword upon you.
  Draw, seem to defend yourself; now quit you well.—   30
  Yield! Come before my father. Light, ho, here!
  Fly, brother.—Torches, torches!—So farewell.
                              [*Exit Edgar.*]
  Some blood drawn on me would beget opinion
  Of my more fierce endeavour. [*Stabs his arm.*] I have seen
    drunkards
  Do more than this in sport.—Father, father!—   35
  Stop, stop! No help?
  [*Enter Gloucester, and Servants with torches.*]
Gloucester: Now, Edmund, where's the villain?
Edmund: Here stood he in the dark, his sharp sword out,
  Mumbling of wicked charms, conjuring the moon
  To stand auspicious mistress.
Gloucester: But where is he?   40
Edmund: Look, sir, I bleed.
Gloucester: Where is the villain, Edmund?
Edmund: Fled this way, sir. When by no means he could—
Gloucester: Pursue him, ho! Go after. [*Exeunt some
    Servants.*] By no means what?
Edmund: Persuade me to the murder of your lordship;
  But that I told him the revenging gods   45
  'Gainst parricides did all the thunder bend;
  Spoke with how manifold and strong a bond
  The child was bound to the father—sir, in fine,
  Seeing how loathly opposite I stood
  To his unnatural purpose, in fell motion   50
  With his prepared sword he charges home
  My unprovided body, launched mine arm;
  And when he saw my best alarumed spirits,
  Bold in the quarrel's right, roused to the encounter,
  Or whether gasted by the noise I made,   55
  Full suddenly he fled.
Gloucester: Let him fly far.
  Not in this land shall he remain uncaught;
  And found—dispatch. The noble Duke my master,
  My worthy arch and patron, comes tonight.

61	*thanks:* gratitude – and reward
62	*to the stake:* to the place of his execution or to death

65	*pight:* determined; *curst:* strong, angry
66	*discover:* denounce, reveal his intentions
67	*unpossessing:* landless, without property
68-70	*If I ... faithed?:* Do you think if I denied your accusations, that any trust, virtue, or value in your character would cause your words to be believed instead of mine?; *faithed?:* believed
72-73	*My very character:* my own handwriting; *turn it all ... practice:* twist matters so that it all seemed to be your idea; *suggestion:* evil instigation; *damned practice:* treachery
74-77	*thou must ... it:* You must assume that people are stupid indeed if they do not think you would benefit from my death; *pregnant:* obvious; *potential:* powerful, compelling

77	*strange:* unnatural; *fastened:* hardened
78	*letter:* Gloucester refers to the letter in Act 1, Scene 2; *I never got him:* I never begot him; i.e., I could not be the father of such a son.

Stage Direction – *Tucket:* a special trumpet call identifying a particular party (here, Cornwall)

80	*ports:* seaports; *villain:* Edgar
81	*picture:* drawing, with a description
84	*natural boy:* Illegitimate children were called this because they were conceived by natural desire.
85	*capable:* able to inherit (his father's property)

87	*I have heard strange news:* i.e., of Edgar's alleged plot
88	*all vengeance comes too short:* Total revenge is not enough.

91	*godson:* Regan seems to suggest that Lear has had some influence on Edgar's character.
92	*He whom my father named?:* the son, whom Lear named Edgar
93	*it:* that Edgar is Lear's godson

By his authority I will proclaim it,   60
That he which finds him shall deserve our thanks,
Bringing the murderous coward to the stake;
He that conceals him, death.
Edmund: When I dissuaded him from his intent
And found him pight to do it, with curst speech   65
I threatened to discover him. He replied,
"Thou unpossessing bastard, dost thou think,
If I would stand against thee, would the reposal
Of any trust, virtue, or worth in thee
Make thy words faithed? No. What I should deny   70
(As this I would; ay, though thou didst produce
My very character), I'd turn it all
To thy suggestion, plot, and damned practice;
And thou must make a dullard of the world,
If they not thought the profits of my death   75
Were very pregnant and potential spirits
To make thee seek it."
Gloucester: O strange and fastened villain!
Would he deny his letter, said he? I never got him.
[*Tucket within.*]
Hark, the Duke's trumpets! I know not why he comes.
All ports I'll bar; the villain shall not scape;   80
The Duke must grant me that. Besides, his picture
I will send far and near, that all the kingdom
May have due note of him, and of my land,
Loyal and natural boy, I'll work the means
To make thee capable.   85
[*Enter Cornwall, Regan, and Attendants.*]
Cornwall: How now, my noble friend? Since I came hither
(Which I can call but now) I have heard strange news.
Regan: If it be true, all vengeance comes too short
Which can pursue the offender. How dost, my lord?
Gloucester: O madam, my old heart is cracked, it's cracked!   90
Regan: What, did my father's godson seek your life?
He whom my father named? Your Edgar?
Gloucester: O lady, lady, shame would have it hid!
Regan: Was he not companion with the riotous knights
That tended upon my father?   95
Gloucester: I know not, madam. 'Tis too bad, too bad!

97	*consort:* company. The word is often used as a term of contempt.
98	*though he were ill affected:* that he would be made disloyal
99	*'Tis they ... death:* They (Lear's riotous knights) have incited him to seek Gloucester's life.
100	*the expense and waste:* the privilege of spending and squandering; *revenues:* income
101	*present:* same
102	*them:* the riotous knights
106	*A childlike office:* a filial duty, obligation of a son
107	*bewray his practice:* reveal his evil schemes (i.e., Edgar's plot)
111-112	*Make your ... please:* Carry out your plans for his capture and use my authority any way you please for that purpose.
113	*virtue and obedience:* virtuous obedience
113-114	*doth this ... itself:* is to be so greatly commended or praised; *ours:* under our protection and patronage
116	*seize on:* engage in our service
117	*however else:* however inadequate I might be in other respects
119	*threading dark-eyed night:* making our way through the darkness as though it were the eye of a needle
120	*Occasions:* situations; *prize:* importance
123	*differences:* disputes, quarrels
124	*answer from our home:* give my answer away from home
125	*From ... dispatch:* are waiting to be sent from here
126-127	*Lay comforts to your bosom:* Be comforted; *bestow your ... businesses:* Give your essential advice to us for our (political) affairs.
128	*Which craves the instant use:* which must be put into effect immediately

Stage Direction – *Flourish:* fanfare of trumpets to mark and honour the exit of important people

Edmund: Yes, madam, he was of that consort.
Regan: No marvel then though he were ill affected.
  'Tis they have put him on the old man's death,
  To have the expense and waste of his revenues.   100
  I have this present evening from my sister
  Been well informed of them, and with such cautions
  That, if they come to sojourn at my house,
  I'll not be there.
Cornwall: Nor I, assure thee, Regan.
  Edmund, I hear that you have shown your father   105
  A childlike office.
Edmund: 'Twas my duty, sir.
Gloucester: He did bewray his practice, and received
  This hurt you see, striving to apprehend him.
Cornwall: Is he pursued?
Gloucester: Ay, my good lord.
Cornwall: If he be taken, he shall never more   110
  Be feared of doing harm. Make your own purpose,
  How in my strength you please. For you, Edmund,
  Whose virtue and obedience doth this instant
  So much commend itself, you shall be ours.
  Natures of such deep trust we shall much need;   115
  You we first seize on.
Edmund: I shall serve you, sir,
  Truly, however else.
Gloucester: For him I thank your Grace.
Cornwall: You know not why we came to visit you—
Regan: Thus out of season, threading dark-eyed night.
  Occasions, noble Gloucester, of some prize,   120
  Wherein we must have use of your advice.
  Our father he hath writ, so hath our sister,
  Of differences, which I best thought it fit
  To answer from our home. The several messengers
  From hence attend dispatch. Our good old friend,   125
  Lay comforts to your bosom, and bestow
  Your needful counsel to our businesses,
  Which craves the instant use.
Gloucester: I serve you, madam.
  Your Graces are right welcome.   [*Exeunt. Flourish.*]

Act 2, Scene 1: Activities

1. Create an editorial cartoon or a panel of cartoons that you think would be appropriate to convey the consequences of Gloucester's response to Edmund's "news."

2. Create a soliloquy for Edmund in which he reviews the plans he has made to trick his father and his brother in order to gain Cornwall's favour. Where would you insert the soliloquy in this scene?

3. From what you have seen of Gloucester so far, what kind of father do you think he is? In your journal, first as Edgar and then as Edmund, tell Gloucester what you think of his attitude towards you.

4. Regan blames Lear's knights for Edgar's strange behaviour. Why do you suppose she does? Write a short speech in which you respond to Regan.

5. Cornwall begins to explain to Gloucester the reasons for his visit (line 118), but it is Regan who finishes the speech. In your journal, write your observations about the relationship between Cornwall and Regan.

   If this was the only segment of the scene between Gloucester, Cornwall, and Regan that you were to observe, what conclusions would you draw about the events that have transpired in the play so far? Prepare a report that makes your observations clear.

For the next scene ...

In your journal describe an experience in which you thought that being frank and honest was the correct approach to solving a problem. What happened?

Act 2, Scene 2

In this scene ...

Outside Gloucester's castle Oswald and Kent meet again, although Oswald does not appear to recognize Kent. Kent is still angry with Oswald for his wretched behaviour to King Lear and attacks him both verbally and physically. The resulting skirmish and Oswald's cries for help bring Cornwall, Regan, Gloucester, and a host of servants to see what is the matter. For his abuse of Oswald and also for his insolence to Cornwall, Kent is placed in the stocks, despite Gloucester's pleas against humiliating a servant of the King. When the others leave, Gloucester remains to offer Kent his sympathy. Although he offers to intercede on Kent's behalf, Kent begs him not to. Left alone, Kent produces a letter that is from Cordelia. Cordelia knows of the role he has assumed and he feels confident she will take action to put things right again. Kent falls asleep, asking fortune to turn her wheel and "smile once more."

Stage Direction – *Without:* outside; *severally:* separately

1	*Good dawning:* equivalent to good morning, but indicative of the fact that it is still dark; *Art of this house?:* Are you a member of this household?
2	*Ay:* Yes
3	*set:* stable
4	*mire:* mud
5	*Prithee:* literally, I pray thee; *if thou ... me:* If you have any courtesy, please tell me.
8	*Lipsbury Pinfold:* an involved pun. "Lipsbury," equivalent to Liptown, means the mouth. A "pinfold" is a corral or pen in which stray cattle are kept. The expression therefore means: If I had you in my mouth (or jaws), or if I had you in my power.
10	*use:* treat
13	*an eater of broken meats:* an eater of scraps
13-22	*A knave ... addition:* Kent is much better at gratuitous insult than at sarcastic humour.
14-17	*three-suited:* Three suits per year were allowed a servant by custom; *hundred-pound:* with small property; *worsted-stocking:* cheap stocking scorned by gentlemen, who wore silk; *lily-livered:* cowardly, white-livered; *action-taking:* going to law instead of meeting an enemy in a duel, cowardly; *glass-gazing:* vain, always gazing into the mirror; *super-serviceable:* going beyond the normal limits of a servant's duty in order to gain favour with the master
17	*finical:* fussy; *one-trunk-inheriting slave:* a servant whose total belongings would fit into one trunk
18	*bawd:* pimp or procurer
19-20	*the composition:* the composite of, the combination; *pander:* pimp
21	*clamorous whining:* noisy wailing, loud crying
22	*addition:* title (all the titles Kent has given him)
24	*rail on:* abuse verbally
25	*brazen-faced:* bold, "nervy"; *varlet:* scoundrel

Scene 2

Without the gates of
Gloucester's castle.
Enter Kent and Oswald the
Steward, severally.

Oswald: Good dawning to thee, friend. Art of this house?
Kent: Ay.
Oswald: Where may we set our horses?
Kent: I' the mire.
Oswald: Prithee, if thou lovest me, tell me.   5
Kent: I love thee not.
Oswald: Why then, I care not for thee.
Kent: If I had thee in Lipsbury Pinfold, I would make thee
　　care for me.
Oswald: Why dost thou use me thus? I know thee not.   10
Kent: Fellow, I know thee.
Oswald: What dost thou know me for?
Kent: A knave, a rascal, an eater of broken meats; a base,
　　proud, shallow, beggarly, three-suited, hundred-
　　pound, filthy, worsted-stocking knave; a lily-livered,   15
　　action-taking, whoreson, glass-gazing, superservicea-
　　ble, finical rogue; one-trunk-inheriting slave; one
　　that wouldst be a bawd in way of good service, and art
　　nothing but the composition of a knave, beggar, cow-
　　ard, pander, and the son and heir of a mongrel bitch;   20
　　one whom I will beat into clamorous whining if thou
　　deny'st the least syllable of thy addition.
Oswald: Why, what a monstrous fellow art thou, thus to
　　rail on one that's neither known of thee nor knows thee!
Kent: What a brazen-faced varlet art thou, to deny thou   25
　　knowest me! Is it two days ago since I tripped up thy
　　heels and beat thee before the King? [*Draws his*
　　sword.] Draw, you rogue! for, though it be night, yet

29-30   *I'll make ... you:* I'll put so many holes in you that you will soak up the moonlight as a piece of bread (sop) soaks up liquid

30   *cullionly:* villainous, base; *barbermonger:* one who is always at the barber's primping himself

33   *Vanity the puppet's part:* Goneril's part. Kent insults Goneril as a vain woman and a mere puppet compared to her father.

34-36   *so carbonado your shanks!:* slash or carve up the parts of the legs between the knee and the ankle; *Come your ways!:* Come on!

38   *neat:* dressed

Stage Direction – *Beats him:* strikes him (humiliatingly) with the flat side of his sword blade

Stage Direction – *Parts them:* separates Kent and Oswald

42   *With you:* I'll fight with you (Edmund) then; *goodman:* a mocking expression implying that Edmund the boy is presumptuous to try to stop Kent the man.

43   *flesh ye:* give you your first lesson

48   *difference?:* dispute, quarrel

49   *scarce in breath:* can scarcely get my breath

50   *No marvel ... valour:* No wonder, you have upset your courage so much with the thought that you may have to use it.

51-52   *disclaims in thee:* denies any part of your making

54-56   *A tailor ... trade:* implies that no stonecutter, or painter – however incompetent – could have produced Oswald

58   *ancient:* old (Kent is disguised)

59   *At suit ... beard:* because of his age

60   *whoreson zed! Thou, unnecessary letter:* The letter "z" is unnecessary in English since *s* can usually serve.

61   *unbolted:* Unbolted mortar was unsifted and lumpy, and had to be trodden with wooden shoes before it could be used.

62   *daub:* to coat or cover; *lakes:* outhouse, latrine, outdoor toilet

63   *Spare my ... wagtail?:* Oswald is bowing obediently, bobbing up and down like a type of bird which moves its tail up and down.

65   *beastly:* disgusting, offensive; *reverence?:* respect for superiors

66   *anger hath a privilege:* You must make allowance for a man who is extremely angry.

the moon shines. I'll make a sop o' the moonshine of
you. You whoreson cullionly barbermonger, draw!   30
Oswald: Away! I have nothing to do with thee.
Kent: Draw, you rascal! You come with letters against the
    King, and take Vanity the puppet's part against the
    royalty of her father. Draw, you rogue, or I'll so car-
    bonado your shanks! Draw, you rascal! Come your   35
    ways!
Oswald: Help, ho! Murder! Help!
Kent: Strike, you slave! Stand, rogue! Stand, you neat slave!
    Strike!   [*Beats him.*]
Oswald: Help, ho! murder! murder!   40
    [*Enter Edmund, with his rapier drawn.*]
Edmund: How now? What's the matter?   [*Parts them.*]
Kent: With you, goodman boy, if you please! Come, I'll
    flesh ye! Come on, young master!
    [*Enter Gloucester, Cornwall, Regan, Servants.*]
Gloucester: Weapons? Arms? What's the matter here?
Cornwall: Keep peace, upon your lives!   45
    He dies that strikes again. What is the matter?
Regan: The messengers from our sister and the King.
Cornwall: What is your difference? Speak.
Oswald: I am scarce in breath, my lord.
Kent: No marvel, you have so bestirred your valour. You   50
    cowardly rascal, nature disclaims in thee; a tailor
    made thee.
Cornwall: Thou art a strange fellow. A tailor make a man?
Kent: A tailor, sir: a stonecutter or a painter could not have
    made him so ill, though they had been but two hours   55
    at the trade.
Cornwall: Speak yet, how grew your quarrel?
Oswald: This ancient ruffian, sir, whose life I have spared
    At suit of his grey beard—
Kent: Thou whoreson zed! Thou unnecessary letter! My   60
    lord, if you'll give me leave, I will tread this unbolted
    villain into mortar and daub the wall of a jakes with
    him. "Spare my grey beard," you wagtail?
Cornwall: Peace, sirrah!
    You beastly knave, know you no reverence?   65
Kent: Yes, sir, but anger hath a privilege.

68   *sword:* the mark of a man

70-71   *oft bite … unloose:* who often bite through the bonds of natural affection, which should be too tight to be untied (possibly recalling the "bond" spoken of by Cordelia previously and that which unites all families as well as societies); *smooth:* flatter; *passion:* outburst

72   *That in … rebel:* that break out in their masters

73   *Being oil to fire:* stimulate anger, as oil feeds a fire; *snow to the colder moods:* encourage feelings of indifference

74   *Renege:* deny; *affirm:* assert

74-75   *and turn … masters:* The body of the halcyon (kingfisher) was thought to be an accurate weather-vane, turning its beak into the wind. Oswald, and those like him, would obey their masters, just as the kingfisher would obey the wind.

76   *Knowing naught … following:* understanding nothing, but following their master like obedient dogs

77   *epileptic:* Oswald's face is twisted into a sort of smile, which fails to hide his fear. He appears about to have a fit.

79   *Goose:* a symbol of stupidity; *Sarum Plain:* Salisbury Plain

80   *Camelot:* site of King Arthur's Court. Kent is saying that he would gladly chase Oswald about, beating him with the flat of his sword, while Oswald utters goose-like shrieks, i.e., "If I had you at my mercy, I'd make you run for your life."

83   *contraries:* opponents

86   *His countenance likes me not:* I just don't like his face.

92-93   *doth … saucy roughness:* adopts a rough insolence

93-94   *constrains the … nature:* forces himself to put on this act or manner of insolence that is contrary to his own nature

98   *Harbour … ends:* have within themselves or conceal more cunning and wicked purposes

99   *silly-ducking:* constantly bowing; *observants:* self-seeking servants

100   *That stretch their duties nicely:* that exert themselves with great conscientiousness

102   *Under the … aspect:* begging the indulgence of your great power

104   *Phœbus' front:* forehead of the sun god

Cornwall: Why art thou angry?
Kent: That such a slave as this should wear a sword,
  Who wears no honesty. Such smiling rogues as these,
  Like rats, oft bite the holy cords atwain   70
  Which are too intrinse to unloose; smooth every passion
  That in the natures of their lords rebel,
  Being oil to fire, snow to the colder moods;
  Renege, affirm, and turn their halcyon beaks
  With every gale and vary of their masters,   75
  Knowing naught (like dogs) but following.
  A plague upon your epileptic visage!
  Smile you my speeches, as I were a fool?
  Goose, if I had you upon Sarum Plain,
  I'd drive ye cackling home to Camelot.   80
Cornwall: What, art thou mad, old fellow?
Gloucester: How fell you out? Say that.
Kent: No contraries hold more antipathy
  Than I and such a knave.
Cornwall: Why dost thou call him knave? What is his fault?   85
Kent: His countenance likes me not.
Cornwall: No more perchance does mine, nor his, nor hers.
Kent: Sir, 'tis my occupation to be plain:
  I have seen better faces in my time
  Than stands on any shoulder that I see   90
  Before me at this instant.
Cornwall: This is some fellow
  Who, having been praised for bluntness, doth affect
  A saucy roughness, and constrains the garb
  Quite from his nature. He cannot flatter, he,
  An honest mind and plain, he must speak truth: 95
  An they will take it, so; if not, he's plain.
  These kind of knaves I know which in this plainness
  Harbour more craft and more corrupter ends
  Than twenty silly-ducking observants
  That stretch their duties nicely.   100
Kent: Sir, in good faith, in sincere verity,
  Under the allowance of your great aspect,
  Whose influence, like the wreath of radiant fire
  On flickering Phœbus' front—
Cornwall: What meanest by this?

105   *dialect:* manner of speaking plainly

106-109   *He that ... it:* Kent means: I assume that someone fooled you in the past with plain words, and therefore made himself a liar, which I would not be, even if I should make you so angry with my bluntness that you would prefer me to flatter you.

112   *late:* recently

113   *upon his misconstruction:* following his (Lear's) misinterpretation of something I said

114   *compact:* in compact with, or in agreement with Lear; *flattering his displeasure:* encouraging Lear's annoyance

116-117   *And put ... worthied him:* and made such a hero of himself in Lear's eyes

118   *attempting ... self-subdued:* attacking or "taking on" Oswald when he was self-controlled

119   *fleshment:* excitement aroused by "fleshing," or first success

120-121   *None of ... fool:* Dishonest people like this always make fools of the mighty or powerful. (Ajax was known as a mighty warrior, with a somewhat slow perception.) Kent's comment enrages Cornwall who assumes, perhaps rightly, that Kent is referring to him.

121   *stocks:* instrument of punishment for minor offences, consisting of a wooden form with holes for hands and feet, and sometimes the head

122   *stubborn:* rough, ungovernable; *ancient:* old; *reverend:* aged

127   *grace and ... master:* both the office and the King as a representative of all the people

133   *being:* since you are; *knave:* servant (hence a menial; one of low status or condition)

135   *away:* out

138   *low correction:* demeaning or humiliating punishment

Kent: To go out of my dialect, which you discommend so   105
　　much. I know, sir, I am no flatterer. He that beguiled
　　you in a plain accent was a plain knave, which, for
　　my part, I will not be, though I should win your dis-
　　pleasure to entreat me to it.
Cornwall: What was the offence you gave him?   110
Oswald: I never gave him any.
　　It pleased the King his master very late
　　To strike at me, upon his misconstruction;
　　When he, compact, and flattering his displeasure,
　　Tripped me behind; being down, insulted, railed   115
　　And put upon him such a deal of man
　　That worthied him, got praises of the King
　　For him attempting who was self-subdued;
　　And, in the fleshment of this dread exploit,
　　Drew on me here again.
Kent: 　　　　　　　　　None of these rogues and
　　cowards   120
　　But Ajax is their fool.
Cornwall: 　　　　　　Fetch forth the stocks!
　　You stubborn ancient knave, you reverend braggart,
　　We'll teach you—
Kent: 　　　　　　Sir, I am too old to learn.
　　Call not your stocks for me. I serve the King,
　　On whose employment I was sent to you.   125
　　You shall do small respect, show too bold malice
　　Against the grace and person of my master,
　　Stocking his messenger.
Cornwall: Fetch forth the stocks! As I have life and honour,
　　There shall he sit till noon.   130
Regan: Till noon? Till night, my lord, and all night too!
Kent: Why, madam, if I were your father's dog,
　　You should not use me so.
Regan: 　　　　　　　　Sir, being his knave, I will.
Cornwall: This is a fellow of the selfsame colour
　　Our sister speaks of. Come, bring away the stocks!   135
　　　　　　　　　　　　　　[*Stocks brought out.*]
Gloucester: Let me beseech your Grace not to do so.
　　His fault is much, and the good King his master
　　Will check him for it. Your purposed low correction

139   *contemnedest:* most despised, most despicable

141   *take it ill:* take it as an insult
142   *so lightly ... messenger:* given so little respect through the humiliation of his servant
143   *answer:* be responsible for

148   *pleasure:* will, desire
150   *rubbed nor stopped:* opposed, resisted. A "rub" in the game of bowls (a game played on grass with round balls, i.e., lawn bowling) is an obstacle which diverts a ball from its proper course; *entreat:* to plead for
153   *grow out at heels:* become worn out (like the heel of a sock or stocking), may come to an end
154   *Give you good morrow:* a salutation: God give you a good tomorrow; equivalent to our expression, "See you in the morning."
156   *that must ... saw:* that must prove the truth of the common saying
157-158 *Thou out ... sun:* a proverb: out of God's blessing into the warm sun, or from good to bad (the sun's heat was thought of as harsh)
159   *beacon:* sun; *globe:* earth
160   *comfortable:* comforting
161-162 *Nothing almost ... misery:* When we are discouraged, any relief seems a miracle. (Kent thinks it a miracle that Cordelia's letter has reached him.)
164   *obscured:* disguised
165-166 *this enormous state:* this unnatural condition; *to give losses their remedies:* to make up or repair losses; *o'erwatched:* worn out
167-168 *Take vantage ... lodging:* take advantage of sleep in order not to see these shameful stocks
169   *Fortune, good ... wheel:* According to legend, the goddess Fortune sits by a wheel from which people are hung, and occasionally turns it. The most fortunate are those at the top; some, less so, are ascending; and the unlucky remainder are descending or at the very bottom of the wheel.

Is such as basest and contemnedest wretches
For pilferings and most common trespasses   140
Are punished with. The King must take it ill
That he, so slightly valued in his messenger,
Should have him thus restrained.
Cornwall: I'll answer that.
Regan: My sister may receive it much more worse,
To have her gentleman abused, assaulted,   145
For following her affairs. Put in his legs.
                              [*Kent is put in the stocks.*]
Come, my good lord, away.
                    [*Exeunt all but Gloucester and Kent.*]
Gloucester: I am sorry for thee, friend. 'Tis the Duke's
    pleasure,
Whose disposition, all the world well knows,
Will not be rubbed nor stopped. I'll entreat for thee.   150
Kent: Pray do not, sir. I have watched and travelled hard.
Some time I shall sleep out, the rest I'll whistle.
A good man's fortune may grow out at heels.
Give you good morrow!
Gloucester: The Duke's to blame in this; 'twill be ill taken.   155
                                              [*Exit.*]
Kent: Good King, that must approve the common saw,
Thou out of heaven's benediction comest
To the warm sun!
Approach, thou beacon to this under globe,
That by thy comfortable beams I may   160
Peruse this letter. Nothing almost sees miracles
But misery. I know 'tis from Cordelia,
Who hath most fortunately been informed
Of my obscured course—and [*Reads.*] "shall find time
From this enormous state, seeking to give   165
Losses their remedies"—All weary and o'erwatched,
Take vantage, heavy eyes, not to behold
This shameful lodging.
Fortune, good night; smile once more, turn thy wheel.
                                        [*Sleeps.*]

Act 2, Scene 2: Activities

1. As Kent, write a soliloquy for the beginning of this scene. It should reveal to the audience why you feel that plain speech and bluntness are important characteristics for a person to maintain, even though the consequences may be unpleasant. Present your soliloquy to your group and ask them to respond to the ideas you have suggested.

2. As Oswald, you are expected to perform certain duties without question in Regan's household. In a letter to a friend in a similar position, give your version of the encounter between yourself and Kent. Include your impressions of Kent and your responses to what you consider to be an unprovoked attack. Were you pleased with Cornwall's swift justice? How do you respond to Kent's accusation that "a tailor made thee" (lines 51–52)?

3. With a partner, prepare a dialogue that might take place between Cornwall and Regan after they have left Kent in the stocks. As Cornwall, what are your concerns about what is happening in your part of the kingdom? As Regan, what course of action have you chosen to keep things in control? Who is the dominant figure in your dialogue? Rehearse your dialogue and present it to your group, to another group, or to the whole class for their responses.

4. Write the letter that Cordelia has sent to Kent. Remember to be consistent with her character as you perceived it in Act 1. Be sure to explain why you have written to Kent and why the letter was not sent to Gloucester. Indicate also what course of action you intend to take and what Kent's role in this action will be.

5. Kent hurls many insults at Oswald (lines 4–22 and 25–30). Without being overtly crude, rewrite these speeches in current English as you might deliver them to someone you perceived as being a modern-day Oswald. Before you write your speech, consider whether you believe Kent's perception of Oswald to be accurate. Could you ever imagine yourself saying these things to anyone? How would you feel if these things were said to you?

6. Kent asks "fortune" to help him (line 169). Edmund also talks about "fortune" (Act 1, Scene 2, lines 118–133). In your group, discuss the difference between the two views of fortune. What are your own views? Do you think "fortune" plays any role at all in human lives? Which view of fortune do you think is most appropriate to the outcome of the play? Record your personal feelings in your journal.

7. Have one member of your group assume the role of Kent in this scene. Have this person write the speech that Kent, who cannot reveal his identity, might have delivered to Oswald. Have another member of the group assume the role of Oswald and respond to Kent's speech, indicating what course of action he might take.

   As a group, listen to the "new" versions and compare them with what actually happened in the play. Which version is more effective? As you make your decision, be sure to consider the entire action of the play so far.

8. Prepare a background story on Oswald or Kent to find out the history of who they are, where they came from, and why they held the positions given to them. Your story may take the form of a short magazine article or a biographical segment of a newspaper account.

For the next scene ...

Has your true identity ever been an obstacle to your safety? If you had to disguise yourself, even from friends and family, how would you do it?

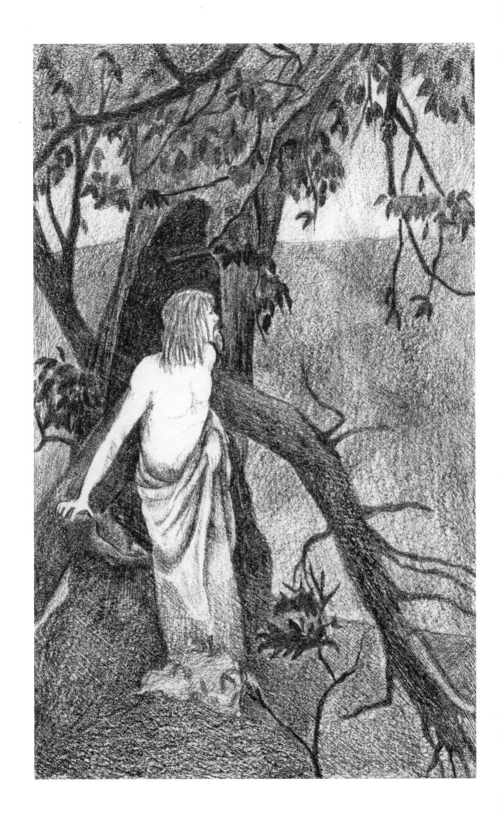

Act 2, Scene 3

In this scene ...

Edgar has heard of the death warrant issued by Gloucester, his father. He decides to disguise himself as a Bedlam beggar in order to escape detection. The beggars, also called Tom O'Bedlams, were patients with mental disabilities who were turned out of Bedlam Hospital (the insane asylum of St. Mary of Bethlehem) to beg for food. Their wanderings about the countryside were commonplace. Edgar will cease to exist; he will now call himself Poor Tom and act like one of the Tom O'Bedlams.

1   *proclaimed:* denounced as a criminal. Proclamations were read publicly.
2   *happy:* lucky, fortunate
3   *port:* seaport. Gloucester alerted all the ports to watch for Edgar.
5   *attend:* await; *taking:* capture; *Whiles ... scape:* until I can escape
6   *am bethought:* have decided
8   *penury:* poverty; *in contempt of man:* to show how worthless man is
10   *elf:* tangle. Matted locks of hair that resulted from infrequent use of a comb were often said to be the work of elves.
11   *presented:* bold; *outface:* defy
12   *winds and ... sky:* the discomfort of exposure to the elements
13   *proof and precedent:* example
14   *Bedlam beggars:* vagrants of the late sixteenth and early seventeenth centuries who were, or pretended to be, discharged inmates of Bedlam Hospital, the insane asylum of St. Mary of Bethlehem
15   *Strike:* stick; *numbed and mortified:* lifeless and deadened
17   *object:* sight
18   *pelting:* paltry, insignificant, worthless; *sheepcotes:* buildings for sheltering sheep
19   *bans:* curses
20   *Enforce their charity:* extort the charity of others; *"Poor Turlygod! Poor Tom!":* Edgar is practising the beggar's cries.
21   *That's something ... am:* As Poor Tom, I may live; as Edgar, I'm dead.

Scene 3

Open country in the neighbourhood of Gloucester's castle.
Enter Edgar.

Edgar: I heard myself proclaimed,
  And by the happy hollow of a tree
  Escaped the hunt. No port is free, no place
  That guard and most unusual vigilance
  Does not attend my taking. Whiles I may scape,   5
  I will preserve myself; and am bethought
  To take the basest and most poorest shape
  That ever penury, in contempt of man,
  Brought near to beast. My face I'll grime with filth,
  Blanket my loins, elf all my hair in knots,   10
  And with presented nakedness outface
  The winds and persecutions of the sky.
  The country gives me proof and precedent
  Of Bedlam beggars, who, with roaring voices,
  Strike in their numbed and mortified bare arms   15
  Pins, wooden pricks, nails, sprigs of rosemary;
  And with this horrible object, from low farms,
  Poor pelting villages, sheepcotes, and mills,
  Sometime with lunatic bans, sometime with prayers,
  Enforce their charity. "Poor Turlygod! Poor Tom!"   20
  That's something yet! Edgar I nothing am.   *[Exit.]*

Act 2, Scene 3: Activities

1. Create a segment for "Crime Stoppers" or "The Ten Most Wanted Men" on television, describing Edgar as a dangerous criminal. Create a police sketch of him and give a physical description (including details of what he was wearing when last seen), the crime of which he is accused, and any other information that might help to identify and apprehend him.

   Alternatively, design the "Wanted" poster that Gloucester promises to send out. In addition, prepare the proclamation that would be read to the public.

2. In groups, discuss why you think Edgar chose the disguise of a Bedlam beggar. Given Edgar's background, how would he know how to act? If Edgar were suddenly transported to this century, what disguise might he adopt? Record the steps you would take to disappear in today's society.

3. You are a director of a modern production of *King Lear*. The actor who is playing Edgar has complained to you that modern-day audiences simply would not understand Tom's speech because it is very artificial. The actor believes that the speech must be cut and modified if it is to be believable. In a director's log, write your responses to his objections, or suggest some cuts that would not damage the overall integrity of the content.

4. When Edgar flees for his life, he becomes "the basest and most poorest shape that ever penury, in contempt of man, brought near to beast" (lines 7–9). With your group, decide what Edgar means and what he is saying about the relationship of human society to nature. What implications do you think this has for events that might unfold? Record your conclusions in a brief magazine article or a news commentary on the topic.

For the next scene ...

In your journal record how you might feel if you were suddenly deserted by those you love and left on your own. What would you do?

Act 2, Scene 4

In this scene ...

Having found Regan absent from her palace, Lear arrives at Gloucester's castle and is immediately confronted by the sight of Kent in the stocks. When Kent explains how he came to be imprisoned, Lear is outraged.

Lear looks for Regan, only to discover that she refuses to see him. When Cornwall and Regan arrive, Kent is set free by Gloucester's intervention. Lear explains that Goneril has cut his retinue in half. He has come to stay with Regan instead, believing that she will be more kind and dutiful than her sister. However, Regan defends Goneril and advises Lear to return to her.

When Goneril arrives, the two sisters attempt to reduce Lear's status to that of a mere dependant. They insist that he can stay with them only if he dismisses all of his knights. Lear, inarticulate with rage and indignation, fears he will go mad. As a fierce storm breaks, Lear rushes out, determined not to give in to his daughters' demands. Regan and Cornwall shut the castle gates to lock him out.

Scene Description — *Gentleman:* The Quarto has "knight," thus one of Lear's train of knights.

1	*they:* Regan and Cornwall
2	*messenger:* Kent
4	*remove:* departure to another residence
6	*Makest thou ... pastime?:* Is this shamefulness something you make a habit of doing to pass the time?
7	*cruel:* a pun, "crewel" being a word for "worsted," a cloth from which garters were made
9	*loins:* waist
10-11	*over-lusty:* too lively, vigorous; also implies "full of sexual desire"; *netherstocks:* stockings. "Wooden netherstocks" is a reference to the stocks themselves.
12	*place:* position, rank
21	*Jupiter:* the supreme deity of the ancient Romans, ruler of gods and humans, and the god of the heavens
22	*Juno:* the wife of Jupiter, the goddess of marriage and childbirth; *durst:* would not dare to
24	*To do ... outrage:* to commit such an offence upon one who is entitled to respect

Scene 4

*Without the gates of Gloucester's
castle; Kent in the stocks.*

Enter Lear, Fool, and Gentleman.

Lear: 'Tis strange that they should so depart from home,
  And not send back my messenger.
Gentleman: As I learned,
  The night before there was no purpose in them
  Of this remove.
Kent: Hail to thee, noble master!
Lear: Ha!   5
  Makest thou this shame thy pastime?
Kent: No, my lord.
Fool: Ha, ha! He wears cruel garters.
    Horses are tied by the head, dogs and bears by the
    neck, monkeys by the loins, and men by the legs.
    When a man's over-lusty at legs, then he wears wooden 10
    netherstocks.
Lear: What's he that hath so much thy place mistook
  To set thee here?
Kent: It is both he and she—
  Your son and daughter.
Lear: No.   15
Kent: Yes.
Lear: No, I say.
Kent: I say yea.
Lear: No, no, they would not!
Kent: Yes, they have.   20
Lear: By Jupiter, I swear no!
Kent: By Juno, I swear ay!
Lear: They durst not do it;
  They could not, would not do it. 'Tis worse than murder
  To do upon respect such violent outrage.

25	*Resolve:* tell; *modest:* reasonable; *which way:* why
26	*usage:* treatment
27	*Coming from us:* inasmuch as you come from us (the royal "we"), the King
28	*commend:* deliver; *letters:* letter
30	*duty:* respect; *reeking post:* sweaty messenger
31	*stewed:* very hot, excited
33	*spite of intermission:* in spite of interrupting my business
34	*presently:* immediately
35	*meinie:* retinue, followers, household; *straight:* immediately
36-37	*attend the ... answer:* Wait until they were ready to answer.
39	*poisoned:* spoiled, made impossible
41	*Displayed so saucily:* behaved so churlishly or insolently
42	*more man than wit:* more courage than judgement
44	*trespass:* the attack on Oswald
46-47	*Winter's not ... way:* Your troubles are not over yet.
48-55	*Fathers that ... year:* Roughly fathers who have no money have blind (uncaring) children. Fathers who are rich have very caring children. Fortune, like a whore, opens her door only when there is someone willing to pay money. But you (Lear) will have more dollars – a pun on the word "dolours," meaning griefs or sadnesses – than you can count in a year.
49	*blind:* to their duties as sons and daughters
50	*bear:* possess; *bags:* bags of money
51	*kind:* only because of the money
52	*arrant:* notorious
53	*turns the key:* opens the door
56-57	*mother swells ... passio:* hysterical suffering that begins as a physical sensation below the heart and rises towards it. The word "mother" is used to indicate emotion – a female trait.
58	*Thy element's:* your proper place is

Resolve me with all modest haste which way   25
Thou mightst deserve or they impose this usage,
Coming from us.
Kent: My lord, when at their home
I did commend your Highness' letters to them,
Ere I was risen from the place that showed
My duty kneeling, came there a reeking post,   30
Stewed in his haste, half breathless, panting forth
From Goneril his mistress salutations;
Delivered letters, spite of intermission,
Which presently they read; on whose contents,
They summoned up their meinie, straight took horse,   35
Commanded me to follow and attend
The leisure of their answer, gave me cold looks,
And meeting here the other messenger,
Whose welcome I perceived had poisoned mine—
Being the very fellow which of late   40
Displayed so saucily against your Highness—
Having more man than wit about me, drew.
He raised the house with loud and coward cries.
Your son and daughter found this trespass worth
The shame which here it suffers.   45
Fool: Winter's not gone yet, if the wild geese fly that
          way.
                    Fathers that wear rags
                        Do make their children blind;
                    But fathers that bear bags   50
                        Shall see their children kind.
                    Fortune, that arrant whore,
                    Ne'er turns the key to the poor.
          But for all this, thou shalt have as many dolours for
          thy daughters as thou canst tell in a year.   55
Lear: O, how this mother swells up toward my heart!
    Hysterica passio! Down, thou climbing sorrow,
    Thy element's below! Where is this daughter?
Kent: With the Earl, sir, here within.
Lear: Follow me not;
    Stay here.   [*Exit.*]   60
Gentleman: Made you no more offence but what you speak of?
Kent: None.

63   *How chance:* why does

67-68   *We'll set ... winter:* The Fool seems to mean that Lear's for-
            tunes have come to an end as do the ant's when winter
            arrives; *All that ... stinking:* All those who possess judge-
            ment accept the testimony given by their own eyes, except
            the blind, who use their sense of smell only, and even a
            blind man in this way could see the truth of the situation
            (that Lear's plight is wretched). This wise saying, and those
            that follow, are meant by the Fool to indicate that he under-
            stands not only that Lear is abandoned, but also, that
            some, like Kent, do not seem to realize how low Lear's for-
            tunes have fallen; *follow their noses:* go straight forward;
            but: except

77-84   *That sir ... perdy:* A rather convoluted argument about loyalty.
            The sense is that the man who serves for personal gain
            serves only for show. He has no inner sense of loyalty and
            serves only because of what he will gain from his master's
            position or rank. Such a person will abandon you when
            things become difficult and leave you to suffer by yourself.
            But I will remain. Let the "wise man" run away, but the ser-
            vant (knave) who runs away turns out in the end to have
            been a fool who is seen by everyone to be contemptible.
            In other words, the faithless man is the true fool; *perdy:* a
            form of oath from the French "par Dieu" meaning "by God"

88   *fetches:* pretexts, pretences (from sailing: a "fetch" or a
            "tack")
89   *images:* very pictures or clearest indications; *revolt and
            flying off:* synonymous words meaning "disloyalty"

91   *quality:* temperament
92   *unremovable and fixed:* synonymous words meaning
            "unyielding" or "inflexible"
94   *Confusion:* ruination
95   *What quality?:* What has his disposition to do with it?
96   *I'd speak:* I simply wish to speak.

98   *Dost thou understand me, man?:* Lear simply cannot grasp
            the idea that he has been deliberately snubbed.

How chance the King comes with so small a number?
Fool: An thou hadst been set i' the stocks for that question,
    thou'dst well deserved it.   65
Kent: Why, fool?
Fool: We'll set thee to school to an ant, to teach thee there's
    no labouring i' the winter. All that follow their noses
    are led by their eyes but blind men, and there's not
    a nose among twenty but can smell him that's stinking. 70
    Let go thy hold when a great wheel runs down a hill,
    lest it break thy neck with following it; but the great
    one that goes upward, let him draw thee after. When
    a wise man gives thee better counsel, give me mine
    again: I would have none but knaves follow it, since 75
    a fool gives it.
        That sir which serves and seeks for gain,
            And follows but for form,
        Will pack when it begins to rain
            And leave thee in the storm.   80
        But I will tarry; the fool will stay,
            And let the wise man fly.
        The knave turns fool that runs away;
            The fool no knave, perdy.
Kent: Where learned you this, fool?   85
Fool: Not i' the stocks, fool.
    [*Enter Lear and Gloucester.*]
Lear: Deny to speak with me? They are sick? they are
    weary?
    They have travelled all the night? Mere fetches—
    The images of revolt and flying off.
    Fetch me a better answer.
Gloucester: My dear lord,   90
    You know the fiery quality of the Duke,
    How unremovable and fixed he is
    In his own course.
Lear: Vengeance! Plague! Death! Confusion!
    Fiery? What quality? Why, Gloucester, Gloucester, 95
    I'd speak with the Duke of Cornwall and his wife.
Gloucester: Well, my good lord, I have informed them so.
Lear: Informed them? Dost thou understand me, man?
Gloucester: Ay, my good lord.

101   *commands, tends service:* Lear commands his daughter's service, and offers his own.

103   *hot:* hot-tempered

104   *May be ... well:* Lear makes excuses for the Duke's snub. He cannot believe that such a thing could happen to a king.

105   *Infirmity:* illness; *neglect all office:* overlook duty

106   *Whereto our health is bound:* that we are bound to carry out when in good health

108   *forbear:* be tolerant, be patient

109   *am fallen out ... will:* am annoyed with my too head-strong impulse

110   *To take:* because I have mistaken

111   *sound:* healthy; *Death on my state:* A curse on my royal power; *Wherefore:* Why? For what reason?

113   *remotion:* avoidance (of me), remoteness from me

114   *practice:* trickery, deceit, a scheme

115   *and's:* and his

118   *cry sleep to death:* make sleep impossible

121-124   *Cry to ... down:* The Fool's comment means that Lear is as naive about Regan and Cornwall as a cockney (a city woman) was about making an eel pie. She did not know enough to kill the eels before cooking them, and as they squirmed about, making the pie a mess, she rapped them over the head – when it was too late.

124-125   *'Twas her ... hay:* Her brother was evidently no more intelligent or practical than his sister: horses don't enjoy greasy hay so it would be silly to give it to them.

126   *Good morrow:* Since it is evening, the greeting is ironical; *Grace:* Majesty

129-131   *If thou ... adultress:* If you are not glad to see me, you can be no daughter of mine.

132   *that:* the matter of the stocks

133   *naught:* wicked (naughty)

Lear: The King would speak with Cornwall; the dear father   100
     Would with his daughter speak, commands, tends
       service.
     Are they informed of this? My breath and blood!
     Fiery? the fiery Duke? Tell the hot Duke that—
     No, but not yet! May be he is not well.
     Infirmity doth still neglect all office   105
     Whereto our health is bound. We are not ourselves
     When nature, being oppressed, commands the mind
     To suffer with the body. I'll forbear;
     And am fallen out with my more headier will,
     To take the indisposed and sickly fit   110
     For the sound man. [*Looks at Kent.*] Death on my state!
       Wherefore
     Should he sit here? This act persuades me
     That this remotion of the Duke and her
     Is practice only. Give me my servant forth.
     Go tell the Duke and's wife I'd speak with them—   115
     Now, presently. Bid them come forth and hear me,
     Or at their chamber door I'll beat the drum
     Till it cry sleep to death.
Gloucester: I would have all well betwixt you.   [*Exit.*]
Lear: O me, my heart, my rising heart! But down!   120
Fool: Cry to it, nuncle, as the cockney did to the eels when
     she put 'em i' the paste alive. She knapped 'em o' the
     coxcombs with a stick and cried "Down, wantons,
     down!" 'Twas her brother that, in pure kindness to
     his horse, buttered his hay.   125
     [*Enter Cornwall, Regan, Gloucester, Servants.*]
Lear: Good morrow to you both.
Cornwall: Hail to your Grace!
                      [*Kent here set at liberty.*]
Regan: I am glad to see your Highness.
Lear: Regan, I think you are; I know what reason
     I have to think so. If thou shouldst not be glad,
     I would divorce me from thy mother's tomb,   130
     Sepulchring an adultress. [*To Kent.*] O, are you free?
     Some other time for that.—Beloved Regan,
     Thy sister's naught. O Regan, she hath tied

134	*like a vulture:* an allusion to the eternal punishment of Prometheus. In the Greek myth he was chained to a rock where, each day, a vulture would tear out his liver and eat it, and each night, it would be restored.
136	*depraved:* wicked. Lear refers to Goneril's character or "quality."
137	*take patience:* have patience
138-139	*you ... duty:* You are less able to determine her worth than she is of neglecting her duty; *scant:* neglect
141	*obligation:* filial obligation, obligation of a son or a daughter to parents
143	*wholesome:* proper
146-147	*Nature in ... confine:* You are on the threshold of death.
148	*discretion ... state:* some discrete person who understands or perceives your mental condition or your dependent condition
150	*make return:* go back
152	*this:* the action Lear immediately performs; *becomes the house:* suits the royal house; i.e., suits my dignity (as a king)
154	*Age is unnecessary:* Old people are useless; i.e., a person has no right to become old (probably spoken ironically).
155	*vouchsafe:* grant; *raiment:* clothing
156	*unsightly tricks:* undignified actions (falling to his knees and whining for charity)
158	*abated me ... train:* reduced my retinue to half
159	*Looked black:* glared; *struck me with her tongue:* abused me with words
160	*Most serpent-like:* like a snake with its flickering tongue (which was thought to be a weapon for stinging)
162	*top:* head; *young bones:* possibly a reference to her unborn children
163	*taking:* infectious
166	*fen-sucked:* sucked up from marshes (by the sun)
167	*fall and blister:* fall upon Goneril and raise blisters on her

Sharp-toothed unkindness, like a vulture, here!
                                [Points to his heart.]
I can scarce speak to thee. Thou'lt not believe   135
With how depraved a quality—O Regan!
Regan: I pray you, sir, take patience. I have hope
    You less know how to value her desert
    Than she to scant her duty.
Lear: Say, how is that?
Regan: I cannot think my sister in the least   140
    Would fail her obligation. If, sir, perchance
    She have restrained the riots of your followers,
    'Tis on such ground, and to such wholesome end,
    As clears her from all blame.
Lear: My curses on her!
Regan: O, sir, you are old!   145
    Nature in you stands on the very verge
    Of her confine. You should be ruled, and led
    By some discretion that discerns your state
    Better than you yourself. Therefore I pray you
    That to our sister you do make return;   150
    Say you have wronged her.
Lear: Ask her forgiveness?
    Do you but mark how this becomes the house:
    [Kneeling.] "Dear daughter, I confess that I am old.
    Age is unnecessary. On my knees I beg
    That you'll vouchsafe me raiment, bed, and food."   155
Regan: Good sir, no more! These are unsightly tricks.
    Return you to my sister.
Lear: [Stands up.]   Never, Regan!
    She hath abated me of half my train;
    Looked black upon me; struck me with her tongue,
    Most serpent-like, upon the very heart.   160
    All the stored vengeances of heaven fall
    On her ingrateful top! Strike her young bones,
    You taking airs, with lameness!
Cornwall: Fie, sir, fie!
Lear: You nimble lightnings, dart your blinding flames
    Into her scornful eyes! Infect her beauty,   165
    You fen-sucked fogs, drawn by the powerful sun,
    To fall and blister!

169 *the rash mood:* the mood of compulsive anger

171 *tender-hefted nature:* disposition governed by tenderness, gentle disposition

175 *bandy:* exchange; literally, bat back and forth (like a tennis ball); *scant my sizes:* reduce my allowances

176 *oppose the bolt:* to close the bolt (or lock) of the door

178 *offices of nature:* duties of a daughter; *bond of childhood:* obligation formed in childhood, a child's duty to her parents

179 *Effects:* actions; *dues of gratitude:* what gratitude is owing to a father

181 *to the purpose:* Come to the point, say what you mean.

Scene Description — *Tucket:* a fanfare or flourish played on a trumpet, thus, "What trumpet's that?"

183 *approves:* confirms

185-186 *easy, borrowed ... follows:* confident pride, borrowed from his mistress Goneril who protects him

187 *varlet:* scoundrel

189 *on't:* of it

190 *sweet sway:* loving authority, gentle rule

191 *Allow:* permit, approve of; *obedience:* your obedience to my wish; *if you yourselves are old:* if you can sympathize with one who is old; if you can understand what it is to be old

192 *Make it your cause:* defend its privileges

196-197 *All's not ... so:* Not everything is an offence just because your lack of judgement and your senility (dotage) make you think it so.

197 *sides:* breast, heart. Lear feels he is bursting with distress.

199 *disorders:* misbehaviour, misconduct

200 *advancement:* promotion, honour (probably ironic)

Regan: O the blest gods! So will you wish on me
  When the rash mood is on.
Lear: No, Regan, thou shalt never have my curse.   170
  Thy tender-hefted nature shall not give
  Thee o'er to harshness. Her eyes are fierce, but thine
  Do comfort and not burn. 'Tis not in thee
  To grudge my pleasures, to cut off my train,
  To bandy hasty words, to scant my sizes,   175
  And, in conclusion, to oppose the bolt
  Against my coming in. Thou better knowest
  The offices of nature, bond of childhood,
  Effects of courtesy, dues of gratitude.
  Thy half of the kingdom hast thou not forgot,   180
  Wherein I thee endowed.
Regan: Good sir, to the purpose.
Lear: Who put my man in the stocks?   *[Tucket within.]*
Cornwall: What trumpet's that?
Regan: I know it—my sister's. This approves her letter
  That she would soon be here.
  [Enter Oswald the Steward.]   Is your lady come?
Lear: This is a slave, whose easy, borrowed pride   185
  Dwells in the fickle grace of her he follows.
  Out, varlet, from my sight!
Cornwall: What means your Grace?
Lear: Who stocked my servant? Regan, I have good hope
  Thou didst not know on't.
  [Enter Goneril.]   Who comes here? O heavens,
  If you do love old men, if your sweet sway   190
  Allow obedience, if you yourselves are old,
  Make it your cause! Send down, and take my part!
  [To Goneril.] Art not ashamed to look upon this beard?—
  O Regan, will you take her by the hand?
Goneril: Why not by the hand, sir? How have I offended?   195
  All's not offence that indiscretion finds
  And dotage terms so.
Lear: O sides, you are too tough!
  Will you yet hold? How came my man i' the stocks?
Cornwall: I set him there, sir, but his own disorders
  Deserved much less advancement.

201   *being weak, seem so:* Since you are powerless, behave as if you are.

204   *train:* retinue
205-206   *I am ... entertainment:* I am not now at home and am unable, therefore, to provide what you require for your comfort.

208   *abjure:* abandon, give up; *roofs:* shelter, to which Lear is entitled
209   *wage:* struggle, fight; *enmity:* hostility
211   *Necessity's sharp pinch:* a summary of the choice he has just announced. It is inevitable that poverty should bring exposure to the cold, the wind, and the rain.
212   *hot-blooded:* passionate; *France:* the King of France
213   *brought:* forced. Since no one has forced Lear to do anything for a long time, he finds the thought of such coercion intolerable.
214   *knee:* bow before; *squire-like:* like a servant
215   *To keep base life afoot:* to keep body and soul together, to keep from starvation
216   *sumpter:* pack-animal, beast of burden
218   *mad:* insane (not angry)

223   *must needs:* am compelled to; *boil:* pus-filled sore
224   *plague sore:* external sign or mark of bubonic plague; *embossed carbuncle:* particularly large boil forming a distinct lump on the surface of the body.
225   *corrupted:* diseased, infected
226   *shame:* Goneril's disgrace as a cruel daughter
227   *Thunder-bearer:* Jupiter
228   *Jove:* Zeus, judge of all humans
229   *Mend:* make amends; *be better:* be a better daughter

233   *give ear, sir, to:* pay attention, listen to
234   *those that ... passion:* who consider reasonably your violent emotion
235   *and so:* Regan breaks off, implying: You are old, and that explains your irrational actions.

Lear: You? Did you?   200
Regan: I pray you, father, being weak, seem so.
  If, till the expiration of your month,
  You will return and sojourn with my sister,
  Dismissing half your train, come then to me.
  I am now from home, and out of that provision   205
  Which shall be needful for your entertainment.
Lear: Return to her, and fifty men dismissed?
  No, rather I abjure all roofs, and choose
  To wage against the enmity o' the air,
  To be a comrade with the wolf and owl—   210
  Necessity's sharp pinch! Return with her?
  Why, the hot-blooded France, that dowerless took
  Our youngest born, I could as well be brought
  To knee his throne, and, squire-like, pension beg
  To keep base life afoot. Return with her?   215
  Persuade me rather to be slave and sumpter
  To this detested groom.   [*Pointing at Oswald.*]
Goneril: At your choice, sir.
Lear: I prithee, daughter, do not make me mad.
  I will not trouble thee, my child; farewell.
  We'll no more meet, no more see one another.   220
  But yet thou art my flesh, my blood, my daughter;
  Or rather a disease that's in my flesh,
  Which I must needs call mine. Thou art a boil,
  A plague sore or embossed carbuncle,
  In my corrupted blood. But I'll not chide thee.   225
  Let shame come when it will, I do not call it.
  I do not bid the Thunder-bearer shoot,
  Nor tell tales of thee to high-judging Jove.
  Mend when thou canst; be better at thy leisure;
  I can be patient; I can stay with Regan,   230
  I and my hundred knights.
Regan: Not altogether so.
  I looked not for you yet, nor am provided
  For your fit welcome. Give ear, sir, to my sister;
  For those that mingle reason with your passion
  Must be content to think you old, and so—   235
  But she knows what she does.

237   *avouch:* maintain, stand by, affirm
238   *well:* enough
239   *sith that:* since; *charge and danger:* expense and risks
        involved in having such large numbers of unruly men about

242   *Hold amity?:* keep peace

245   *slack ye:* be neglectful of you, fall short of their duty

247   *spy:* see, perceive
248   *but:* only
249   *notice:* recognition
250   *I gave you all:* I gave you everything; *And in ... it:* You gave
        up your kingdom just in time (because you are old and
        senile).
251   *depositaries:* trustees. Lear thought that his rule was given
        in trust to his daughters, and that all the privileges of his
        office would remain as they had been. Goneril and Regan,
        of course, put no such limit on their inheritance.
252-253 *kept a reservation:* reserved the right; *to be ... number:* to
        be served by my original one hundred knights
256-258 *Those wicked ... wicked:* Some wicked persons (like
        Goneril) look pleasing by comparison when others (like
        Regan) are even more wicked; *not being ... praise:* It is in
        Goneril's favour that she is not as bad as Regan.

261   *What need you:* what need have you of
262   *twice so many:* fifty (of my servants)

264-265 *O, reason not the need:* Do not examine the exact need;
        Our basest ... superfluous: Even the poorest beggars have
        things that they do not actually need.
266-267 *Allow not ... beast's:* If you allow a person no more than
        what is absolutely necessary, that person is no better than
        an animal.
268-270 *If only ... thee warm:* If warmth alone were all you require of
        clothing, then your dazzling dress is obviously unnecessary,
        since gorgeousness is not naturally essential.

Lear: Is this well spoken?
Regan: I dare avouch it, sir. What, fifty followers?
   Is it not well? What should you need of more?
   Yea, or so many, sith that both charge and danger
   Speak 'gainst so great a number? How in one house   240
   Should many people, under two commands,
   Hold amity? 'Tis hard; almost impossible.
Goneril: Why might not you, my lord, receive attendance
   From those that she calls servants, or from mine?
Regan: Why not, my lord? If then they chanced to slack
      ye,   245
   We could control them. If you will come to me
   (For now I spy a danger), I entreat you
   To bring but five-and-twenty. To no more
   Will I give place or notice.
Lear: I gave you all—
Regan: And in good time you gave it!   250
Lear: Made you my guardians, my depositaries;
   But kept a reservation to be followed
   With such a number. What, must I come to you
   With five-and-twenty, Regan? Said you so?
Regan: And speak it again, my lord. No more with me.   255
Lear: Those wicked creatures yet do look well-favoured
   When others are more wicked; not being the worst
   Stands in some rank of praise. [*To Goneril.*] I'll go with
      thee.
   Thy fifty yet doth double five-and-twenty,
   And thou art twice her love.
Goneril: Hear me, my lord.   260
   What need you five-and-twenty, ten, or five,
   To follow in a house where twice so many
   Have a command to tend you?
Regan: What need one?
Lear: O, reason not the need! Our basest beggars
   Are in the poorest thing superfluous.   265
   Allow not nature more than nature needs,
   Man's life is cheap as beast's. Thou art a lady:
   If only to go warm were gorgeous,
   Why, nature needs not what thou gorgeous wearest,

270-271   *But, for ... I need:* As Lear is about to explain the difference between true need and frivolous need, he stops to pray for his own need at the moment – patience.

275-276   *fool me ... anger:* Do not make such a fool of me that I will take all this meekly; give me anger fitting a noble mind.

277   *women's weapons, water drops:* tears

Stage Direction – *Sounds of an approaching storm:* The storm and Lear's madness approach together.

285   *flaws:* pieces, fragments
286   *or ere:* before

289   *bestowed:* lodged, sheltered
290   *blame:* fault; *hath put himself from rest:* has caused his own frustration and disturbed state of mind
291   *taste his folly:* endure the effects of his foolish actions
292   *his particular:* himself alone

297   *will I know not whither:* I do not know where he intends to go.
298   *give him way:* let him go; *leads himself:* does as he wishes, and will not be hindered

301   *Do sorely ruffle:* are very blustery

Which scarcely keeps thee warm. But, for true need—   270
You heavens, give me that patience, patience I need!
You see me here, you gods, a poor old man,
As full of grief as age; wretched in both.
If it be you that stirs these daughters' hearts
Against their father, fool me not so much   275
To bear it tamely; touch me with noble anger,
And let not women's weapons, water drops,
Stain my man's cheeks! No, you unnatural hags!
I will have such revenges on you both
That all the world shall—I will do such things—   280
What they are yet, I know not; but they shall be
The terrors of the earth! You think I'll weep.
No, I'll not weep.   [*Sounds of an approaching storm.*]
I have full cause of weeping, but this heart
Shall break into a hundred thousand flaws   285
Or ere I'll weep. O fool, I shall go mad!
                [*Exeunt Lear, Gloucester, Kent, and Fool.*]
Cornwall: Let us withdraw, 'twill be a storm.
Regan: This house is little; the old man and's people
    Cannot be well bestowed.
Goneril: 'Tis his own blame; hath put himself from rest   290
    And must needs taste his folly.
Regan: For his particular, I'll receive him gladly,
    But not one follower.
Goneril: So am I purposed.
    Where is my Lord of Gloucester?
Cornwall: Followed the old man forth.
    [*Enter Gloucester.*]   He is returned.   295
Gloucester: The King is in high rage.
Cornwall: Whither is he going?
Gloucester: He calls to horse, but will I know not whither.
Cornwall: 'Tis best to give him way, he leads himself.
Goneril: My lord, entreat him by no means to stay.
Gloucester: Alack, the night comes on, and the bleak winds   300
    Do sorely ruffle. For many miles about
    There's scarce a bush.
Regan: O, sir, to wilful men
    The injuries that they themselves procure

304	*Must be their schoolmasters:* must teach them wisdom
305	*desperate train:* violent group of followers
306	*incense:* provoke
307	*To have his ear abused:* to be misled by evil advisers and their stories (abuse means to deceive); *wisdom bids fear:* It would be wise to fear (the "desperate train").

Must be their schoolmasters. Shut up your doors.
He is attended with a desperate train,   305
And what they may incense him to, being apt
To have his ear abused, wisdom bids fear.
Cornwall: Shut up your doors, my lord; 'tis a wild night.
My Regan counsels well. Come out o' the storm.

            [*Exeunt.*]

Act 2, Scene 4: Activities

1. The Fool delivers two puzzling speeches in this scene (lines 46–55 and 67–84). In groups, determine what the functions of these speeches are. Write a new speech for the Fool that would combine these two speeches. Insert your speech into the scene in an appropriate place, and share it with others in the class. Remember to compose your speech so that your audience will understand its context.

2. In this scene, King Lear appears bewildered by Regan's absence from her home and by Kent's imprisonment. Discuss with your group why you think Lear cannot comprehend what is happening. If you were Kent in this scene, what might you say to Lear who seems to be more interested in his own plight than in yours? Where would you place this speech?

3. In your journal, record your responses to Lear's behaviour in this scene, remembering that he is a former king, a father, and an ordinary human being. If you had an opportunity to speak to Lear at this point, what would you say to him?

4. With your group, discuss how you feel about Regan's treatment of her father in this scene. Do you feel she is justified? Prepare an argument that Regan might use to defend her position if she were interviewed on a current affairs program on television. Conduct the interview for other groups in the class.

5. Regan implies that suffering is a good teacher (lines 302–04). With your group, discuss whether or not you agree with her. Cite as many current examples as you feel appropriate, as well as any significant examples from the play so far. Write the argument you would use in support of your conclusion, and choose one character from the play to hear your reasoning. How do you think he or she would respond?

Act 2: Consider the Whole Act

1. Imagine that you are Gloucester's official court chronicler or historian, and you are keeping a chronicle of the events in the kingdom since Lear's abdication. Though you are loyal to Gloucester and his family, in your records you want to hint at the people who you think are, or are not, trustworthy. Write your chronicle of events so that your readers can guess at your suspicion. Remember that these notes may be used to provide information to Cordelia at some later date.

2. In Scene 4, when Kent asks the Fool why Lear now has so few followers, he is told that men desert leaders when they sense that fortune has turned against them. As a member of Lear's retinue, how would you respond to this criticism? Create a brief dialogue between you and another of Lear's knights in which you give your thoughts on this issue.

3. Cornwall makes a number of brief appearances in this act. With a partner or in your group, determine what you think Cornwall understands about the events that have occurred in this act. What do you think motivates him? Is he in control of events or is his wife the motivator for his actions? What is your opinion of Cornwall as a character? What sorts of things do you think he is capable of doing?

4. If you were given the opportunity to add one more illustration to this text that would best capture the essence of Act 2, what would you draw? Sketch or describe your illustration and compare it with those already included with the act.

5. Create a chart, listing on one side the factors and events that suggest the collapse of Lear's former kingdom and, on the other, those that suggest that total collapse may not occur. From the evidence on your chart, predict the action that could possibly transpire. You may wish to add to your chart as the play unfolds.

6. Prepare a list of five or six questions that you would like to ask one character from this act. Make sure that your questions are worded in such a way that they will get full responses. Ask a classmate to assume the character you have chosen and interview him or her, using your prepared questions. You have five minutes to conduct your interview. Did you learn what you wanted to? What other questions do you wish you had asked?

7. There are a number of repeated words and images in this act that help both to underscore key ideas and to reinforce characterization. Brainstorm with your group and make a list of these words and images. Decide whether these words and images help to identify characters as either clearly good or clearly evil. From your list, decide which words and images are better related to themes than to characters. What do you think the most important themes are?

Keep your list current as the play progresses and decide whether or not the observations you have made are consistent throughout. Feel free to alter your point of view as you continue.

8. You have been asked to make a one-page summary of the action, the characters, and the main themes of the play so far. You will use this summary as the basis of a children's story based on *King Lear.* You must make certain that your summary is very clear, easy to follow, and easy to understand. Write your summary and share it with others in the class. How do the summaries differ? How do you account for these differences? After reading several summaries, make an entry in your journal in which you decide whether or not there is such a thing as the "right" story.

9. Lear keeps recounting the good he has done and the gratitude that is owed to him. Do you think his self-assessment is justified? Does doing good necessarily lead to gratitude? In your written analysis of King Lear, decide how he should have behaved and determine to what extent he is the engineer of his own misfortune. It may help to discuss this with your group before you make your decisions.

10. Choose a speech that you would like to recite. Before you do that, read it several times to get a sense of it and how it should sound. Become the character you have adopted and deliver the speech, from memory, to the class. In your journal, you might want to recount the experience.

For the next scene ...

When a country is in social and political turmoil, many things we take for granted are no longer true. From what you know about such conditions, what are some of the codes of behaviour that no longer apply?

Act 3, Scene 1

In this scene ...

In the barren countryside, Kent meets one of Lear's gentlemen. Kent learns that Lear is wandering about in the raging storm, accompanied only by the Fool.

Kent tells the gentleman that a dispute is brewing between Albany and Cornwall and that Cordelia and France have been kept informed of the situation by their spies. The King of France is now sending troops to invade England and to rescue Lear. Kent sends the gentleman to Dover with a message for Cordelia, and gives him a ring with which he can identify himself. Kent and the gentleman separate in search of Lear.

2	*minded like ... unquietly:* with an unquiet (uneasy) mind
4	*Contending with the fretful elements:* struggling with the weather
6	*curled waters:* waves; *main:* land
7	*things:* everything, the order of the world; specifically, Lear's misfortunes
8	*blasts:* winds; *eyeless:* unseeing, blind
9	*make nothing of:* show no respect for
10	*his little world of man:* man's microcosm, in the sense that man is himself a little world
11	*to-and-fro-conflicting:* swaying around in angry conflict
12	*cub-drawn:* hungry. Literally, with udders sucked dry by cubs; *couch:* remain in shelter
13	*belly-pinched:* gaunt and ravenous
14	*unbonneted:* hatless
15	*And bids ... all:* and invites any destructive force to take his life. A gambler, recklessly staking everything he or she has left, might call "Take all."
16-17	*labours to ... injuries:* works hard at joking to relieve the pain caused by Lear's heart-breaking situation
18	*upon the ... note:* on the strength or guarantee of the fact that I know you
19	*Commend:* entrust; *a dear thing:* an important matter; *division:* discord, disunity
20-21	*(Although as ... cunning):* although the appearance of discord is cunningly concealed
22-23	*that their ... high?:* that fate has raised to a position of great power; *who seem no less:* who appear nothing more or less
24	*speculations:* synonym for "spies"
25	*Intelligent of our state:* giving information about our government
26	*snuffs and packings:* resentments and (consequent) plottings
27-28	*hard rein ... King:* arbitrary and cruel way in which they have treated Lear

Act 3, Scene 1

A heath.

Storm still. Enter Kent and a
Gentleman, severally.

Kent: Who's there, besides foul weather?
Gentleman: One minded like the weather, most unquietly.
Kent: I know you. Where's the King?
Gentleman: Contending with the fretful elements;
  Bids the wind blow the earth into the sea,   5
  Or swell the curled waters 'bove the main,
  That things might change or cease; tears his white hair,
  Which the impetuous blasts, with eyeless rage,
  Catch in their fury and make nothing of;
  Strives in his little world of man to outscorn   10
  The to-and-fro-conflicting wind and rain.
  This night, wherein the cub-drawn bear would couch,
  The lion and the belly-pinched wolf
  Keep their fur dry, unbonneted he runs,
  And bids what will take all.
Kent: But who is with him?   15
Gentleman: None but the fool, who labours to outjest
  His heart-struck injuries.
Kent: Sir, I do know you,
  And dare upon the warrant of my note
  Commend a dear thing to you. There is division
  (Although as yet the face of it is covered   20
  With mutual cunning) 'twixt Albany and Cornwall;
  Who have (as who have not, that their great stars
  Throned and set high?) servants, who seem no less,
  Which are to France the spies and speculations
  Intelligent of our state. What hath been seen,   25
  Either in snuffs and packings of the Dukes,
  Or the hard rein which both of them have borne
  Against the old kind King, or something deeper,

29	*furnishings:* outward evidences, trimmings, pretexts. Kent's sentence remains unfinished.
30	*power:* army
31	*scattered:* divided
32	*Wise in our negligence:* knowing that we are ill-prepared; *have secret feet:* having obtained a secret foothold
33	*at point:* on the point of, ready to
35	*If on ... far:* if you dare to trust me as far as
36	*make your speed:* hurry
37	*making:* for making; *just:* accurate
38	*bemadding:* maddening
39	*plain:* complain of
41	*assurance:* reliable information
42	*office:* assignment, duty
45	*my out-wall:* my outer wall, exterior, or what I appear to be. Kent is in the disguise of a servant.
52	*to effect:* in their importance
53-54	*(in which ... this):* in which your task or effort lies this way (as he has just been instructed by Kent), while mine lies in this direction; *lights on:* discovers
55	*Holla:* shout for, summon

Whereof, perchance, these are but furnishings—
But, true it is, from France there comes a power   30
Into this scattered kingdom, who already,
Wise in our negligence, have secret feet
In some of our best ports and are at point
To show their open banner. Now to you:
If on my credit you dare build so far   35
To make your speed to Dover, you shall find
Some that will thank you, making just report
Of how unnatural and bemadding sorrow
The King hath cause to plain.
I am a gentleman of blood and breeding,   40
And from some knowledge and assurance offer
This office to you.
Gentleman: I will talk further with you.
Kent: No, do not.
For confirmation that I am much more
Than my out-wall, open this purse and take   45
What it contains. If you shall see Cordelia
As fear not but you shall, show her this ring,
And she will tell you who that fellow is
That yet you do not know. Fie on this storm!
I will go seek the King.   50
Gentleman: Give me your hand. Have you no more to say?
Kent: Few words, but, to effect, more than all yet:
That, when we have found the King (in which your pain
That way, I'll this), he that first lights on him
Holla the other.   [*Exeunt severally.*] 55

Act 3, Scene 1: Activities

1. Kent obviously knows a great deal more about what is going on in the kingdom than he has told Lear's gentleman. Assume the two have had a fuller conversation and, with a partner, create their brief but pointed dialogue. What is Kent's role in the invasion plot? What are his plans and motives? Is he completely open and honest with Lear's gentleman? Does the gentleman trust him?

   Enact your conversation for the class.

2. In this scene, Kent reveals enough to have himself killed. Who is the man to whom he is talking? What can you tell about him and his motives? Role-play a television interview with this mystery man, the source of some important information about impending events. Find out who he is and what he is up to.

3. There appears to be no coherent sense of geography in this play. Draw a map of the action so far in terms of "who went where." Use this scene as the centre of your map and position everyone else in locations that make sense for you.

4. If this scene were accidentally left out, how might the play as you see it unfolding be altered by this omission? Discuss your ideas before you write and present them.

For the next scene ...

In your journal, recount an instance in which you encountered an elderly person in a position much worse than your own. What thoughts went through your mind? What thoughts do you think were going through that person's mind? What feeling do you have about becoming elderly yourself?

Act 3, Scene 2

In this scene ...

In another part of the heath, Lear stands raging at the storm. The Fool attempts to make him take shelter, but Lear pays no attention. When Kent finds them, he persuades Lear to seek out a hovel that is close by. Lear agrees, fearing for his sanity. Kent decides to return to Gloucester's castle to persuade Goneril and Regan that they should allow Lear to return.

1	*Blow, winds ... blow:* Old maps were often decorated with faces drawn in the act of furiously blowing air or wind.
2	*cataracts:* the floodgates of the heavens; *hurricanoes:* waterspouts
3	*cocks:* weather-vanes on the peaks of buildings
4	*thought-executing:* killing with the speed of thought
5	*Vaunt-couriers:* forerunners (from the French "avant coureurs"); *oak-cleaving:* strong enough to split an oak
7	*Strike flat ... world:* flatten the earth
8	*Nature's molds:* shapes into which all things are first poured in their creation, i.e., the creative force of Nature, which has cheated Lear by giving him such ungrateful daughters; *germens:* seeds; *spill:* destroy, kill
10	*court holy water:* flattering words (a proverbial or popular phrase). Flatter your daughters into giving you shelter for the night.
11-12	*ask thy daughters' blessing:* Apologize and come to terms with your daughters.
14	*thy bellyful:* Since the storm is personified, the sense is "to your heart's content," or until you have had enough.
15	*Nor:* neither
16-18	*I tax ... subscription:* Lear feels no bitterness at the storm, which owes him nothing. He implies that what the storm can do to him is nothing compared with what has been done to him by his daughters.
21	*servile ministers:* slave-like or cringing servants
22-23	*pernicious:* evil; *join your high-engendered battles:* combine your heavenly (and hence, all-powerful) battalions
25	*put's:* put his
26	*headpiece:* a pun: hat and brain. Lear should have brains enough to take shelter from the storm.
27-30	*The codpiece ... many:* The man who satisfies his sexual drives before he has a roof over his head will end up a lice-infested beggar; *codpiece:* a cover for the male genitals, worn on the outside of tight fitting hose. Here, it symbolizes sexual lust.

Scene 2

Another part of the heath.
Storm still. Enter Lear and Fool.

Lear: Blow, winds, and crack your cheeks! rage! blow!
   You cataracts and hurricanoes, spout
   Till you have drenched our steeples, drowned the cocks!
   You sulph'rous and thought-executing fires,
   Vaunt-couriers of oak-cleaving thunderbolts,   5
   Singe my white head! And thou, all-shaking thunder,
   Strike flat the thick rotundity o' the world,
   Crack Nature's molds, all germens spill at once,
   That make ingrateful man!
Fool: O nuncle, court holy water in a dry house is better   10
   than this rain water out o' door. Good nuncle, in; ask
   thy daughters' blessing! Here's a night pities neither
   wise men nor fools.
Lear: Rumble thy bellyful! Spit, fire! Spout, rain!
   Nor rain, wind, thunder, fire are my daughters.   15
   I tax not you, you elements, with unkindness.
   I never gave you kingdom, called you children,
   You owe me no subscription. Then let fall
   Your horrible pleasure. Here I stand your slave,
   A poor, infirm, weak, and despised old man.   20
   But yet I call you servile ministers,
   That will with two pernicious daughters join
   Your high-engendered battles 'gainst a head
   So old and white as this! O, ho! 'Tis foul!
Fool: He that has a house to put's head in has a good   25
   headpiece.
            The codpiece that will house
               Before the head has any,
            The head and he shall louse:
               So beggars marry many.   30

31-34	*The man ... wake:* The man who pays more attention to an unimportant part of his body (his toe) rather than to an important one (his brain) will suffer harm from the part he considered significant. The implication is that Lear has brought this trouble on himself by failing to see things in the proper order of importance.
35-36	*For there ... glass:* A reference to vanity – possibly that of Goneril and Regan or, perhaps, a reference to their practised hypocrisy.
37	*pattern:* example
40	*grace:* the King's grace or the King himself; *codpiece:* The Fool refers to himself. He leaves Kent to decide which is the wise man and which the fool.
44	*Gallow ... dark:* terrify even the creatures that walk at night
45	*keep:* stay inside; *Since... man:* Kent is 48 and therefore reflecting.
48	*carry:* bear, endure
50	*pudder:* turmoil
53	*Unwhipped of:* unpunished by; *bloody:* murderous
54	*simular:* simulator, pretender
55	*incestuous:* lustful after child, sibling, or parent – a desire considered abhorrent in all societies; *Caitiff:* villain
56	*covert:* secret; *seeming:* pretence, hypocrisy fitted for the purpose
57	*practised:* plotted against; *guilts:* crimes
58-59	*Rive your concealing continents:* Shatter the containers hiding you; *summoners:* church officers who called offenders before the church courts. Here, the summoners are the vengeances against sinful man, represented by the storm; *cry these dreadful summoners grace:* beg for mercy from (the storm)
62	*lend:* give, afford
63	*hard house:* cruel palace (of Gloucester)
65	*Which:* the owners of which
66	*to come in:* entry, welcome
67	*scanted:* missing

   The man that makes his toe
    What he his heart should make
   Shall of corn cry woe,
    And turn his sleep to wake.
 For there was never yet fair woman but she made   35
 mouths in a glass.
 [*Enter Kent.*]
Lear: No, I will be the pattern of all patience;
 I will say nothing.
Kent: Who's there?
Fool: Marry, here's grace and a codpiece; that's a wise man   40
 and a fool.
Kent: Alas, sir, are you here? Things that love night
 Love not such nights as these. The wrathful skies
 Gallow the very wanderers of the dark
 And make them keep their caves. Since I was man,   45
 Such sheets of fire, such bursts of horrid thunder,
 Such groans of roaring wind and rain, I never
 Remember to have heard. Man's nature cannot carry
 The affliction nor the fear.
Lear: Let the great gods,
 That keep this dreadful pudder o'er our heads,   50
 Find out their enemies now. Tremble, thou wretch,
 That hast within thee undivulged crimes
 Unwhipped of justice. Hide thee, thou bloody hand;
 Thou perjured, and thou simular of virtue
 That are incestuous. Caitiff, to pieces shake   55
 That under covert and convenient seeming
 Hast practised on man's life. Close pent-up guilts,
 Rive your concealing continents, and cry
 These dreadful summoners grace. I am a man
 More sinned against than sinning.
Kent: Alack, bareheaded?   60
 Gracious my lord, hard by here is a hovel;
 Some friendship will it lend you 'gainst the tempest.
 Repose you there, while I to this hard house
 (More harder than the stones whereof 'tis raised,
 Which even but now, demanding after you,   65
 Denied me to come in) return, and force
 Their scanted courtesy.

70	*art:* Lear refers to the art of alchemy, which contrived to turn base metals into gold. He is pointing out that necessity has a strange way of changing us.
71	*vile:* paltry (such as mere straw for bedding)
74-77	*He that ... day:* The Fool's song is an adaptation of a song in *Twelfth Night.* The meaning is that a fool must be content with whatever fortune brings, which will be poor because he is a fool. He may be referring to himself, or to Lear, or to both.
78	*True:* Lear agrees with the Fool; *bring:* show us the way
79	*brave ... a courtesan:* a good night to cool the lust of a courtier's (a well-to-do servant of the court) mistress
81	*more in word than matter:* better in preaching than in conduct
81-94	*When priests ... feet:* The Fool speaks of a series of prophecies that are based upon common events, and pretends that they will probably never happen. Lines 81-84 refer to the actual state at affairs; lines 85-90 refer to the ideal state of affairs.
82	*malt:* an ingredient of beer and ale
83	*their tailors' tutors:* teach their tailors how to make clothes
84	*No heretics ... suitors:* accepted religious belief. They were frequently burned at the stake. The Fool is punning: "burned" means suffering from the pox (syphilis).
86	*squire:* boy apprenticed to a knight to learn the art of knighthood
88	*cutpurses:* thieves (who cut purse strings and make off with the purse)
89	*When usurers tell:* when those who charge outrageous interest for loans count (their money)
90	*bawds:* See line 79, a variant of courtesan or prostitute; *do churches build:* as a sign of repentance
91	*Albion:* Britain
92	*confusion:* ruin
93	*who:* if anyone
94	*That going ... feet:* that feet shall be used for walking, with an obvious pun on "used"
95	*Merlin:* the magician of King Arthur's Court. The general setting of *King Lear* is early England before the time of King Arthur.

Lear: My wits begin to turn.
  Come on, my boy. How dost, my boy? Art cold?
  I am cold myself. Where is this straw, my fellow?
  The art of our necessities is strange,   70
  And can make vile things precious. Come, your hovel.
  Poor fool and knave, I have one part in my heart
  That's sorry yet for thee.
Fool [*Sings.*]:
         He that has and a little tiny wit,
            With hey, ho, the wind and the ram,   75
         Must make content with his fortunes fit,
            Though the rain it raineth every day.
Lear: True, boy. Come, bring us to this hovel.
                      [*Exeunt Lear and Kent.*]
Fool: This is a brave night to cool a courtesan. I'll speak a
  prophecy ere I go: 80
       When priests are more in word than matter;
       When brewers mar their malt with water;
       When nobles are their tailors' tutors,
       No heretics burned, but wenches' suitors;
       When every case in law is right;   85
       No squire in debt nor no poor knight;
       When slanders do not live in tongues;
       Nor cutpurses come not to throngs;
       When usurers tell their gold i' the field;
       And bawds and whores do churches build: 90
       Then shall the realm of Albion
       Come to great confusion.
       Then comes the time, who lives to see't,
       That going shall be used with feet.
  This prophecy Merlin shall make, for I live before his   95
  time.   [*Exit.*]

Act 3, Scene 2: Activities

1. One of the ways Shakespeare establishes mood in *King Lear* is to generate an oppressive atmosphere full of storms and darkness. With your group, find a number of particularly effective images that help to reinforce this sense of gloom and indicate, where possible, how the various characters respond to it. As a member of the audience for the first performance of the play, what effect did it have on you? In a journal entry, decide what role mood or atmosphere has in the overall impact of a drama.

2. Many of the Fool's comments and songs contain obscene references. Why do you think the Fool might speak this way? Is he simply crude? insane? trying to make a point of some kind? Is Shakespeare using the Fool simply to amuse the audience?

   In groups, discuss your ideas about the Fool's role. In your journal, record whether or not you think the Fool is necessary in the play.

3. Physical action can reflect the turmoil going on in a character's mind. In the opening of this scene, Lear rages that the entire universe should be destroyed. Read the first 24 lines as Lear, moving about the room. Add gestures as the intensity increases, and modulate your voice to fit your mood. What do you do to create a general feeling of anger and distress? Before you rehearse your delivery, you might wish to copy out the speech and determine what lines may be key to movement and where gestures might occur.

For the next scene ...

In your journal, recall an incident in which you tried to help two parties resolve a problem, but became the villain in the eyes of both parties. Do you think you were used by one or the other party? How was the situation resolved?

Act 3, Scene 3

In this scene ...

Gloucester trusts Edmund so implicitly that he reveals to him the contents of a letter that gives details of the invading army that has already landed in England. In addition, Gloucester tells Edmund that he is determined to help Lear despite Cornwall's commands against it.

Edmund decides to inform Cornwall that his father is a traitor. He believes that this information will induce Cornwall (who has confiscated Gloucester's possessions) to give them to Edmund.

Scene Description — The quarto adds "with lights" to suggest a night scene in Gloucester's house.

1-2	*unnatural dealing:* cruel treatment given to Lear; *leave:* permission
2	*pity:* take pity on, help
4	*perpetual displeasure:* permanent hostility
5	*sustain:* care for, as in provide with necessities
8	*Go to:* roughly equivalent to "That's enough."
9	*worse matter:* i.e., the French invasion
10	*'tis dangerous to be spoken:* It's dangerous to divulge the contents in speaking.
11	*closet:* private room or, perhaps, cupboard
12	*home:* completely, to the utmost
13	*power:* army; *footed:* landed (from France); *incline to:* support
14	*look him:* look for him; *privily relieve:* secretly aid
15	*charity:* kind treatment
19	*toward:* imminent, about to happen
21	*courtesy:* service; *forbid:* forbidden
22	*Instantly know:* from Edmund
23	*a fair deserving:* a service that should bring me the reward I deserve; *draw me:* bring to me

Scene 3

Inside Gloucester's castle.
Enter Gloucester and Edmund.

Gloucester: Alack, alack, Edmund, I like not this unnatural
dealing! When I desired their leave that I might pity
him, they took from me the use of mine own house;
charged me on pain of perpetual displeasure neither
to speak of him, entreat for him, nor any way sustain   5
him.
Edmund: Most savage and unnatural!
Gloucester: Go to; say you nothing. There is division between
the Dukes, and a worse matter than that. I have received a letter this night—'tis dangerous to be spoken—   10
I have locked the letter in my closet. These injuries
the King now bears will be revenged home; there is part
of a power already footed; we must incline to the
King. I will look him and privily relieve him. Go you
and maintain talk with the Duke, that my charity   15
be not of him perceived. If he ask for me, I am ill and
gone to bed. If I die for it, as no less is threatened
me, the King my old master must be relieved. There
are strange things toward, Edmund. Pray you be
careful.   [*Exit.*]   20
Edmund: This courtesy, forbid thee, shall the Duke
Instantly know, and of that letter too.
This seems a fair deserving, and must draw me
That which my father loses—no less than all.
The younger rises when the old doth fall.   [*Exit.*]   25

Act 3, Scene 3: Activities

1. Many critics have argued that Shakespeare wrote some scenes simply to give actors time to prepare for the action that follows. This scene is often cited as an example of this argument. In groups, discuss whether or not you think this scene is necessary to the sense of the play. Does it present any new information? Does it add any new insights to your understanding of the play? Before making your decision, review the scene with your group. Consider the difference between the text and a performance of this scene on stage. How long might it take to present this scene?

2. Some people have said that this scene is repetitive and boring. Do you agree? Discuss your ideas with your group and explain your position in a brief essay.

3. Edmund hopes to gain "that which my father loses" by means of duplicity. Discuss with your group why Edmund seems to have been so successful in his plan. Create an editorial or an editorial cartoon that expresses your views on deceitfulness as a means of achieving your goals.

For the next scene ...

In your journal, describe an example of human life in the most degraded form imaginable that you have either witnessed first-hand or encountered in the media. What, in your opinion, caused the situation? Do you believe that people in such degraded conditions need society's help or do you feel that they must help themselves?

Act 3, Scene 4

In this scene ...

Kent, Lear, and the Fool arrive outside the hovel. Despite Kent's pleas, Lear refuses to enter. Seemingly impervious to the storm, he rages at his two daughters for their treatment of him. He tells Kent that he wishes to remain outside and pray.

As the Fool goes inside, Lear addresses the "poor naked wretches" (line 28) of the world whom he feels he has neglected. Suddenly Edgar, disguised as Poor Tom, speaks from inside the hovel. Lear, now quite mad, thinks the beggar has been brought to his fate by ungrateful daughters – he feels that only daughters as cruel as his own could reduce a man to such a pitiful condition. Faced with this image of "unaccommodated man," Lear asks, "Is man no more than this?" In sympathy with the beggar, Lear tears off his own clothes.

Gloucester enters to offer Lear shelter. Lear eventually agrees to follow him but insists on taking Poor Tom along. Gloucester reveals to Kent that Goneril and Regan are seeking Lear's death.

1	*the place:* i.e., the hovel
2	*The tyranny ... night's:* the harshness of the night in the open air
3	*nature:* human strength
4	*Wilt break my heart?:* Possibly Lear addressing his own heart or Lear thinking that if he remains in the storm he will be distracted from thinking about the ingratitude that has happened to him which would break his heart.
6	*'tis much:* that it at all matters; *contentious:* contending (in the sense of contending or struggling against humans)
7	*Invades:* soaks
8-9	*But where ... felt:* Where a greater illness is established, a lesser one is scarcely noticed.
11-12	*i' the mouth:* face to face; *When the ... delicate:* When the mind is untroubled, the body is sensitive.
14	*Save what beats there:* except what troubles my heart – the ungratefulness of Goneril and Regan; *Filial ingratitude:* ungratefulness of children
16	*home:* to the fullest extent
20	*frank:* generous
21	*that way:* in thinking of those things; *shun:* avoid
25	*On things would:* on things that would

Scene 4

Before a hovel on the heath.
Storm still. Enter Lear, Kent,
and Fool.

Kent: Here is the place, my lord. Good my lord, enter.
　The tyranny of the open night's too rough
　For nature to endure.
Lear: 　　　　　　　Let me alone.
Kent: Good my lord, enter here.
Lear: 　　　　　　　　Wilt break my heart?
Kent: I had rather break mine own. Good my lord, enter.　　5
Lear: Thou thinkest 'tis much that this contentious storm
　Invades us to the skin. So 'tis to thee;
　But where the greater malady is fixed,
　The lesser is scarce felt. Thou'dst shun a bear;
　But if thy flight lay toward the roaring sea,　　10
　Thou'dst meet the bear i' the mouth. When the mind's
　　free,
　The body's delicate. The tempest in my mind
　Doth from my senses take all feeling else
　Save what beats there. Filial ingratitude!
　Is it not as this mouth should tear this hand　　15
　For lifting food to it? But I will punish home!
　No, I will weep no more. In such a night
　To shut me out! Pour on; I will endure.
　In such a night as this! O Regan, Goneril!
　Your old kind father, whose frank heart gave all!　　20
　O, that way madness lies; let me shun that!
　No more of that.
Kent: 　　　　　　Good my lord, enter here.
Lear: Prithee go in thyself; seek thine own ease.
　This tempest will not give me leave to ponder
　On things would hurt me more. But I'll go in.　　25

26	*You houseless poverty:* you poor, homeless fellow. Here, the abstract is used for the concrete.
27	*pray:* Lear prays to the poor, not to the gods.
29	*bide:* endure; *pelting:* relentless pouring
31	*looped and windowed raggedness:* ragged clothing full of gaping holes.
33	*this:* this condition of the poor, to which I have been reduced; *Take physic, pomp:* Cure yourselves, you great ones. Lear then gives the remedy.
35-36	*shake the ... just:* Cast away what you do not need (the "superflux" or superfluity) and give it to the poor, and show that there is more justice in life than we think.
37	*Fathom and half:* Edgar uses the call of the sailor sound, which is made to sound the depth of water in the hold of a sinking ship.
46	*Humh:* Edgar shivers from the cold and damp.
48	*Didst thou ... daughters?:* Lear, in his madness, thinks that any misfortune evidently as great as Poor Tom's could only have been inflicted by daughters as ungrateful as his own.
50-61	*Who gives ... there:* Edgar is begging for charity, but he is not entirely coherent. We must remember that he is playing a part.
53	*laid knives under his pillow:* for killing himself; *halters in his pew:* ropes with which to hang himself from a porch
54	*ratsbane:* rat poison; *porridge:* broth, soup
55	*bay:* brown; *trotting horse:* horse trained to move gently; *four-inched:* very narrow
56-57	*course:* chase; *for:* as; *Bless thy five wits:* May God bless your faculties. The five wits were imagination, common wit, estimation, fantasy, and memory. These are not to be confused with the five senses.
57	*O, do ... de:* Edgar shudders from the cold.
58	*Bless thee:* May God protect you; *star-blasting:* being struck by a wandering star; *taking:* being struck by disease, infection
60-61	*There could ... there:* Edgar pretends to clutch at a spirit or devil that haunts him and torments his body.

[*To the Fool.*] In, boy; go first.—You houseless poverty—
Nay, get thee in. I'll pray, and then I'll sleep.
[*The Fool enters the hovel.*]
Poor naked wretches, wheresoe'er you are,
That bide the pelting of this pitiless storm,
How shall your houseless heads and unfed sides, 30
Your looped and windowed raggedness, defend you
From seasons such as these? O, I have ta'en
Too little care of this! Take physic, pomp;
Expose thyself to feel what wretches feel,
That thou may'st shake the superflux to them 35
And show the heavens more just.
Edgar: [*Within.*] Fathom and half, fathom and half! Poor
Tom!
[*Re-enter Fool.*]
Fool: Come not in here, nuncle, here's a spirit. Help me,
help me! 40
Kent: Give me thy hand. Who's there?
Fool: A spirit, a spirit! He says his name's poor Tom.
Kent: What art thou that dost grumble there i' the straw?
Come forth.
[*Enter Edgar.*]
Edgar: Away! the foul fiend follows me! Through the sharp 45
hawthorn blow the winds. Humh! Go to thy bed, and
warm thee.
Lear: Didst thou give all to thy two daughters? And art
thou come to this?
Edgar: Who gives anything to poor Tom? Whom the foul 50
fiend hath led through fire and through flame,
through ford and whirlpool, o'er bog and quagmire;
that hath laid knives under his pillow and halters in his
pew, set ratsbane by his porridge, made him proud
of heart, to ride on a bay trotting horse over four-inched 55
bridges, to course his own shadow for a traitor. Bless
thy five wits! Tom's acold. O, do de, do de, do de.
Bless thee from whirlwinds, star-blasting, and taking!
Do poor Tom some charity, whom the foul fiend
vexes. There could I have him now, and there, and 60
there again, and there! [*Storm still.*]

69   *Death, traitor:* Lear would condemn Kent to death for daring to suggest that anything but filial ingratitude could have caused Poor Tom's plight; *subdued nature:* reduced his powers

72   *little mercy on their flesh?:* a reference either to Edgar's horrid state or to his own flesh, in which he possibly has stuck pins and thorns

73   *Judicious:* fitting, appropriate, suitable; *this flesh:* Lear himself; *begot:* fathered

74   *pelican:* thought to feed its young with its own blood

75-76   *Pillicock Hill:* The word "pillicock" is suggested to Edgar by the word "pelican." "Pillicock" was a term of endearment meaning, roughly, "darling"; *Alow, alow, loo, loo:* a cry used to call a hawk

78-81   *Take heed ... acold:* Edgar is apparently reciting a catechism (a means of religious instruction using questions and answers about aspects of religious doctrine); *keep thy word's justice:* Literally, be as just in deeds as you are in words. Here the sense is, keep the word; *commit not ... spouse:* Do not commit adultery with another man's wife.

83   *A servingman:* either a lover or a servant who uses his good looks to advantage

89-90   *out-paramoured the Turk:* had more mistresses than the Sultan of Turkey

90-91   *light of ear:* ready to listen to any malicious talk; *hog in sloth:* as lazy as a pig. Sloth was one of the Seven Deadly Sins.

92-94   *Let not ... woman:* Do not fall in love with a woman as soon as you hear her shoes creak or her skirts rustle.

95   *plackets:* An opening, in the side-seam of a woman's dress or skirt, that made it easier to put the garment on. A placket was also used as a synonym for a loose woman; *lender's books:* a money-lender's record book

96-98   *Still through ... wind:* Edgar's words are probably the refrain of a song or a poem; *suum, mun, hey, no, nonny:* possibly the sound of the wind; *Dolphin my boy, my boy:* Dolphin was a common name for a horse; *sessa:* a term used with horses, like "giddy-up"

99   *answer:* bear the brunt of

100   *extremity:* severity

Lear: Have his daughters brought him to this pass?
  Couldst thou save nothing? Wouldst thou give 'em all?
Fool: Nay, he reserved a blanket, else we had been all
    shamed.   65
Lear: Now all the plagues that in the pendulous air
  Hang fated o'er men's faults light on thy daughters!
Kent: He hath no daughters, sir.
Lear: Death, traitor! Nothing could have subdued nature
  To such a lowness but his unkind daughters.   70
  Is it the fashion that discarded fathers
  Should have thus little mercy on their flesh?
  Judicious punishment! 'Twas this flesh begot
  Those pelican daughters.
Edgar: Pillicock sat on Pillicock Hill. Alow, alow,   75
    loo, loo!
Fool: This cold night will turn us all to fools and madmen.
Edgar: Take heed o' the foul fiend; obey thy parents; keep
    thy word's justice; swear not; commit not with man's
    sworn spouse; set not thy sweet heart on proud array.   80
    Tom's acold.
Lear: What hast thou been?
Edgar: A servingman, proud in heart and mind; that curled
    my hair, wore gloves in my cap; served the lust of my
    mistress' heart and did the act of darkness with her;   85
    swore as many oaths as I spake words, and broke
    them in the sweet face of heaven; one that slept in the
    contriving of lust, and waked to do it. Wine loved I
    deeply, dice dearly; and in woman out-paramoured
    the Turk. False of heart, light of ear, bloody of hand;   90
    hog in sloth, fox in stealth, wolf in greediness, dog in
    madness, lion in prey. Let not the creaking of shoes
    nor the rustling of silks betray thy poor heart to
    woman. Keep thy foot out of brothels, thy hand out
    of plackets, thy pen from lender's books, and defy the   95
    foul fiend. Still through the hawthorn blows the cold
    wind; says suum, mun, hey, no, nonny. Dolphin my
    boy, my boy, sessa! Let him trot by.   [*Storm still.*]
Lear: Thou wert better in thy grave than to answer with
    thy uncovered body this extremity of the skies. Is man   100

165

103-104   *cat:* the civet-cat, whose glands function like those of the
           skunk and provide the base for the best perfume; *on's:* of
           us; *sophisticated:* made artificial, wearing clothes that are
           not a part of themselves. Lear comments on the contrast
           between Edgar, who has taken nothing from the animals for
           himself, and Lear, Kent, and the Fool, who are all fully
           clothed.
104   *unaccommodated:* unsheltered, unprotected
105   *forked:* two-legged
106   *lendings:* borrowed articles (his clothing)

Stage Direction – *Tearing his garments:* Lear tears at his clothing,
trying to remove it, to be "natural."

107   *naughty:* awful
108-110   *Now a ... cold:* Just as a flame in a barren field will not
           cause a widespread fire, so the lust in a wicked old man's
           heart will not give energy, warmth or potency to his body.
110   *a walking fire:* Gloucester, carrying his torch
111-113   *Flibbertigibbet:* an Elizabethan devil; *curfew:* 9 p.m.; *first
           cock:* midnight; *the web and the pin:* eye cataract
114   *white:* unripened
115-119   *Swithold footed ... thee:* St. Withold travelled around the
           world three times, met the demon Nightmare and her nine
           children, ordered her to dismount from the spirits she was
           riding, and to promise never to trouble anyone again.

125   *todpole:* tadpole; *wall-newt:* wall lizard; *water:* water newt

127   *sallets:* salads; *old rat and the ditch-dog:* dead rat and dog
           carcass found in a ditch
128   *green mantle:* greenish scum; *standing:* stagnant
129   *tithing:* parish or district. A district contained ten families.
           Elizabethan law required that vagrants be publicly whipped
           and sent off to another district; *stock-punished:* put into the
           stocks
130   *three suits:* the allowance of a servant
134   *my follower:* my attending fiend or familiar; *Smulkin:* name
           of another Elizabethan devil

137   *Modo ... Mahu:* powerful Elizabethan devils

no more than this? Consider him well. Thou owest
the worm no silk, the beast no hide, the sheep no wool,
the cat no perfume. Ha! Here's three on's are sophis-
ticated! Thou art the thing itself; unaccommodated man
is no more but such a poor, bare, forked animal as   105
thou art. Off, off, you lendings! Come, unbutton here.
         [*Tearing his garments.*]
Fool: Prithee, nuncle, be contented! 'Tis a naughty night
to swim in. Now a little fire in a wild field were like an
old lecher's heart—a small spark, all the rest on's
body cold. Look, here comes a walking fire.   110
[*Enter Gloucester with a torch.*]
Edgar: This is the foul Flibbertigibbet. He begins at curfew,
and walks till the first cock. He gives the web and the
pin, squints the eye, and makes the harelip; mildews
the white wheat, and hurts the poor creature of earth.
  Swithold footed thrice the 'old;   115
  He met the nightmare, and her nine fold;
    Bid her alight
    And her troth plight,
  And aroint thee, witch, aroint thee!
Kent: How fares your Grace?   120
Lear: What's he?
Kent: Who's there? What is't you seek?
Gloucester: What are you there? Your names?
Edgar: Poor Tom, that eats the swimming frog, the toad,
  the todpole, the wall-newt and the water; that in the   125
fury of his heart, when the foul fiend rages, eats cow-
dung for sallets, swallows the old rat and the ditch-dog,
drinks the green mantle of the standing pool; who is
whipped from tithing to tithing, and stock-punished and
imprisoned; who hath had three suits to his back, six   130
shirts to his body, horse to ride, and weapon to wear;
  But mice and rats, and such small deer,
  Have been Tom's food for seven long year.
Beware my follower. Peace, Smulkin! Peace, thou fiend!
Gloucester: What, hath your Grace no better company?   135
Edgar: The prince of darkness is a gentleman!
  Modo he's called, and Mahu.

138	*Our flesh and blood:* our children – Edgar, Goneril and Regan. Gloucester links all of these people together because he considers them to be villains; *is grown:* has become
139	*gets:* begets, is the father of, causes
141	*suffer:* permit, allow
147	*philosopher:* scientist. In Elizabethan English, "philosophy" meant science or the accumulation of knowledge.
148	*What is ... thunder?:* a scientific question, frequently discussed before the facts were known.
150	*learned Theban:* learned Greek, a scholar
151	*study?:* particular field of study or research
152	*prevent:* avoid, keep ahead of; *vermin:* small, parasitic animals
154	*Importune:* beg, implore. Pronounced with the stress on "por."
160	*outlawed from my blood:* outcast from my family as a criminal
164	*cry you mercy, sir:* I beg your pardon. (Lear did not hear Gloucester.)
170	*soothe him:* Let him have his way.

Gloucester: Our flesh and blood, my lord, is grown so vile,
  That it doth hate what gets it.
Edgar: Poor Tom's acold.   140
Gloucester: Go in with me. My duty cannot suffer
  T' obey in all your daughters' hard commands.
  Though their injunction be to bar my doors
  And let this tyrannous night take hold upon you,
  Yet have I ventured to come seek you out   145
  And bring you where both fire and food is ready.
Lear: First let me talk with this philosopher.
  What is the cause of thunder?
Kent: Good my lord, take his offer; go into the house.
Lear: I'll talk a word with this same learned Theban.   150
  What is your study?
Edgar: How to prevent the fiend and to kill vermin.
Lear: Let me ask you one word in private.
Kent: Importune him once more to go, my lord.
  His wits begin to unsettle.
Gloucester: Canst thou blame him?   155
                    [*Storm still.*]
  His daughters seek his death. Ah, that good Kent!
  He said it would be thus—poor banished man!
  Thou sayest the King grows mad: I'll tell thee, friend,
  I am almost mad myself. I had a son,
  Now outlawed from my blood. He sought my life   160
  But lately, very late. I loved him, friend—
  No father his son dearer. True to tell thee,
  The grief hath crazed my wits. What a night's this!
  I do beseech your Grace—
Lear: O, cry you mercy, sir.
  Noble philosopher, your company.   165
Edgar: Tom's acold.
Gloucester: In, fellow, there, into the hovel; keep thee warm.
Lear: Come, let's in all.
Kent: This way, my lord.
Lear: With him!
  I will keep still with my philosopher.
Kent: Good my lord, soothe him; let him take the fellow.   170

171   *Take him you on:* This may refer either to Poor Tom or to the Fool. If Tom, he is taken to the hovel and Kent goes elsewhere with the King and the others.

173   *Athenian:* philosopher, thinker

175   *Child:* a candidate for knighthood; *Rowland:* nephew of Charlemagne and the chief knight of his time, according to legends; *Child Rowland ... came:* probably a line from a lost ballad

176   *word:* motto; *still:* ever, always

177-178   *Fie, foh ... man:* a couplet from "Jack the Giant Killer," which is madly unsuitable for a chivalrous knight to use as a motto for his coat of arms.

Gloucester: Take him you on.
Kent: Sirrah, come on; go along with us.
Lear: Come, good Athenian.
Gloucester: No words, no words! hush.
Edgar: Child Rowland to the dark tower came;   175
    His word was still
               Fie, foh, and fum!
               I smell the blood of a British man.
                                  [Exeunt.]

Act 3, Scene 4: Activities

1. Choose one of the following:

   a) Create a crossword puzzle using only words that appear in the glossary in this scene. Keep your puzzle simple – twenty words at most, and exchange it with another group. Follow standard crossword-puzzle format to avoid confusion.

   b) Extract Edgar's speeches and paraphrase them. Make special note of the key ideas and visual images they contain. Create a shortened version of these speeches in modern English and present it as a monologue to the class. Make sure that, while your speech may sound like nonsense, it communicates meaning to an astute listener.

2. Prepare a two-minute dramatization of one important part of this scene. You might choose to use a reader's theatre presentation in which you read the text, using facial expressions and gestures to give meaning and feeling to the words you read.

   Make sure you communicate essentials of the plot, conflict, and theme in your presentation. Perform your reading with a partner or with a group.

3. Select a modern piece of music, or portions of one, that you think best captures the mood of this scene. Tape the music and play it for your group or the whole class. Be sure to identify the portion of the scene you are illustrating. Discuss the effectiveness of each choice.

4. Write a detailed description or draw a picture of how you think Edgar as a Bedlam beggar appears in this scene.

5. As a director for this scene, decide how you might present this scene to create dramatic effect on your audience. Make diagrams to show where you would place characters in relation to each other. Decide what effects you want to create and how you would do this. Share your ideas with your classmates.

6. Write a poem or piece of prose that captures the mood, the weather, and the action in this scene. Share your selection with a partner or your group, and select the words and phrases that you feel most effectively convey the scene's atmosphere. Record your final version and present it to the class.

For the next scene ...

Why do you think loyalty is so important to people and betrayal is so upsetting?

Act 3, Scene 5

In this scene ...

In this brief scene, we learn that Edmund continues to be successful. He has informed Cornwall that his father plans to support France. As a reward for this information, he has been granted the earldom of Gloucester. Cornwall commands Edmund to find his father so that punishment can be administered. Edmund hopes he will find Gloucester helping Lear, which will cast even greater suspicion on his father.

1	*I will have my revenge:* Edmund has told Cornwall that Gloucester intends to help Lear and to support the invading French army; *his house:* Gloucester's castle
2	*censured:* judged; *nature:* human nature, the natural bond between father and son
3	*loyalty:* to Cornwall, rather than his father; *fears me:* makes me worry
6	*provoking merit:* something deserved that motivates action; *reprovable badness:* wickedness deserving punishment. Cornwall claims that it was not only the evil in Edgar that made him plot against his father. Gloucester's evil was also to blame although Edgar's wickedness was a motivating factor.
8-9	*repent to be just:* feel remorse for doing the right thing; *approves:* proves
10	*an intelligent party:* a well-informed person, spy; *to the advantages of:* on behalf of
11	*That … or not I:* I wish that this treason did not exist, and that I was not (the detector).
16	*True or false:* The letter itself is evidence enough; the exact facts do not matter.
18	*apprehension:* arrest
19	*comforting:* aiding
20	*stuff:* reinforce, strengthen; *his suspicion:* the suspicion that already rests on Gloucester

Scene 5

Inside Gloucester's castle.
Enter Cornwall and Edmund.

Cornwall: I will have my revenge ere I depart his house.
Edmund: How, my lord, I may be censured, that nature thus
    gives way to loyalty, something fears me to think of.
Cornwall: I now perceive it was not altogether your broth-
    er's evil disposition made him seek his death; but a   5
    provoking merit, set a-work by a reprovable badness
    in himself.
Edmund: How malicious is my fortune that I must repent
    to be just! This is the letter he spoke of, which approves
    him an intelligent party to the advantages of France.   10
    O heavens! That this treason were not, or not I the
    detector!
Cornwall: Go with me to the Duchess.
Edmund: If the matter of this paper be certain, you have
    mighty business in hand.   15
Cornwall: True or false, it hath made thee Earl of Gloucester.
    Seek out where thy father is, that he may be ready
    for our apprehension.
Edmund: [*Aside.*] If I find him comforting the King, it will
    stuff his suspicion more fully. [*Aloud.*] I will persevere   20
    in my course of loyalty, though the conflict be sore
    between that and my blood.
Cornwall: I will lay trust upon thee, and thou shalt find a
    dearer father in my love.   [*Exeunt.*]

Act 3, Scene 5: Activities

1. Imagine that you knew nothing whatsoever about events in King Lear's England and you happened to overhear this exchange between Cornwall and Edmund. What would you assume was going on? As a loyal subject of the King, what would you do? Who would you tell about what you overheard? Record your responses in your journal.

2. As Cornwall, write a diary entry explaining why you trust Edmund implicitly.

3. You have discovered a lost soliloquy given by Edmund at the end of this scene. In the soliloquy, Edmund reveals that he has no intentions of being satisfied with the title of Earl of Gloucester. Write the soliloquy in modern English, revealing what other schemes you have devised and how you (as Edmund) will attempt to accomplish them.

For the next scene ...

How would you define justice? Does justice mean bringing to trial all people who have committed wrongs so that the court may identify their crimes and make them repent? Is justice a form of revenge? Do you think our justice system saves wrongdoers by reprimanding them for the sins they have committed? How do you think a judge's definition of justice might be similar to or different from your own?

Act 3, Scene 6

In this scene ...

Lear is taking shelter in the outbuilding or farmhouse provided by Gloucester. Overcome with a desire for revenge, he insists that his daughters be tried for their sins against him. He convenes a court with Edgar, Kent, and the Fool as judges and proceeds to try two stools which he sees as his daughters. Throughout the trial, Edgar sings irrelevant songs and the Fool clowns through the part he is given to play. Finally, Edgar is so overwhelmed by pity that he cannot continue.

Kent persuades the old King to lie down and rest, but as Lear is settling down, Gloucester brings the news that there is a plot against Lear's life. He tells Kent to take Lear to Dover where friends will assist him. Kent and the Fool carry Lear away. Left alone, Edgar comments on the extent of Lear's suffering and hopes the King will escape.

After this point in the play, the Fool is not seen again.

6   *Frateretto:* another devil's name; *Nero:* Nero was condemned to playing the fiddle in hell; Edgar may be confus-
ing Nero with Trajan, who was doomed to fish for frogs in
hell.

7   *innocent:* fool

10   *yeoman:* a freeholder, i.e., one who owned his own land but
was lower in status than a gentleman

12-14   *No, he's ... him:* This statement has been explained as a reference by Shakespeare to his own efforts to acquire a coat
of arms for his father. To Edgar, the words would convey
only nonsense. Lear understands them in the light of his
own experience.

15   *To have a thousand:* Lear exaggerates the number of his
offspring in the vehemence of his desire to torture them;
spits: iron rods used to pierce meat in order to turn it over
a fire and roast it

16   *hizzing:* hissing (from the heat)

19   *horse's health:* likely the seller's account of the health of the
horse

20   *arraign them straight:* bring his daughters to trial immediately. Lear is now intent on bringing his daughters to trial
instead of to torture, as he first decided. He is at the height
of his madness here.

21   *justicer:* judge

22-23   *sapient:* wise; *she-foxes:* symbols of cunning deception and
ingratitude

24   *he:* a fiend; or Lear

25   *eyes:* watchers, spectators; *madam?:* Edgar pretends to
address Goneril and Regan, turning to the two stools that
Lear thinks are his daughters.

26   *Come o'er ... me:* Edgar sings the first line of an old song in
which the singer calls upon his love to come closer to him
across a brook ("bourn").

Scene 6

An outbuilding near
Gloucester's castle.
Enter Gloucester and Kent.

Gloucester: Here is better than the open air; take it thank-
fully. I will piece out the comfort with what addition I
can. I will not be long from you.

Kent: All the power of his wits have given way to his impatience. The gods reward your kindness!   5

                                      [Exit Gloucester.]

[Enter Lear, Edgar, and Fool.]

Edgar: Fraterretto calls me, and tells me Nero is an angler
in the lake of darkness. Pray, innocent, and beware
the foul fiend.

Fool: Prithee, nuncle, tell me whether a madman be a
gentleman or a yeoman.   10

Lear: A king, a king!

Fool: No, he's a yeoman that has a gentleman to his son;
for he's a mad yeoman that sees his son a gentleman
before him.

Lear: To have a thousand with red burning spits   15
Come hizzing in upon 'em—

Edgar: The foul fiend bites my back.

Fool: He's mad that trusts in the tameness of a wolf, a
horse's health, a boy's love, or a whore's oath.

Lear: It shall be done; I will arraign them straight.   20
[*To Edgar.*] Come, sit thou here, most learned justicer.
[*To the Fool.*] Thou, sapient sir, sit here. Now, you she-
foxes!

Edgar: Look, where he stands and glares! Wantest thou
eyes at trial, madam?   25
Come o'er the bourn, Bessy, to me.

27-29   *Her boat ... thee:* The Fool completes the song, modifying the lines, perhaps to imply that the case of Goneril and Regan is not a sound one.

31   *nightingale:* Edgar believes that the Fool's voice is that of a fiend disguised as a nightingale; *Hoppedance:* another Elizabethan devil; *in Tom's belly:* a reference to a rumbling caused by hunger
32   *white herring:* unsmoked or fresh herring; *Croak not:* another reference to his rumbling stomach
34   *How do you:* How do you feel?; *amazed:* dumbfounded, stunned
36   *evidence:* witnesses to testify against Goneril and Regan – an abstract term used for the concrete
38   *yoke fellow of equity:* partner in law
39   *Bench:* take your place on the bench; *o' the commission:* of those commissioned as justices or law officers
42-45   *Sleepest or harm:* the words of an old song; *And for one blast:* and if you take time to play just one tune (on the shepherd's pipe); *minikin:* little, dainty

46   *Purr:* Edgar pretends to see a fiend in the form of a cat.
47   *Arraign:* try
48   *kicked:* an action conceived in Lear's tortured imagination

52   *Cry you mercy:* I beg your pardon; *joint-stool:* a low stool of three or four legs that were carefully fitted into the seat. The whole phrase is an apology for not noticing someone, equivalent to "I didn't know you were there."
53   *another:* Regan; *warped:* twisted by evil thoughts
54   *store:* substance; *on;* of; *Stop her there:* Lear imagines Regan is escaping from the court.
55   *Corruption in the place:* There is evil in this court (because Regan is being allowed to escape).
58   *Sir:* He addresses Lear.

61   *counterfeiting:* pretending
62-63   *The little ... me:* Lear imagines that even his own pets have turned against him.
64   *throw his head:* perhaps throw a hat or a similar gesture

Fool: Her boat hath a leak,
             And she must not speak
             Why she dares not come over to thee.
Edgar: The foul fiend haunts poor Tom in the voice of a   30
    nightingale. Hoppedance cries in Tom's belly for two
    white herring. Croak not, black angel; I have no food
    for thee.
Kent: How do you, sir? Stand you not so amazed.
    Will you lie down and rest upon the cushions?   35
Lear: I'll see their trial first. Bring in their evidence.
    [*To Edgar.*] Thou, robed man of justice, take thy place.
    [*To the Fool.*] And thou, his yokefellow of equity,
    Bench by his side. [*To Kent.*] You are o' the commission,
    Sit you too.   40
Edgar: Let us deal justly.
             Sleepest or wakest thou, jolly shepherd?
                Thy sheep be in the corn;
             And for one blast of thy minikin mouth
                Thy sheep shall take no harm.   45
    Purr! the cat is grey.
Lear: Arraign her first. 'Tis Goneril. I here take my oath
    before this honourable assembly, she kicked the poor
    King her father.
Fool: Come hither, mistress. Is your name Goneril?   50
Lear: She cannot deny it.
Fool: Cry you mercy, I took you for a joint-stool.
Lear: And here's another, whose warped looks proclaim
    What store her heart is made on. Stop her there!
    Arms, arms! Sword! Fire! Corruption in the place!   55
    False justicer, why hast thou let her scape?
Edgar: Bless thy five wits!
Kent: O pity! Sir, where is the patience now
    That you so oft have boasted to retain?
Edgar: [*Aside.*] My tears begin to take his part so much   60
    They mar my counterfeiting.
Lear: The little dogs and all,
    Tray, Blanch, and Sweetheart, see, they bark at me.
Edgar: Tom will throw his head at them. Avaunt, you curs!

74   *thy horn is dry:* An animal horn was apparently used by
        Bedlam beggars for drinking.
75   *anatomize:* dissect; *breeds:* is growing
77   *entertain:* engage
78   *hundred:* his former group of knights
79   *Persian:* Persian clothing was a symbol of gorgeous attire.
        Lear turns Edgar's rags into rich garments.

82   *curtains:* There are none, of course, and no cushions – only
        straw.
83   *So, so:* words spoken as he settles down, as his delirium
        subsides; *supper i' the morning:* Lear remembers that he
        has had no meal.
84   *And I'll ... noon:* The Fool, jokingly, takes Lear at his word
        and decides that, if breakfast is at supper time, bedtime
        must surely be noon.

89   *litter:* a type of stretcher. Some litters had a tent-like cover-
        ing that would shelter the person being carried.
90   *drive:* The litter was probably designed to be suspended
        between two horses, in tandem, one at each end of the
        litter. Gloucester is also urging great haste.

94   *Stand in assured loss:* are certain to be lost; *Take up:* Lift
        up the litter.

96   *Oppressed nature sleeps:* Lear, overwhelmed by a deep
        hurt, has fallen into a deep sleep.
97   *balmed:* comforted, helped to cure, healed
98   *convenience:* circumstances, the present situation
99   *Stand in hard cure:* will be difficult to cure

Be thy mouth or black or white,   65
Tooth that poisons if it bite;
Mastiff, greyhound, mongrel grim,
Hound or spaniel, brach or lym,
Bobtail tyke or trundle-tail—
Tom will make him weep and wail;   70
For, with throwing thus my head,
Dogs leap the hatch, and all are fled.
Do de, de, de. Sessa! Come, march to wakes and
fairs and market towns. Poor Tom, thy horn is dry.
Lear: Then let them anatomize Regan. See what breeds about 75
her heart. Is there any cause in nature that makes
these hard hearts? [*To Edgar.*] You, sir, I entertain
for one of my hundred; only I do not like the fashion
of your garments. You'll say they are Persian; but let
them be changed.   80
Kent: Now, good my lord, lie here and rest awhile.
Lear: Make no noise, make no noise; draw the curtains.
So, so. We'll go to supper i' the morning.
Fool: And I'll go to bed at noon.
[*Enter Gloucester.*]
Gloucester: Come hither, friend. Where is the King my
master?   85
Kent: Here, sir; but trouble him not; his wits are gone.
Gloucester: Good friend, I prithee take him in thy arms.
I have o'erheard a plot of death upon him.
There is a litter ready; lay him in it
And drive toward Dover, friend, where thou shalt meet 90
Both welcome and protection. Take up thy master.
If thou shouldst daily half an hour, his life,
With thine, and all that offer to defend him,
Stand in assured loss. Take up, take up!
And follow me, that will to some provision   95
Give thee quick conduct.
Kent: Oppressed nature sleeps.
This rest might yet have balmed thy broken sinews
Which, if convenience will not allow,
Stand in hard cure. [*To the Fool.*] Come, help to bear
thy master.
Thou must not stay behind.

101   *our betters:* those like Lear; *our woes:* the same sort of ills
        that we ordinary people must endure
102   *We scarcely ... foes:* We scarcely think our misfortunes are
        serious.
103   *Who alone ... mind:* "Alone" and "most" are the words to be
        emphasized. The one who suffers alone suffers most deeply.
104   *free:* carefree; *happy shows:* all appearances of happiness
105   *sufferance:* misery; *o'erskip:* avoid
106   *mates:* companions, company; *bearing fellowship:* when the
        endurance of misfortune is made bearable by companionship
107   *portable:* bearable, endurable
108   *When that ... bow:* when what afflicts me also afflicts the
        King
109   *He childed as I fathered:* He had children as cruel as the
        father I had (and our sorrows are therefore the same).
110-111 *Mark the high noises:* Pay attention to the disagreements
        among those who are powerful in the country; *thyself
        bewray ... thee:* Reveal yourself when false opinion that
        deforms you is reversed by your own proof that restores
        (reconciles) you to your true character; *bewray:* throw off
113   *What will ... King:* Whatever else may occur tonight, may
        the King escape safely!
114   *Lurk:* hide

Gloucester: Come, come, away! 100
[*Exeunt all but Edgar.*]
Edgar: When we our betters see bearing our woes,
We scarcely think our miseries our foes.
Who alone suffers suffers most i' the mind,
Leaving free things and happy shows behind;
But then the mind much sufferance doth o'erskip 105
When grief hath mates, and bearing fellowship.
How light and portable my pain seems now,
When that which makes me bend makes the King bow,
He childed as I fathered! Tom, away!
Mark the high noises, and thyself bewray 110
When false opinion, whose wrong thoughts defile thee,
In thy just proof repeals and reconciles thee.
What will hap more tonight, safe scape the King!
Lurk, lurk. [*Exit.*]

Act 3, Scene 6: Activities

1. The Fool makes his last appearance in this scene. In your journal, explain why, in your opinion, he disappears. What happens to him? Do you think there may be a piece missing from the play? If you were the Fool and had one last speech, what would you say? To whom would you address it? Write your speech and present it to your group for their reaction.

2. What is it about Kent that makes him persist in attempting to help Lear? Is it just loyalty or is there some other purpose? Write your conclusions as an aside to the audience.

3. Review the scene to observe what speeches characters make when they are *not* talking to each other. What speeches do they make when they *are* talking to each other? What (if any) pattern do you note? Discuss your ideas.

   If you were presenting this scene to an audience, what (if any) changes would you make? Why?

4. Edgar says referring to Lear, "He childed as I fathered!" (line 109). Discuss with your group what this puzzling line means and what it implies about what might ultimately happen in the rest of the play. Chart your prediction as the play unfolds.

5. Put your least favourite characters on trial using actions from this scene as evidence. For example, you may wish to enact Lear's trial of his daughters using real people instead of stools. Other class members can serve as witnesses, lawyers, prosecutor, defendant, judge, jury, and court personnel. You have only 15 minutes per character so it is essential to be well organized and that the characters on trial behave appropriately to the text.

For the next scene ...

Recall the most horrible scene you have ever encountered, either in real life or in the media. What made this scene horrible for you? How do you define "horror"?

In your opinion, is there any purpose in displaying horrifying scenes for people to watch? What do you think is the effect of these scenes on the people who watch them?

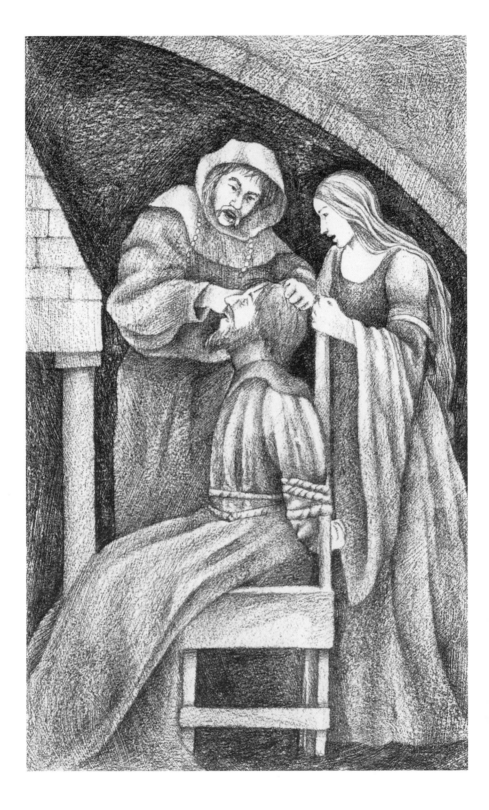

Act 3, Scene 7

In this scene ...

Cornwall gives Goneril and Edmund instructions to inform the Duke of Albany of the arrival of the French army. Oswald enters to tell Cornwall that Lear and his party, advised by Gloucester, have escaped to Dover.

After Goneril and Edmund leave, Gloucester is arrested and brought before Cornwall. When Gloucester admits to having warned Lear, Cornwall gouges out one of his eyes. One of Cornwall's own servants protests this cruelty and fatally wounds Cornwall in the fight that ensues. Regan stabs the servant and Cornwall then gouges out Gloucester's other eye. Gloucester asks for Edmund and is told that he is Gloucester's betrayer. Thus, at the moment of his blinding, Gloucester sees his sons in their true roles and prays for forgiveness.

Gloucester is thrown outside his castle gates and told to "smell his way to Dover." One of Cornwall's servants chooses to follow Gloucester and to have Poor Tom lead him to safety.

1   *post:* hurry
2   *letter:* taken by Edmund from Gloucester's private room or
           perhaps his cabinet

5   *Pluck out his eyes:* a medieval penalty for rape because
           sight incited adultery
7   *sister:* sister-in-law

9-11   *Advise the ... preparation:* Tell Albany, to whose palace you
           are going, to make the swiftest possible preparation for war;
           festinate: urgent; *preparation:* for war; *We are ... like:* We
           will do the same.
11   *posts:* letters, messages; *intelligent:* giving information

14   *hence:* from here

16   *Hot questrists:* eager, anxious searchers
17   *lord's:* Gloucester's.

22   *Pinion:* tie his arms; *thief:* The word had a stronger sense
           than it has now.

Scene 7

Inside Gloucester's castle.
Enter Cornwall, Regan, Goneril,
Edmund the Bastard, and Servants.

Cornwall: [*To Goneril.*] Post speedily to my lord your hus-
    band, show him this letter. The army of France is
    landed.—Seek out the traitor Gloucester.
                    [*Exeunt some of the Servants.*]
Regan: Hang him instantly.
Goneril: Pluck out his eyes.   5
Cornwall: Leave him to my displeasure. Edmund, keep you
    our sister company. The revenges we are bound to
    take upon your traitorous father are not fit for your
    beholding. Advise the Duke where you are going, to
    a most festinate preparation. We are bound to the   10
    like. Our posts shall be swift and intelligent betwixt
    us. Farewell, dear sister; farewell, my Lord of Gloucester.
    [*Enter Oswald the Steward.*]
    How now? Where's the King?
Oswald: My Lord of Gloucester hath conveyed him hence.
    Some five or six and thirty of his knights,   15
    Hot questrists after him, met him at gate;
    Who, with some other of the lord's dependants,
    Are gone with him toward Dover, where they boast
    To have well-armed friends.
Cornwall: Get horses for your mistress.
Goneril: Farewell, sweet lord, and sister.   20
Cornwall: Edmund, farewell.
             [*Exeunt Goneril, Edmund, and Oswald.*]
            Go seek the traitor Gloucester,
    Pinion him like a thief, bring him before us.
                   [*Exeunt other Servants.*]

23-25   *Though well ... justice:* although we may not truly pass judgement on him without some form of trial; *our power ... wrath:* My power as Duke will enable me to satisfy the anger I feel towards him.
26   *blame:* criticize

27   *fox:* i.e., crafty person
28   *corky:* stiff, dry, withered (by age)

30   *foul play:* injustice

31   *Hard:* tightly
32   *none:* no traitor

34   *ignobly done:* dishonourable, mean

36   *white:* Regan looks at the hairs of Gloucester's beard and observes, mockingly, that they are white and symbolic of purity; *Naughty:* wicked, evil
37   *ravish:* pluck, tear
38   *quicken:* come alive; *host:* Gloucester protests against the dishonouring of the age-old rule that courtesy between host and guest is inviolable.
39   *hospitable favours:* my face, which has an expression of hospitality on it
40   *ruffle:* do violence to
41   *late:* lately, recently
42   *simple-answered:* straightforward
43   *confederacy:* unauthorized alliance or agreement, conspiracy
44   *footed:* landed
47   *guessingly set down:* written down without firm knowledge
48   *of a neutral heart:* taking neither side

49   *Cunning:* Now he is using cunning; *And false:* and he is false as well

52   *Wherefore:* why; *charged at peril:* ordered on pain of death

Though well we may not pass upon his life
Without the form of justice, yet our power
Shall do a court'sy to our wrath, which men   25
May blame, but not control.
[*Enter Gloucester, brought in by two or three.*]
                          Who's there? The traitor?
Regan: Ingrateful fox! 'Tis he.
Cornwall: Bind fast his corky arms.
Gloucester: What mean your Graces? Good my friends,
    consider
You are my guests. Do me no foul play, friends.   30
Cornwall: Bind him, I say.   [*Servants bind him.*]
Regan: Hard, hard. O filthy traitor!
Gloucester: Unmerciful lady as you are, I am none.
Cornwall: To this chair bind him. Villain, thou shalt find—
                     [*Regan pulls his beard.*]
Gloucester: By the kind gods, 'tis most ignobly done
    To pluck me by the beard.   35
Regan: So white, and such a traitor!
Gloucester: Naughty lady,
    These hairs which thou dost ravish from my chin
    Will quicken, and accuse thee. I am your host.
    With robber's hands my hospitable favours
    You should not ruffle thus. What will you do?   40
Cornwall: Come, sir, what letters had you late from France?
Regan: Be simple-answered, for we know the truth.
Cornwall: And what confederacy have you with the traitors
    Late footed in the kingdom?
Regan: To whose hands you have sent the lunatic King? 45
    Speak.
Gloucester: I have a letter guessingly set down,
    Which came from one that's of a neutral heart,
    And not from one opposed.
Cornwall: Cunning.
Regan: And false.
Cornwall: Where hast thou sent the King?   50
Gloucester: To Dover.
Regan: Wherefore to Dover? Wast thou not charged at
    peril—

54-55   *I am ... course:* I am like a bear chained to a post and must endure as best I can – a reference to bear-baiting, in which bears were attacked by dogs.

59   *anointed:* blessed with holy oil at his coronation. Therefore, to attack the King is sacrilege); *rash:* slash, as with a tusk, like a boar

61-62   *hell-black night:* night as black as hell itself; *would have ... fires:* would have risen in one great wave and extinguished the fire of the stars

63   *holp the heavens rain:* helped the heavens to rain (with his tears)

64   *If:* even if; *dern:* dreadful

65   *turn the key:* open the door (and let them in)

66   *All cruels else subscribe:* Disregard all other cruelties, i.e., other than those inflicted upon Lear, since all others are less diabolical.

67   *winged vengeance:* the vengeance of the gods, vengeance like a bird of prey

72   *One side will mock another:* An eye remaining would make the eyeless socket look worse; *The other too:* Gouge out the other eye as well.

76   *How now:* What do you think you are doing?

78   *shake it on this quarrel:* insult you to provoke an immediate quarrel over this cause – Gloucester's treatment

79   *villain:* used here in the double sense of scoundrel and serf

80   *Nay, then:* a denial that he is a serf; *come on:* an invitation to fight; *take the chance of anger:* take the risk of fighting when angry (and therefore, rash)

81   *peasant:* Regan interprets Cornwall's punning use of "villain."

Stage Direction – *takes a ... behind:* stabs him in the back,

83   *mischief:* injury

84   *Lest:* in case that; *vile jelly:* Gloucester's remaining eye

85   *lustre:* brightness of the living eye

Cornwall: Wherefore to Dover? Let him answer that.
Gloucester: I am tied to the stake, and I must stand the
    course.   55
Regan: Wherefore to Dover?
Gloucester: Because I would not see thy cruel nails
    Pluck out his poor old eyes; nor thy fierce sister
    In his anointed flesh rash boarish fangs.
    The sea, with such a storm as his bare head   60
    In hell-black night endured, would have buoyed up
    And quenched the stelled fires.
    Yet, poor old heart, he holp the heavens to rain.
    If wolves had at thy gate howled that dern time,
    Thou shouldst have said, "Good porter, turn the key."   65
    All cruels else subscribe: but I shall see
    The winged vengeance overtake such children.
Cornwall: See it shalt thou never. Fellows, hold the chair.
    Upon these eyes of thine I'll set my foot.
Gloucester: He that will think to live till he be old,   70
    Give me some help!—O cruel! O you gods!
                     [Gloucester's eye is put out.]
Regan: One side will mock another. The other too!
Cornwall: If you see vengeance—
First Servant: Hold your hand, my lord!
    I have served you ever since I was a child,
    But better service have I never done you   75
    Than now to bid you hold.
Regan: How now, you dog?
First Servant: If you did wear a beard upon your chin,
    I'd shake it on this quarrel.
Regan: What do you mean?
Cornwall: My villain!   *[They draw and fight.]*
First Servant: Nay, then, come on, and take the chance of
    anger.   80
Regan: Give me thy sword. A peasant stand up thus?
          [She takes a sword and runs at him behind.]
First Servant: O, I am slain! My lord, you have one eye
    left
    To see some mischief on him. O!   *[He dies.]*
Cornwall: Lest it see more, prevent it. Out, vile jelly!
    Where is thy lustre now?   85

87	*enkindle:* summon up; *sparks of nature:* feelings of filial affection
88	*quit:* repay, requite, avenge; *Out:* an interjection, expressing hatred; abbreviated from "Out upon you!"
90-91	"That" and "who" have the same antecedent: "he" (line 87); *overture:* disclosure, revelation
92	*abused:* wronged
93	*that:* Edgar's banishment; *prosper him:* May he (Edgar) prosper.
95	*How look you?:* How are you feeling?
96	*hurt:* wound
97	*slave:* the servant who attempted to defend Gloucester
98	*apace:* quickly, freely
99	*Untimely:* at the wrong time in my life
101-103	*If she ... monsters:* If she lives to a ripe age and dies a normal death, then all women will become wicked (since they will not have to fear punishment for their crimes).
104	*bedlam:* Edgar, evidently known to the servant
105-106	*His roguish ... anything:* Since the Bedlam beggar is mad, he will not be called to account and can, therefore, safely lead Gloucester.

Gloucester: All dark and comfortless! Where's my son
    Edmund?
    Edmund, enkindle all the sparks of nature
    To quit this horrid act.
Regan: Out, treacherous villain!
    Thou callest on him that hates thee. It was he
    That made the overture of thy treasons to us,   90
    Who is too good to pity thee.
Gloucester: O my follies! Then Edgar was abused.
    Kind gods, forgive me that, and prosper him!
Regan: Go thrust him out at gates, and let him smell
    His way to Dover.   *[Exit a Servant with Gloucester.]*
             How is't, my lord? How look you?   95
Cornwall: I have received a hurt. Follow me, lady.
    Turn out that eyeless villain. Throw this slave
    Upon the dunghill. Regan, I bleed apace.
    Untimely comes this hurt. Give me your arm.
             [Exit Cornwall, led by Regan.]
Second Servant: I'll never care what wickedness I do,   100
    If this man come to good.
Third Servant: If she live long,
    And in the end meet the old course of death,
    Women will all turn monsters.
Second Servant: Let's follow the old Earl, and get the bedlam
    To lead him where he would. His roguish madness   105
    Allows itself to anything.
Third Servant: Go thou. I'll fetch some flax and whites of
    eggs
    apply to his bleeding face. Now heaven help him!
             [Exeunt.]

Act 3, Scene 7: Activities

1. Discuss with your group how you would stage the blinding of Gloucester. Would you make the act of blinding graphic or would you rely on the imagination of the audience to create their own images of horror? In your decision, consider the purpose of the scene in general rather than focusing on the act of blinding itself.

2. Whenever characters in this play ask for divine assistance, they meet either with indifference or with outright hostility.

   In Act 3, Scene 6, Kent thanks Gloucester for his kindness to Lear by saying, "The gods reward your kindness" (line 5). In this scene Gloucester is brutally maimed. In your journal, consider whether or not the gods play any role in this play. You may wish to share some of your ideas with others in a group.

3. Sensational headlines in tabloid newspapers always want to capture the lurid, the outrageous, and the bizarre. Create your own headlines for Gloucester's ousting into the raging storm based on Regan's statement "Go thrust him out at gates, and let him smell his way to Dover" (lines 94–95). Follow your headline with the story that might accompany it.

4. Irony is a figure of speech in which the literal meaning of an expression is the opposite of that intended, particularly when the expression understates the effect intended. One example of irony occurs in line 30. Select as many other examples as you can from this scene and, in a group discussion, determine what effect they have on the scene. Do you believe that the irony is always deliberate on the part of the speaker? What effect would the removal of all the irony have on the scene?

Act 3: Consider the Whole Act

1. There are obvious parallels between what happens to Lear and what happens to Gloucester. Divide a page in half; on one side, list what happens to Lear in this act and, on the other, what happens to Gloucester. With your group, discuss what you think is the purpose of this parallelism. Do you think it is a deliberate dramatic device or just an accident of the plot?

2. While exploring the heath, you come across an ancient artifact, a button, that you think might have belonged to one of the characters, possibly Lear himself. This artifact allows you to transport yourself to the time of the play and enter part of a scene. Where would you suddenly find yourself, and who would you meet? You are allowed one speech to a character that you hope will change the outcome of the play significantly. Write the speech you will deliver to that character. What is the response? How do you identify yourself? Does your intervention change things? Record why or why not.

3. There is an expression, "Children and fools tell the truth." From your observation of the characters in this act, who would you say are "children" and who would you say are "fools"? Share your observations with others in the class. Write an editorial explaining your interpretation of the expression for publication in a magazine.

4. You are Edmund. In a television interview, you are asked to explain your actions. Role-play the interview for the class. Explain what you have done and the reasons for your actions. How do you defend your choices? Did you have any alternative?

5. There are numerous ways in which Shakespeare develops characters in this scene. Create a chart with three headings: "Physical Appearance," "Actions," and "Personality Traits." Fill in the chart for each character. Share your discoveries with a partner and add any details that you have missed. Write a character sketch of the figure you find to be the most complete.

6. Nobody really knows how this play was originally staged. Select a scene you are particularly intrigued by and create specific stage directions that detail how it should appear on stage. With your group, present your version of the staging for the rest of the class and explain your choice.

7. Change the setting of one scene in this act to the present time. This means you may have to adjust the characters and probably parts of the plot. Sketch what you might do and what your point is in doing it. In your journal, decide whether or not it is a good idea to adapt a Renaissance play to conform to a contemporary setting.

8. There are many short scenes in this act that could easily be extended: scenes 1, 3, and 5, for example. Suppose you decide to extend one of these scenes. In a short essay, consider how logical it is to do so, what the extension would add to the act as a whole, and how your extension would blend with the next scene. Or, compare the effect on the audience of these three short, rapid scenes to the effect created by modern film editing.

9. In scenes 6 and 7, alliances form: Gloucester with Lear and Edmund with Goneril and Regan. Many see these scenes as the turning point of the play: opposites line up and affinities are established. With your group, discuss whether there is an actual turning point in a play, and why or why not there particular scenes should qualify. If they do not, then write a persuasive argument that clarifies what you think propels the play to its inevitable end.

10. If you decided to produce this play as a pop musical using contemporary songs, which ones would you choose and why? Select a scene segment you find compelling in some way, and insert a song to express the emotions or actions of the characters. Rehearse the segment inserting the song at the appropriate time and place, and present it to the class. You may have to explain your choices.

For the next scene ...

In your opinion, is it possible for a seemingly insensitive person to change? Have you ever known someone who did just that? If so, what do you think prompted the person to change? Write your ideas in a journal entry.

Act 4, Scene 1

In this scene ...

Edgar believes his fortunes have reached their lowest possible ebb and that anything that happens from this point on is bound to be a change for the better. No sooner does he express this belief than his blind father appears, led by another old man.

Gloucester tells the old man to leave, saying in despair that, since he had nowhere to go, he has no need of direction. His one wish is to meet his son Edgar again. Edgar realizes that, in fact, he has not yet seen the worst.

Meeting Poor Tom, Gloucester asks the old man to bring the beggar some clothes, and asks Poor Tom to lead him to Dover. He is planning to end his misery by jumping off one of the cliffs there. Edgar, still in disguise, consents to guide him.

1-2   *better thus ... flattered:* better as a Bedlam beggar and aware of being despised, than to live unaware that one is despised in the midst of flattery

2-5   *To be ... best:* When one's fortunes are at the very worst, there is only hope for the better; thus, the creature whose fortune is at the lowest ebb has everything to hope for and nothing to fear; *esperance:* hope

6   *The worst returns to laughter:* The worst circumstances can only change to those inspiring laughter.

7   *unsubstantial:* having little substance, not being able to sustain human life

8   *wretch:* Edgar himself

9   *Owes nothing to:* has nothing to fear from

10-12   *poorly led?:* led by a poor old man or led like a poor man (beggar); *World, world ... age:* O, world, if the strange changes in our fortunes did not make us hate you, we should not surrender to old age and death.

14   *fourscore:* eighty

19-21   *I stumbled ... commodites:* When I was in full possession of my faculties, I was careless (stumbled). Very often, we observe that our own faculties (means) make us feel over-confident (secure us), and our very weaknesses (defects) prove to be beneficial in causing us to take notice of our circumstances.

22   *The food ... wrath:* the object or victim of your deceived father's anger

23-24   *Might I ... again:* If only I might live to touch you, I'd feel as if my sight were restored.

24   *How now?:* What's that?

Act 4, Scene 1

The heath.

Enter Edgar.

Edgar: Yet better thus, and known to be contemned,
   Than still contemned and flattered. To be worst,
   The lowest and most dejected thing of fortune,
   Stands still in esperance, lives not in fear.
   The lamentable change is from the best;   5
   The worst returns to laughter. Welcome then,
   Thou unsubstantial air that I embrace!
   The wretch that thou hast blown unto the worst
   Owes nothing to thy blasts.
   [*Enter Gloucester, led by an Old Man.*]
                           But who comes here?
   My father, poorly led? World, world, O world!   10
   But that thy strange mutations make us hate thee,
   Life would not yield to age.
Old Man: O my good lord,
   I have been your tenant, and your father's tenant,
   These fourscore years.
Gloucester: Away, get thee away! Good friend, be gone.   15
   Thy comforts can do me no good at all;
   Thee they may hurt.
Old Man: You cannot see your way.
Gloucester: I have no way, and therefore want no eyes;
   I stumbled when I saw. Full oft 'tis seen
   Our means secure us, and our mere defects   20
   Prove our commodities. O dear son Edgar,
   The food of thy abused father's wrath;
   Might I but live to see thee in my touch,
   I'd say I had eyes again!
Old Man: How now? Who's there?

26	*I am ... was:* Edgar sees his father's pitiful condition and realizes that circumstances are worse than ever.
27-28	*The worst ... worst:* The worst has not befallen us as long as we can assure ourselves that it is the worst. Thus, we are not without hope.
31	*He has some reason:* He seems to have some intelligence.
33	*a worm:* a thing of no consequence
34	*Came then ... mind:* either because he saw something of Edgar beneath his disguise or because he thought that Edgar must have become a homeless wanderer
35	*scarce:* scarcely; *friends:* friendly
36	*wanton:* carelessly playful
37	*How should this be?:* "Why should this be the case?", "How did he come to forgive me?", or "How did he lose his eyes?"
38-39	*Bad is ... others:* It is bad business (trade) that I must disguise myself as a Bedlamite, making myself and others angry, when my father is in such sorrow.
43	*I' the way:* on the path or track; *ancient love:* love dating from earlier days
44	*covering:* clothing
45	*entreat:* humbly request
46	*'Tis the ... blind:* It is the curse of our time that the leaders of the country are mad and that the people whom they lead are blind.
47	*thy pleasure:* what you please
48	*Above the rest:* above all
49	*'parel:* apparel, clothing
50	*Come on't what will:* no matter what happens to me
52	*daub it:* pretend. The metaphor is taken from the skill of plastering.

Edgar: [*Aside.*] O gods! Who is't can say, "I am at the
    worst"?   25
    I am worse than e'er I was.
Old Man: 'Tis poor mad Tom.
Edgar: [*Aside.*] And worse I may be yet. The worst is not
    So long as we can say, "This is the worst."
Old Man: Fellow, where goest?
Gloucester: Is it a beggarman?
Old Man: Madman and beggar too.   30
Gloucester: He has some reason, else he could not beg.
    I' the last night's storm I such a fellow saw,
    Which made me think a man a worm. My son
    Came then into my mind, and yet my mind
    Was then scarce friends with him. I have heard more
    since.   35
    As flies to wanton boys are we to the gods.
    They kill us for their sport.
Edgar: [*Aside.*]   How should this be?
    Bad is the trade that must play fool to sorrow,
    Angering itself and others.—Bless thee, master!
Gloucester: Is that the naked fellow?
Old Man: Ay, my lord.   40
Gloucester: Get thee away. If for my sake
    Thou wilt o'ertake us hence a mile or twain
    I' the way toward Dover, do it for ancient love;
    And bring some covering for this naked soul,
    Which I'll entreat to lead me.
Old Man: Alack, sir, he is mad!   45
Gloucester: 'Tis the time's plague when madmen lead the
    blind.
    Do as I bid thee, or rather do thy pleasure.
    Above the rest, be gone.
Old Man: I'll bring him the best 'parel that I have,
    Come on't what will.   [*Exit.*]   50
Gloucester: Sirrah, naked fellow—
Edgar: Poor Tom's acold. [*Aside.*] I cannot daub it
    further.
Gloucester: Come hither, fellow.
Edgar: [*Aside.*] And yet I must.—Bless thy sweet eyes, they   55
    bleed.

58   *horseway:* a path used by horseback riders

61   *Obidicut:* another Elizabethan devil

63-64   *mopping and mowing:* grimacing and making faces
64   *possesses:* possesses the souls of
65   *heavens' plagues:* afflictions, misfortunes of the gods

67-68   *humbled to all strokes:* reduced to the lowest kind of mis-
          ery; *That I ... still:* The fact that I am wretched makes you
          appear happier than I. May the gods continue to inflict this
          kind of punishment – to make my suffering the common
          experience of the powerful whenever they abuse their
          power.
69-72   *Let the ... excess:* Let the pampered man who treats the
          commands of the gods as if these commands were his
          slaves, and who will not see the truth because he is insensi-
          tive, feel your power quickly. If this were done, the man with
          excessive wealth would be willing to distribute it more justly.
75   *bending:* overhanging
76   *fearfully:* in such a manner as to inspire terror; *the con-
          firmed deep:* the channel; the Strait of Dover
78-79   *And I'll ... me:* and I will reward you (lessen your misery) by
          giving you something of value that I have on my person.

Gloucester: Knowest thou the way to Dover?

Edgar: Both stile and gate, horseway and footpath. Poor
    Tom hath been scared out of his good wits. Bless thee,
    good man's son, from the foul fiend! Five fiends have   60
    been in poor Tom at once: of lust, as Obidicut; Hob-
    bididence, prince of dumbness; Mahu, of stealing;
    Modo, of murder; Flibbertigibbet, of mopping and
    mowing, who since possesses chambermaids and waiting
    women. So, bless thee, master!   65

Gloucester: Here, take this purse, thou whom the heavens'
    plagues
    Have humbled to all strokes. That I am wretched
    Makes thee the happier. Heavens, deal so still!
    Let the superfluous and lust-dieted man,
    That slaves your ordinance, that will not see   70
    Because he does not feel, feel your power quickly;
    So distribution should undo excess,
    And each man have enough. Dost thou know Dover?

Edgar: Ay, master.

Gloucester: There is a cliff, whose high and bending head   75
    Looks fearfully in the confirmed deep.
    Bring me but to the very brim of it,
    And I'll repair the misery thou dost bear
    With something rich about me. From that place
    I shall no leading need.

Edgar: Give me thy arm.   80
    Poor Tom shall lead thee.   [*Exeunt.*]

Act 4, Scene 1: Activities

1. As Edgar imagine that you are being interviewed by a television host about your behaviour and attitudes in this scene. You are asked the following questions:

   • Since your father was blind when you met him, why did you continue to remain disguised?

   • Since you already heard him express a desire to see you again, why didn't you tell him who you were?

   With a partner, role-play this interview for others in the class.

2. You have been asked to make a presentation to a group on the topic of "divine justice." Brainstorm with a group to gather ideas on your topic, based on the events of the play so far and this scene in particular. Prepare your presentation and deliver it to another group, making your argument as concise, yet thorough, as you can.

   Based on what you have discovered, what do you think Shakespeare might have thought about "divine justice"? If you could ask him three questions on this topic, what would they be?

3. One of the issues raised towards the end of the scene is the unfair distribution of wealth. With your group, consider what is said about affluent people in this scene. Do you agree or disagree with Gloucester's opinion? Write a short article for a business magazine in which you use the play as the basis for your economic ideas. Share your article with classmates for their responses.

4. Gloucester's solution to his problem is to commit suicide by jumping off a cliff. In groups, discuss what you think of this as a solution. Why do you think Edgar still conceals his identity from his father, and why can't Edgar be of more help to him? Report your findings to the rest of the class.

For the next scene ...

What does physical courage mean to you? What does moral courage mean? Can a person who is considered to be passive show physical and/or moral courage? Discuss your ideas with classmates.

Act 4, Scene 2

In this scene ...

Edmund and Goneril meet outside the Duke of Albany's palace. Oswald brings news that the Duke's behaviour has changed greatly, and that the Duke has reacted oddly to the news of Gloucester's supposed treason. Goneril interprets the change in his behaviour as cowardice in the face of the French invasion. She sends Edmund back to Cornwall to warn him to speed his efforts to prepare his army. Before Edmund leaves, she declares her love for him and hints that she will be calling on Edmund to murder Albany.

Albany enters and confronts Goneril, condemning her for her cruelty to Lear. As they argue, a messenger delivers the news of Gloucester's blinding and Cornwall's death. Albany is horrified, particularly when he learns of Edmund's part in the torture of his own father. Goneril, on the other hand, is excited by the news of Cornwall's death. She thinks that she and Edmund will now be able to seize Regan's part of the kingdom. However, she is also troubled by the thought that Regan may steal Edmund from her, now that Cornwall is dead.

1	*Welcome:* i.e., to my palace; *our mild husband:* Goneril reveals to Edmund her true feeling towards her husband.
2	*your master?:* Albany
3	*so changed:* The ruthlessness of Goneril and Regan have appalled Albany, but he seems incapable of positive action.
7	*loyal service:* denouncing his father to Cornwall; *son:* Edmund
8	*sot:* blockhead, fool
9	*I had ... out:* I had seen good as evil, and evil as good.
10-11	*What most ... offensive:* Oswald asserts that it is Albany, not himself, who has reversed good and evil.
11	*Then shall ... further:* You will not accompany me at this point.
12	*cowish terror:* cowardly fear
13	*undertake:* transform conviction into action; *feel:* notice or appear to notice. He will ignore wrongs that demand some responsible action from him.
14-15	*Our wishes ... effects:* The desire we have for each other may possibly be fulfilled.
17-18	*I must ... hands:* I must take my husband's sword and present him with a distaff (a staff used for spinning and associated, therefore, with women); *This trusty servant:* Oswald
19	*pass between us:* be our intermediary or go-between; *like:* likely
20	*(If you ... behalf):* if you have the initiative to advance yourself. (Goneril implies that Edmund should kill Albany.)

Stage Direction – *favour:* trinket (recognizing Edmund as her lover)

22	*Decline your head:* Bend your head (to be kissed or to put a chain around his neck).
23	*Would stretch ... air:* would raise your spirits to the skies. Goneril changes from the formal "your" to the intimate "thy" and "thee."
24	*Conceive:* understand (what I am suggesting about our future – without Albany)

Scene 2

*Outside the Duke of
Albany's palace.
Enter Goneril and Edmund
the Bastard.*

Goneril: Welcome, my lord. I marvel our mild husband
  Not met us on the way.
  [*Enter Oswald the Steward.*]
                  Now where's your master?
Oswald: Madam, within, but never man so changed.
  I told him of the army that was landed:
  He smiled at it. I told him you were coming: 5
  His answer was, "The worse." Of Gloucester's treachery
  And of the loyal service of his son
  When I informed him, then he called me sot
  And told me I had turned the wrong side out.
  What most he should dislike seems pleasant to him;   10
  What like, offensive.
Goneril: [*To Edmund.*] Then shall you go no further.
  It is the cowish terror of his spirit,
  That dares not undertake. He'll not feel wrongs
  Which tie him to an answer. Our wishes on the way
  May prove effects. Back, Edmund, to my brother.   15
  Hasten his musters and conduct his powers.
  I must change arms at home and give the distaff
  Into my husband's hands. This trusty servant
  Shall pass between us. Ere long you are like to hear
  (If you dare venture in your own behalf)   20
  A mistress's command. Wear this;   [*Gives a favour.*]
                  Spare speech;
  Decline your head: this kiss, if it durst speak,
  Would stretch thy spirits up into the air.
  Conceive, and fare thee well.

28   *A fool usurps my body:* My husband enjoys my body (but Edmund possesses my heart).

29   *I have ... whistle:* This line is evidently based on an old proverb: It is a poor dog that is not worth the whistling.

31   *I fear your disposition:* I am appalled at your character.
32   *nature ... origin:* character that despises its source, i.e., Lear (whom Albany admires)
33   *Cannot be ... itself:* cannot be kept within set limits
34   *sliver and disbranch:* be cut off
35-36   *material sap:* essential nourishment – in this case, the characteristics Goneril should have received from Lear; *perforce:* of necessity, necessarily; *must wither ... use:* must be as a dead branch, fit only for burning (or for death)
37   *text:* Goneril means: A sermon from you is not worth hearing, since the text is foolish.
39   *savour:* relish, have a liking for
42   *Whose reverence ... lick:* who would be (affectionately) licked even by a bear that is being tugged along via a head harness
43   *madded:* driven mad
44   *brother:* brother-in-law (Cornwall)
45   *him:* Lear
46   *If that:* if; *visible spirits:* avenging spirits in visible form
47   *offences:* offenders
49-50   *Humanity must ... deep:* People will devour one another, like the creatures of the ocean; *Milk-livered:* cowardly

51   *a cheek for blows:* See Matthew 5:39; *a head for wrongs:* a head that would endure injustices against it
52-53   *Who hast ... suffering:* who has no insight to tell you what should be accepted honourably and what should not
54-55   *Fools do ... mischief:* Only fools pity the villains who are punished before they have committed evil acts; *Where's thy drum?:* i.e., your war drum

Edmund: Yours in the ranks of death!   *[Exit.]*
Goneril: My most dear
    Gloucester!   25
    O, the difference of man and man!
    To thee a woman's services are due;
    A fool usurps my body.
Oswald: Madam, here comes my lord.
                                    [Exit.]

    [Enter Albany.]
Goneril: I have been worth the whistle.
Albany: O Goneril,
    You are not worth the dust which the rude wind   30
    Blows in your face! I fear your disposition.
    That nature which contemns it origin
    Cannot be bordered certain in itself.
    She that herself will sliver and disbranch
    From her material sap, perforce must wither   35
    And come to deadly use.
Goneril: No more! The text is foolish.
Albany: Wisdom and goodness to the vile seem vile;
    Filths savour but themselves. What have you done?
    Tigers, not daughters, what have you performed?   40
    A father, and a gracious aged man,
    Whose reverence even the head-lugged bear would lick,
    Most barbarous, most degenerate, have you madded.
    Could my good brother suffer you to do it?
    A man, a prince, by him so benefited!   45
    If that the heavens do not their visible spirits
    Send quickly down to tame these vile offences,
    It will come,
    Humanity must perforce prey on itself,
    Like monsters of the deep.
Goneril: Milk-livered man!   50
    That bearest a cheek for blows, a head for wrongs;
    Who hast not in thy brows an eye discerning
    Thine honour from thy suffering; that not knowest
    Fools do those villains pity who are punished
    Ere they have done their mischief. Where's thy drum?   55
    France spreads his banners in our noiseless land,
    With plumed helm thy state begins to threat,

58   *a moral fool:* a fool who moralizes when action is necessary

59   *See thyself:* See yourself as others see you.
60-61   *Proper deformity ... woman:* Physical or moral deformity, expected in a fiend, looks much more horrid in woman, where it is not expected.
62   *changed:* transformed; *self-covered:* with your real self covered with a woman's body
63   *Bemonster:* Do not change your appearance into that of a fiend; *Were't my fitness:* if it were proper to me
64   *blood:* impulses
66   *Howe'er:* in whatever ways

68   *Marry:* By the Virgin Mary; *your manhood – mew:* Confine (or coop up) your feeble manhood until it is strong enough for a man's work. Alternatively, Goneril may be making a scornful sound, imitating a cat's cry, in an expression of contempt.

73   *bred:* reared, brought up; *thrilled with remorse:* moved or excited by compassion
74   *Opposed against:* tried to prevent; *bending:* turning, directing
76   *amongst them felled him dead:* Among the lot of them, they killed him.
77   *harmful stroke:* fatal wound
78   *plucked him after:* drew him along to death after the murdered servant
79   *justicers:* judges, dispenses of justice, gods; *neither crimes:* crimes on earth, crimes committed here and now

84-86   *But being ... life:* But since Regan is now a widow, and my lover Edmund is with her, my dreams of a life with Edmund may be shattered, and escape from my hated life with Albany may be impossible.
87   *tart:* sour, unpleasant
88   *son:* Edmund

Whiles thou, a moral fool, sittest still, and cries
"Alack, why does he so?"
Albany: See thyself, devil!
Proper deformity shows not in the fiend   60
So horrid as in woman.
Goneril: O vain fool!
Albany: Thou changed and self-covered thing, for shame!
Bemonster not thy feature! Were't my fitness
To let these hands obey my blood,
They are apt enough to dislocate and tear   65
Thy flesh and bones. Howe'er thou art a fiend,
A woman's shape doth shield thee.
Goneril: Marry, your manhood—mew!
[*Enter a Gentleman.*]
Albany: What news?
Gentleman: O, my good lord, the Duke of Cornwall's dead,   70
Slain by his servant, going to put out
The other eye of Gloucester.
Albany: Gloucester's eyes?
Gentleman: A servant that he bred, thrilled with remorse,
Opposed against the act, bending his sword
To his great master; who, there at enraged,   75
Flew on him, and amongst them felled him dead;
But not without that harmful stroke which since
Hath plucked him after.
Albany: This shows you are above,
You justicers, that these our nether crimes
So speedily can venge! But O poor Gloucester!   80
Lost he his other eye?
Gentleman: Both, both, my lord.
This letter, madam, craves a speedy answer.
'Tis from your sister.
Goneril: [*Aside.*]   One way I like this well;
But being widow, and my Gloucester with her,
May all the building in my fancy pluck   85
Upon my hateful life. Another way
The news is not so tart.—I'll read, and answer.   [*Exit.*]
Albany: Where was his son when they did take his eyes?
Gentleman: Come with my lady hither.
Albany: He is not here.

90   *back:* on his way back

93-94   *And quit ... course:* and left deliberately so that those dealing with Gloucester might have a freer hand in punishment

Gentleman: No, my good lord; I met him back again. 90
Albany: Knows he the wickedness?
Gentleman: Ay, my good lord: 'twas he informed against
    him,
  And quit the house on purpose, that their punishment
  Might have the freer course.
Albany: Gloucester, I live
  To thank thee for the love thou show'dst the King, 95
  And to revenge thine eyes. Come hither, friend.
  Tell me what more thou knowest.   *[Exeunt.]*

Act 4, Scene 2: Activities

1. As Albany, write a diary entry explaining why it took you so long to understand what was happening both in your own life and in the kingdom in general. How do you respond to the accusations of cowardice levelled at you? What were your motivations for marrying Goneril? What did you really think of Cornwall? Are you motivated by a desire for revenge? Explain.

2. Goneril and Edmund believe that human beings design their own fates. Albany believes the opposite. Do you agree with Goneril and Edmund or with Albany? Using the three characters and their situations to illustrate your point of view, share your response with others. You might create a short tale with a moral (a fable) or create a comic strip to illustrate your philosophy.

3. The medieval convention of courtly love – the chivalric relationship between a knight and a lady – followed a strict etiquette. Goneril and Edmund use the language of courtly love with each other in this scene. Do you think this suits their behaviour so far in the play?

   Write a short scene suitable for a daytime soap opera in which you show the two of them together in an intimate conversation.

For the next scene ...

What do you think could be worth soldiers risking their lives for?

Act 4, Scene 3

In this scene ...

Kent arrives at the French camp near Dover only to discover that the King has been recalled to France to deal with an emergency. The army has been left in control of the Marshal of France under the guidance of Cordelia, who remains in England.

Kent learns that Cordelia is distressed over the plight of her father and, reveals that, although Lear knows she is in Dover, he refuses to see her out of guilt for the wrongs he has done her.

As the scene closes, Kent is told that the combined forces of Albany and Cornwall are approaching.

1   *gone back:* i.e., to France

3   *imperfect:* unfinished
4   *imports:* portends (indicates beforehand, as an omen
           does), signifies
6   *required:* requested
7   *general?:* as general, in charge of the army

9   *pierce:* impel; move

12   *trilled:* trickled or rolled
13   *delicate:* lovely
13-15   *It seemed ... her:* It appeared that she was in control of her
           feelings ("passion") which seemed to be trying to control her.

16-17   *Patience and ... goodliest:* Her self-control struggled with
           her sorrow as to which would give her the most appropriate
           (or beautiful) expression.
19   *A better way:* i.e., of expressing the ideas; *smilets:* little
           smiles
21   *guests:* tears (visiting her eyes)
22   *As pearls from diamonds dropped:* a courtly and therefore
           exaggerated compliment from the messenger, who com-
           pares her tears to pearls and her eyes to diamonds
23-24   *Sorrow would ... it:* Sorrow would be a prized jewel if it was
           as becoming to others (made them as attractive).
24   *Made she no verbal question?:* Did she say nothing apart
           from what you gathered from her tears?
25   *Faith:* in faith (a mild oath); *heaved:* spoke with difficulty

Scene 3

The French camp near Dover.
Enter Kent and a Gentleman.

Kent: Why the King of France is so suddenly gone back;
    know you no reason?
Gentleman: Something he left imperfect in the state, which
    since his coming forth is thought of, which imports
    to the kingdom so much fear and danger that his per-   5
    sonal return was most required and necessary.
Kent: Who hath he left behind him general?
Gentleman: The Marshal of France, Monsieur La Far.
Kent: Did your letters pierce the Queen to any demonstration
    of grief?   10
Gentleman: Ay, sir. She took them, read them in my
    presence,
    And now and then an ample tear trilled down
    Her delicate cheek. It seemed she was a queen
    Over her passion, who, most rebel-like,
    Sought to be king o'er her.
Kent: O, then it moved her?   15
Gentleman: Not to a rage. Patience and sorrow strove
    Who should express her goodliest. You have seen
    Sunshine and rain at once: her smiles and tears
    Were like. A better way: those happy smilets
    That played on her ripe lip seemed not to know   20
    What guests were in her eyes, which parted thence
    As pearls from diamonds dropped. In brief,
    Sorrow would be a rarity most beloved,
    If all could so become it.
Kent: Made she no verbal question?
Gentleman: Faith, once or twice she heaved the name of
    father
    Pantingly forth, as if it pressed her heart;   25
    Cried, "Sisters, sisters! Shame of ladies! Sisters!

29	*Let pity not be believed:* Let it not be believed that pity can exist in a world that sees such deeds, and let it not be believed for the sake of human pity.
29-31	*There she ... moistened:* The general sense is that Cordelia's emotion was calmed by a great outburst of tears, but probably also that the outbursts of tears punctuated her exclamations.
31-32	*Then away ... alone:* Then she simply gave way to her feelings of grief.
32-33	*It is ... conditions:* The stars themselves control our characters.
34-35	*Else one ... issues:* Otherwise, the same husband and wife could not produce children so utterly unalike.
39	*in his better tune:* when he is comparatively rational
41	*yield to see:* submit to seeing
42	*sovereign:* overwhelming; *elbows:* jogs his elbow, reminds him of what he did to Cordelia
43	*stripped her from his benediction:* cut her off from his blessings
44	*foreign casualties:* hazards encountered in foreign countries
45	*dog-hearted:* cruel, fierce, pitiless
48	*powers:* armies
49	*afoot:* on the march
51	*Some dear cause:* an important matter
52	*Will in ... awhile:* will occupy my time and conceal my true identity
53	*aright:* in my true character
54	*Lending me this acquaintance:* for having been acquainted with me

Kent! Father! Sisters! What, i' the storm? I' the night?
Let pity not be believed!" There she shook
The holy water from her heavenly eyes,   30
And clamour moistened. Then away she started
To deal with grief alone.
Kent: It is the stars,
The stars above us, govern our conditions;
Else one self mate and make could not beget
Such different issues. You spoke not with her since?   35
Gentleman: No.
Kent: Was this before the King returned?
Gentleman: No, since.
Kent: Well, sir, the poor distressed Lear's i' the town;
Who sometime, in his better tune, remembers
What we are come about, and by no means   40
Will yield to see his daughter.
Gentleman: Why, good sir?
Kent: A sovereign shame so elbows him; his own unkindness,
That stripped her from his benediction, turned her
To foreign casualties, gave her dear rights
To his dog-hearted daughters—these things sting   45
His mind so venomously that burning shame
Detains him from Cordelia.
Gentleman: Alack, poor gentleman!
Kent: Of Albany's and Cornwall's powers you heard not?
Gentleman: 'Tis so; they are afoot.
Kent: Well, sir, I'll bring you to our master Lear   50
And leave you to attend him. Some dear cause
Will in concealment wrap me up awhile.
When I am known aright, you shall not grieve
Lending me this acquaintance. I pray you go
Along with me.   *[Exeunt.]*   55

Act 4, Scene 3: Activities

1. This scene is frequently omitted from productions of *King Lear*. With your group, prepare an argument as to whether you, as directors, would cut the scene or leave it in the play. Present your argument to classmates.

2. As the person in charge of the French troops, what qualities do you think Cordelia might have that are not revealed to us? In your group, reread the descriptions of Cordelia in this scene.

   a) Create a written portrait of her from your observations.

   b) Using your written description, make a sketch of Cordelia that could be used as an illustration for this scene.

3. You are the King of France. Before you return to your country, you leave Cordelia a letter explaining how you feel about your leaving, the situation in which you are leaving her, and your feelings toward her. Write that letter in your journal.

   In a brief statement, describe the relationship between Cordelia and her husband. Share your statement with others in the class.

4. A "ghost" scene is one that does not appear in the play, but could have. It is the one that could have been there but isn't. Write a brief scene that you think should have been in this play that explains action that actually happened. As a director, write to the play's producer and present your argument for including your "ghost" scene. How would you justify doing so?

For the next scene ...

In your journal, describe a friend, relative, or neighbour who is considered to be an epitome of patience, compassion, and goodness. You may wish to share your portrait with others.

Act 4, Scene 4

In this scene ...

Cordelia sends her soldiers to search for her father, who is wandering aimlessly in the countryside, dressed in garlands of weeds and wild flowers. A doctor comforts her with the reassurance that Lear can be cured with rest and relaxation. Cordelia is concerned, however, that he will die before she can find and help him.

A messenger enters to warn of the approach of the British forces. Cordelia is prepared to meet this army, but makes it clear that her French forces are entering into this war only to aid her father, not to gain political control.

3   *rank:* luxuriant; *fumiter:* fumitory, a plant with bitter leaves. Its juice was used to help in cases of hypochondria and jaundice; *furrow-weeds:* weeds that spring up in the furrows of plowed land

4   *hardocks:* white burdocks; *hemlock:* swamp hemlock, a deadly poisonous weed used as a narcotic; *nettles:* weeds with fine stinging needles

5   *Darnel:* hurtful weed

5-6   *idle weeds ... corn:* worthless rather than sustaining as is corn which provides us with food

6   *century:* force of one hundred soldiers

8-9   *What can ... sense?:* What power has man's accumulated knowledge in restoring his impaired faculties?

10   *He ... worth:* Whoever cures him can take all of my material possessions.

11   *means:* a way

13   *That to provoke:* to cause that (sleep)

14   *simples operative:* effective medicinal plants (called simples, because they were not compounds)

15   *eye of anguish:* eye of one suffering from deep sorrow; *secrets:* remedies, once regarded as the special secrets of the physician

16   *All you ... earth:* a more impressive way of referring to the secrets; *virtues:* here, medicinal plants

17   *Spring:* grow; *aidant and remediate:* as aids and remedies

19   *rage:* insane frenzy

20   *wants:* lacks; *the means:* here, the reason, the rationality; *lead:* guide, control

21   *hitherward:* this way, in this direction

22-23   *Our preparation ... them:* Our troops are ready to meet them.

23-24   *O dear ... about:* Likely a reference to *Luke* 2:49: "I must go about my father's business."

Scene 4

Same.

Enter, with Drum and Colours,
Cordelia, Doctor, and Soldiers.

Cordelia: Alack, 'tis he! Why, he was met even now
  As mad as the vexed sea, singing aloud,
  Crowned with rank fumiter and furrow-weeds,
  With hardocks, hemlock, nettles, cuckoo-flowers,
  Darnel, and all the idle weeds that grow   5
  In our sustaining corn. A century send forth.
  Search every acre in the high-grown field
  And bring him to our eye. [*Exit an Officer.*] What can man's wisdom
  In the restoring his bereaved sense?
  He that helps him take all my outward worth.   10
Doctor: There is means, madam.
  Our foster nurse of nature is repose,
  The which he lacks. That to provoke in him
  Are many simples operative, whose power
  Will close the eye of anguish.
Cordelia: All blest secrets,   15
  All you unpublished virtues of the earth,
  Spring with my tears! be aidant and remediate
  In the good man's distress! Seek, seek for him!
  Lest his ungoverned rage dissolve the life
  That wants the means to lead it.
  [*Enter Messenger.*]
Messenger: News, madam.   20
  The British powers are marching hitherward.
Cordelia: 'Tis known before. Our preparation stands
  In expectation of them. O dear father,
  It is thy business that I go about.

25-26   *Therefore great ... pitied:* For that reason, the King of
           France has taken pity on my mourning and my importunate
           (urging) tears.
27   *blown:* mighty; *arms incite:* provoke us to war

Therefore great France   25
My mourning and importuned tears hath pitied.
No blown ambition doth our arms incite,
But love, dear love, and our aged father's right.
Soon may I hear and see him!   [*Exeunt.*]

Act 4, Scene 4: Activities

1. In this scene we learn that Lear is wearing weeds and wild flowers. Some of these are fumiter, hardocks, nettles, and darnell. Find out what these look like, what they smell like, and if they have special properties, such as a medical cure. Decide why Lear is dressed in such a manner. Who dressed him? What is he thinking about?

2. Cordelia and a doctor discuss possible cures for Lear. Research with your group what sorts of cures were used for madness in Elizabethan times and prescribe a cure of your own.

3. As Cordelia, you are concerned that you will be accused of using the rescue of Lear as an excuse for taking over Britain. Prepare a written defence that Cordelia could present to a court of law, if necessary.

For the next scene ...

What experience have you had with sibling rivalry? Describe one in your journal. Is competition more keen between siblings than it is between unrelated people? If so, what might be the reason for this?

Act 4, Scene 5

In this scene ...

Regan is hoping to read the letter that Goneril has sent with Oswald to Edmund. She is clearly looking for evidence that Goneril and Edmund are having an affair. Regan tells Oswald that she and Edmund are lovers and, because she is already a widow, Edmund is more likely to marry her than Goneril.

Goneril also tells Oswald that Edmund, meanwhile, has gone to find and kill his father. Gloucester, now a potential object of pity, might turn public opinion against the lovers and endanger their common cause. Oswald, who has previously shunned violence, now eagerly agrees to join the hunt for Gloucester, on Regan's instructions.

1	*brother's:* brother-in-law's, i.e., Albany's; *powers:* army
2	*ado:* fuss; probably said sarcastically. Oswald is really Goneril's servant and has little to do with Albany.
3	*Your sister ... soldier:* because of Albany's reluctance to take arms against Lear. "Soldier" is pronounced as three syllables.
6	*What might ... him?:* The topic of the letter was obviously discussed before the beginning of the scene. Regan probably suspects that the letter is a love letter; *import:* indicate, signify—both, "What might my sister's letter contain," and "What is the purpose of writing to him?"
8	*is posted:* has ridden off in haste; *serious matter:* important business. This is information that Oswald must have given to Regan previously.
9	*ignorance:* foolishness, lack of judgement of the political consequences
10	*Where:* wherever
12	*In pity of his misery:* the comment is intentional irony; *dispatch:* take
13	*nighted:* darkened, because of his blindness; *descry:* discover
18	*charged my duty:* gave me strict instructions
20	*Transport her purposes:* carry her instructions; *Belike:* probably
21	*Some things ... what:* Regan conveys her suspicion that Goneril and Edmund are lovers; *I'll love thee much:* I'll reward you generously.
22	*Madam, I had rather:* Oswald refuses to give up the letter.
25	*eliads:* loving looks
26	*her bosom:* in her confidence

Scene 5

Inside Gloucester's castle.

*Enter Regan and Oswald
the Steward.*

Regan: But are my brother's powers set forth?
Oswald: Ay, madam.
Regan: Himself in person there?
Oswald: Madam, with much ado:
   Your sister is the better soldier.
Regan: Lord Edmund spake not with your lord at home?
Oswald: No, madam.   5
Regan: What might import my sister's letter to him?
Oswald: I know not, lady.
Regan: Faith, he is posted hence on serious matter.
   It was great ignorance, Gloucester's eyes being out,
   To let him live. Where he arrives he moves   10
   All hearts against us. Edmund, I think, is gone,
   In pity of his misery, to dispatch
   His nighted life; moreover, to descry
   The strength o' the enemy.
Oswald: I must needs after him, madam, with my letter.   15
Regan: Our troops set forth tomorrow. Stay with us.
   The ways are dangerous.
Oswald: I may not, madam.
   My lady charged my duty in this business.
Regan: Why should she write to Edmund? Might not you
   Transport her purposes by word? Belike,   20
   Some things—I know not what—I'll love thee much—
   Let me unseal the letter.
Oswald: Madam, I had rather—
Regan: I know your lady does not love her husband;
   I am sure of that; and at her late being here
   She gave strange eliads and most speaking looks   25
   To noble Edmund. I know you are of her bosom.

29	*take this note:* take note of this (not a reference to her letter)
30	*talked:* talked about marriage, or, have come to an understanding
31	*convenient:* fitting
32	*You may gather more:* You may assume more (that we are already lovers).
33	*this:* a love-token or trinket, like that Goneril gave Edmund
34	*thus much:* what I have already told you
35	*call her wisdom to her:* have the good sense to accept the situation
38	*Preferment:* promotion

Oswald: I, madam?
Regan: I speak in understanding. Y'are! I know't.
    Therefore I do advise you take this note.
    My lord is dead; Edmund and I have talked,   30
    And more convenient is he for my hand
    Than for your lady's. You may gather more.
    If you do find him, pray you give him this;
    And when your mistress hears thus much from you,
    I pray desire her call her wisdom to her.   35
    So fare you well.
    If you do chance to hear of that blind traitor,
    Preferment falls on him that cuts him off.
Oswald: Would I could meet him, madam! I should show
    What party I do follow.
Regan: Fare thee well.   [*Exeunt.*]   40

Act 4, Scene 5: Activities

1. This scene shows the development of what we commonly call a "love triangle." In groups, determine how the triangle came about, what events you can assume have taken place, and who you think is to blame.

   Such triangles are common in television shows and in movies. How do they usually turn out, from your observations? How do you think this one will turn out?

2. Suddenly, it has become important to kill Gloucester. You are a reporter preparing for a six o'clock newscast. How will you handle the Gloucester story? Will you be sympathetic to Gloucester's plight or openly hostile towards him? Make a video of your broadcast to share with the class. Remember that you are broadcasting to a country that is essentially leaderless.

3. This scene presents many new developments. With your group, discuss what these are. Make a prediction about how this will all turn out in terms of allegiances and relationships. Discuss your conclusions with the others in the class.

For the next scene ...

In your journal, recall an incident in your life that made
you feel there was no justice in the world. How did you
respond? Have your views on the world's justice
changed as a result of your experience? Comment.

Act 4, Scene 6

In this scene ...

Edgar has led Gloucester to some fields near Dover. He tells his father that they have climbed to the top of a cliff. Believing this to be true, Gloucester thanks Edgar, gives him a purse containing a jewel, and dismisses him. Then Gloucester jumps off what he believes to be the cliff. Although he does not fall far, he faints, overwhelmed by his action. When he revives, he is greeted by Edgar pretending to be a peasant who has seen Gloucester fall. Edgar convinces Gloucester that his survival is a miracle, a sign from the gods that they want him to live. As a result, Gloucester determines that he must endure his suffering until the gods decide that he should die.

Lear now enters, wearing garlands of wild flowers. He raves about the hypocrisy of human beings and decides, in garbled speech, that all of humanity is guilty of sin and that suffering is the lot for all of us. When one of Cordelia's gentlemen attempts to take him in charge, Lear flees.

Oswald appears, delighted to have found Gloucester. Before he can murder the blind man, however, he is attacked by Edgar and killed in the course of their duel. Before he dies, Oswald asks Edgar to take a letter he is carrying to Edmund. Edgar reads the letter in which Goneril confirms her plot with Edmund to murder Albany. Edgar vows to inform Albany and then leads Gloucester away to a friend who will take care of him.

2	*labour:* i.e., at going uphill
3	*Methinks:* it seems to me; *the ground is even:* The ground is indeed even. Edgar has only pretended to lead his blind father to where the cliff is "Horrible steep"; *Horrible:* terrifyingly
4	*Hark:* listen
5-6	*Why, then ... anguish:* Then your other senses must be dulled by pain caused by the loss of your eyes.
7-8	*Methinks thy ... didst:* Edgar uses several different accents during his period of disguise (see Act 4, Scene 1, lines 52-55). Apparently, he has dropped part of his assumed character.
10	*Methinks y'are better spoken:* You speak with a better accent (than you did before).
13	*choughs:* jackdaws, birds that were common on the cliffs (pronounced "chuffs")
14	*gross:* large
15	*sampire:* sampire or *herbe de Saint Pierre,* a plant used with vinegar to produce a meat relish and gathered from the cliff face at Dover by men suspended on a rope from the top of the cliff, hence, Edgar's comment "Dreadful trade!"
18	*bark:* ship
19	*Diminished to her cock:* reduced in size (by the distance) to seem no bigger then her cockboat, the small boat used by the crew to reach shore from the ship; *her cock, a buoy:* the tiny cockboat is similarly reduced in size to that of a buoy
20	*surge:* surf, breaking waves
21	*unnumbered:* numberless; *idle:* moved by a continuous agitation for no purpose; *pebble:* pebbles
23-24	*the deficient ... headlong:* And my sight failing me, I fall headlong down the cliff.

Scene 6

Open country near Dover.
Enter Gloucester, and Edgar,
clothed as a countryman.

Gloucester: When shall I come to the top of that same hill?
Edgar: You do climb up it now. Look how we labour.
Gloucester: Methinks the ground is even.
Edgar: Horrible steep.
  Hark, do you hear the sea?
Gloucester: No, truly.
Edgar: Why, then, your other senses grow imperfect   5
  By your eyes' anguish.
Gloucester: So may it be indeed.
  Methinks thy voice is altered, and thou speakest
  In better phrase and matter than thou didst.
Edgar: Y'are much deceived. In nothing am I changed
  But in my garments.
Gloucester: Methinks y'are better spoken.   10
Edgar: Come on, sir; here's the place. Stand still. How
      fearful
  And dizzy 'tis to cast one's eyes so low!
  The crows and choughs that wing the midway air
  Show scarce so gross as beetles. Halfway down
  Hangs one that gathers sampire—dreadful trade!   15
  Methinks he seems no bigger than his head.
  The fishermen that walk upon the beach
  Appear like mice; and yond tall anchoring bark,
  Diminished to her cock; her cock, a buoy
  Almost too small for sight. The murmuring surge   20
  That on the unnumbered idle pebble chafes
  Cannot be heard so high. I'll look no more,
  Lest my brain turn, and the deficient sight
  Topple down headlong.

27   *leap upright:* He is so close to the cliff that if he jumped
            straight up in the air, he still could fall over the edge.

29   *Fairies:* possibly a reference to a superstition that hidden
            treasure is guarded by fairies

33-34   *Why I ... it:* The reason that I humour my father's despair is
            to cure it – a necessary explanation for the audience, who
            would otherwise be puzzled by Edgar's behaviour.

38   *fall to quarrel with:* rebel against; *opposeless:* not to be
            opposed, not to be resisted, irresistible
39   *My snuff ... nature:* the darkened and hated remainder of
            my life
42-44   *how conceit ... theft:* how imagination may be robbing life's
            treasury of all its strength when life itself surrenders or con-
            sents (yields) to the theft. Edgar is fearful that, even though
            his father has not jumped off the cliff, simply imagining the
            fall may be enough of a shock to kill him.
45   *this:* the act of apparent suicide; *had thought been past:*
            i.e., he would have been dead and therefore past or
            beyond thinking (thought)
46   *Ho you ... Speak:* Edgar tries to rouse Gloucester, who has
            fallen down on the ground from a slight height.
47   *pass:* die
49   *Hadst thou:* if you had; *aught:* anything; *gossamer:* thread
            of a spider's web
50   *precipating:* falling
51   *Thou'dst:* you would have; *shivered:* shattered
52   *Hast heavy substance:* are of normal weight, subject to
            gravity; *art sound:* are uninjured
53   *Ten masts at each:* ten masts of a tall ship, one on top of
            the other
54   *fell:* fallen
57   *bourn:* boundary of the sea (the cliffs at Dover are com-
            posed of chalk)

Gloucester: Set me where you stand.
Edgar: Give me your hand; you are now within a foot   25
   Of the extreme verge; for all beneath the moon
   Would I not leap upright.
Gloucester: Let go my hand.
   Here, friend, 's another purse; in it a jewel
   Well worth a poor man's taking. Fairies and gods
   Prosper it with thee! Go thou further off;   30
   Bid me farewell, and let me hear thee going.
Edgar: Now fare ye well, good sir.
Gloucester: With all my heart.
Edgar: [Aside.] Why I do trifle thus with this despair
   Is done to cure it.
Gloucester: O you mighty gods!   [He kneels.]
   This world I do renounce, and, in your sights,   35
   Shake patiently my great affliction off.
   If I could bear it longer and not fall
   To quarrel with your great opposeless wills,
   My snuff and loathed part of nature should
   Burn itself out. If Edgar live, O, bless him!   40
   Now, fellow, fare thee well.
                     [He falls forward and faints.]
Edgar: Gone, sir, farewell.—
   And yet I know not how conceit may rob
   The treasury of life when life itself
   Yields to the theft. Had he been where he thought,
   By this had thought been past.—Alive or dead?   45
   Ho you, sir! Friend! Hear you, sir? Speak!—
   Thus might he pass indeed. Yet he revives.
   What are you, sir?
Gloucester: Away, and let me die.
Edgar: Hadst thou been aught but gossamer, feathers, air,
   So many fathom down precipitating,   50
   Thou'dst shivered like an egg; but thou dost breathe;
   Hast heavy substance; bleedest not; speakest; art sound.
   Ten masts at each make not the altitude
   Which thou hast perpendicularly fell.
   Thy life's a miracle. Speak yet again.   55
Gloucester: But have I fallen, or no?
Edgar: From the dread summit of this chalky bourn.

58	*a-height:* on high, to the height above; *shrill-gorged:* shrill-throated, shrill-voiced
61-64	*Is wretchedness ... death?:* Am I, in my misfortune, to be deprived of the benefit of death? *'Twas yet ... will:* After all, it was some comfort to know that in my unhappiness I could cheat the tyrant's (Cornwall's) tyranny and foil his aims by suicide.
65	*Up – so:* Edgar is straining to get Gloucester to his feet again; *Feel you:* either "Can you use?" or "Have you any feeling in?"
66	*above all strangeness:* the strangest thing I have ever seen
67-68	*Upon the ... you?:* Edgar pretends to be a new rescuer. He is no longer the Bedlam beggar who led Gloucester to the cliff.
69-72	*As I ... fiend:* Edgar further confuses Gloucester by convincing him that a fiend, not Poor Tom, led him to the cliff, and that the gods pitied him and saved him; *whelked:* twisted; *enridged:* furrowed
73-74	*Think that ... thee:* Believe that the most glorious gods, who make themselves honoured by performing miracles impossible to men, have saved you (from the fiend).
77	*die:* disappear. Gloucester determines to bear his suffering until affliction itself recognizes he has been hurt enough and dies.
79	*"The fiend, the fiend":* Edgar's words during his pretended madness
80	*free:* i.e., free from despair
81-82	*The safer ... thus:* The sane judgement of a man would not permit him to dress in this fashion. Edgar implies that the man he sees must be mad because of his strange dress.
83	*touch:* charge, arrest; *coining:* making counterfeit money. The king in early days coined all the legal money of the realm.
86	*Nature's above ... respect:* A born (or natural) king is superior to one dependent upon legal supports.
86-87	*press money:* money paid by those forced (pressed) into military service so they can avoid a serving

Look up a-height. The shrill-gorged lark so far
Cannot be seen or heard. Do but look up.
Gloucester: Alack, I have no eyes!   60
   Is wretchedness deprived that benefit
   To end itself by death? 'Twas yet some comfort
   When misery could beguile the tyrant's rage
   And frustrate his proud will.
Edgar: Give me your arm.
   Up—so. How is't? Feel you your legs? You stand.   65
Gloucester: Too well, too well.
Edgar: This is above all strangeness.
   Upon the crown o' the cliff what thing was that
   Which parted from you?
Gloucester: A poor unfortunate beggar.
Edgar: As I stood here below, methought his eyes
   Were two full moons; he had a thousand noses,   70
   Horns whelked and waved like the enridged sea:
   It was some fiend; therefore, thou happy father,
   Think that the clearest gods, who make them honours
   Of men's impossibilities, have preserved thee.
Gloucester: I do remember now. Henceforth I'll bear   75
   Affliction till it do cry out itself,
   "Enough, enough," and die. That thing you speak of,
   I took it for a man. Often 'twould say,
   "The fiend, the fiend"—he led me to that place.
Edgar: Bear free and patient thoughts.
   [*Enter Lear, mad, garlanded with wild flowers.*]
                            But who comes here?   80
   The safer sense will ne'er accommodate
   His master thus.
Lear: No, they cannot touch me for coining;
   I am the King himself.
Edgar: O thou side-piercing sight!   85
Lear: Nature's above art in that respect. There's your press
   money. That fellow handles his bow like a crowkeeper.
   Draw me a clothier's yard. Look, look, a mouse! Peace,
   peace; this piece of toasted cheese will do it. There's
   my gauntlet; I'll prove it on a giant. Bring up the   90
   brown bills. O, well flown, bird! I' the clout, i' the
   clout! Hewgh! Give the word.

93	*Sweet marjoram:* wild flower; also a remedy for mental illness
94	*Pass:* move on, go ahead
96-98	*Ha! Goneril with a white beard?:* Lear mistakes Gloucester for Goneril; *They flattered ... there:* They flattered me by telling me I had white hair and was therefore wise, although I proved myself foolish.
99-100	*"Ay" and "no" ... divinity:* Lear now understands that just because his followers agreed with everything he claimed, this did not make him divine.
101	*chatter:* shiver with cold
102	*peace:* stop, go silent, keep quiet
103	*men:* women. It appears that Lear confuses the two.
105	*ague:* fever
106	*trick:* individual peculiarity or intonation
109	*cause?:* charge or offence that brought you to court to be judged
111	*Die for adultery?:* Adultery was not a capital offence in Elizabethan England nor in the imagined time of the play.
112	*gilded:* deceptively and superficially beautiful
113	*lecher:* copulate
117	*To it:* Go to it; *luxury:* lust; *pell-mell:* in disorder or confusion
119	*forks:* legs; *presages snow:* promises chastity, seems to be frigidly chaste.
120	*minces virtue:* coyly affects the timidity of virtue
121	*To hear of pleasure's name:* even to hear the word "pleasure"
122	*fitchew:* polecat (weasel) – prostitute
123	*riotous:* unrestrained
124	*Centaurs:* legendary creatures half-horse and half-human
126-127	*But to ... fiend's:* Down to the waist, they belong to the gods; below the waist, to the devil.

Edgar: Sweet marjoram.
Lear: Pass.
Gloucester: I know that voice.   95
Lear: Ha! Goneril with a white beard? They flattered me
    like a dog, and told me I had white hairs in my beard
    ere the black ones were there. To say "ay" and "no"
    to everything that I said! "Ay" and "no" too was no
    good divinity. When the rain came to wet me once,   100
    and the wind to make me chatter; when the thunder
    would not peace at my bidding; there I found 'em,
    there I smelt 'em out. Go to, they are not men o' their
    words! They told me I was everything. 'Tis a lie—I
    am not ague-proof.   105
Gloucester: The trick of that voice I do well remember.
    Is't not the King?
Lear: Ay, every inch a king!
    When I do stare, see how the subject quakes.
    I pardon that man's life. What was thy cause?
    Adultery?   110
    Thou shalt not die. Die for adultery? No.
    The wren goes to it, and the small gilded fly
    Does lecher in my sight.
    Let copulation thrive; for Gloucester's bastard son
    Was kinder to his father than my daughters   115
    Got 'tween the lawful sheets.
    To it, luxury, pell-mell! For I lack soldiers.
    Behold yond simpering dame,
    Whose face between her forks presages snow,
    That minces virtue, and does shake the head   120
    To hear of pleasure's name.
    The fitchew nor the soiled horse goes to it
    With a more riotous appetite.
    Down from the waist they are Centaurs,
    Though women all above.   125
    But to the girdle do the gods inherit,
    Beneath is all the fiend's.
        There's hell, there's darkness, there is the sulphurous
        pit; burning, scalding, stench, consumption. Fie, fie,
        fie! Pah, pah! Give me an ounce of civet; good apoth-   130
        ecary, sweeten my imagination. There's money for thee.

133	*mortality:* death or existence (or the bitter experience of life)
134-135	*O ruined ... naught:* What a masterpiece of nature (Lear) is ruined! In such a way will the universe eventually be worn down to nothing.
137	*blind Cupid:* the god of love, whose image was used commonly in Shakespeare's day on signs for brothels
138	*this challenge:* summons (probably imagined); *mark:* observe; *penning:* handwriting
140	*I would ... report:* I would not believe this if it had been reported to me; *is:* is so
143	*case of eyes?:* eye socket
144	*are you there with me?:* Are you like me in that respect?
145-146	*in a heavy case:* in a serious condition; *light:* empty
148	*feelingly:* by touch, by pain
151	*justice:* judge; *rails upon:* scolds, lectures; *simple:* ordinary
152	*handy-dandy:* take your choice (from a children's game in which one child hides a prize in one of his or her closed hands and another guesses which hand holds the prize)
153-158	*Thou hast ... office:* Lear says that anyone in power is obeyed regardless of his character.
156	*creature:* beggar
159	*beadle:* parish constable; *hold thy bloody hand:* Restrain yourself from giving out punishment.
162	*usurer:* one who lends money at an exhorbitant rate of interest; *cozener:* cheat
164	*Robes and ... all:* fine dress of those in office hides all evil
164-166	*Plate sin ... it:* Dress a sinner in expensive clothing and he will be untouched by the law; dress him in rags and the law fails him.
167	*None does ... 'em:* No person shall be considered guilty. I will authorize all to act as they wish.
169	*glass eyes:* glasses – an anachronism
170	*scurvy politician:* vile trickster

Gloucester: O, let me kiss that hand!
Lear: Let me wipe it first; it smells of mortality.
Gloucester: O ruined piece of nature! This great world
    Shall so wear out to naught. Dost thou know me?   135
Lear: I remember thine eyes well enough. Dost thou squint
    at me? No, do thy worst, blind Cupid! I'll not love.
    Read thou this challenge; mark but the penning of it.
Gloucester: Were all thy letters suns, I could not see.
Edgar: [*Aside.*] I would not take this from report. It is,   140
    And my heart breaks at it.
Lear: Read.
Gloucester: What, with the case of eyes?
Lear: O, ho, are you there with me? No eyes in your head,
    nor no money in your purse? Your eyes are in a heavy   145
    case, your purse in a light. Yet you see how this
    world goes.
Gloucester: I see it feelingly.
Lear: What, art mad? A man may see how this world goes
    with no eyes. Look with thine ears. See how yond   150
    justice rails upon yond simple thief. Hark in thine
    ear. Change places and, handy-dandy, which is the
    justice, which is the thief? Thou hast seen a farmer's
    dog bark at a beggar?
Gloucester: Ay, sir.   155
Lear: And the creature run from the cur? There thou mightst
    behold the great image of authority: a dog's obeyed
    in office.
    Thou rascal beadle, hold thy bloody hand!
    Why dost thou lash that whore? Strip thine own back.   160
    Thou hotly lusts to use her in that kind
    For which thou whippest her. The usurer hangs the
    cozener.
    Through tattered clothes small vices do appear;
    Robes and furred gowns hide all. Plate sin with gold,
    And the strong lance of justice hurtless breaks;   165
    Arm it in rags, a pygmy's straw does pierce it.
    None does offend, none, I say, none; I'll able 'em:
    Take that of me, my friend, who have the power
    To seal th' accuser's lips. Get thee glass eyes
    And, like a scurvy politician, seem   170

172 *So:* said as his boots come off – an expression of relief. Lear thinks that he has just completed a journey or tour of inspection.

173 *matter and impertinency:* sense and incoherence

175-176 *If thou ... Gloucester:* Lear's mind clears for a moment, and he recognizes his old supporter.

177 *We came crying hither:* We come into the world crying.

179 *mark:* Listen carefully.

182 *this great stage:* this great world; *This' a good block:* This is a stylish hat.

183 *a delicate stratagem:* a very difficult plan

184 *felt:* material of specially matted fur from which hats are made, and a fanciful means by which a whole troop of horses could be made to move quietly; *put't in proof:* put in to the test

185 *stolen upon:* with a troop of felt-shod horses; *sons-in-law:* Albany and Cornwall

186 *kill, kill ... kill:* a cry used by soldiers, meaning "No mercy."

189 *What, a prisoner?:* Lear feels he has been taken prisoner.

190 *The natural fool of fortune:* a plaything of fortune

192 *cut:* wounded

193 *seconds?:* supporters

194 *Why, this ... salt:* This would make any man weep.

195-196 *To use ... dust:* to weep more copiously; *bravely:* in fine dress

197 *smug:* trim, neat

198 *masters:* gentlemen

200 *Then there's life in't:* Then there's still hope; *an:* if

201 *Sa, sa, sa, sa:* a hunting cry to urge on the hounds

204 *general:* universal

205 *twain:* a pair

206 *speed you:* God bless you; *What's your will?:* What do you wish?

To see the things thou dost not. Now, now, now, now!
Pull off my boots. Harder, harder! So.
Edgar: O, matter and impertinency mixed!
Reason in madness!
Lear: If thou wilt weep my fortunes, take my eyes.   175
I know thee well enough; thy name is Gloucester.
Thou must be patient. We came crying hither;
Thou knowest, the first time that we smell the air
We wawl and cry. I will preach to thee: mark.
Gloucester: Alack, alack the day!   180
Lear: When we are born, we cry that we are come
To this great stage of fools. This' a good block.
It were a delicate stratagem to shoe
A troop of horse with felt. I'll put't in proof,
And when I have stolen upon these sons-in-law,   185
Then kill, kill, kill, kill, kill, kill!
[*Enter a Gentleman with Attendants.*]
Gentleman: O, here he is! Lay hand upon him.—Sir,
Your most dear daughter—
Lear: No rescue? What, a prisoner? I am even
The natural fool of fortune. Use me well;   190
You shall have ransom. Let me have surgeons;
I am cut to the brains.
Gentleman: You shall have anything.
Lear: No seconds? All myself?
Why, this would make a man a man of salt,
To use his eyes for garden waterpots,   195
Ay, and laying autumn's dust. I will die bravely,
Like a smug bridegroom. What! I will be jovial.
Come, come, I am king; masters, know you that?
Gentleman: You are a royal one, and we obey you.
Lear: Then there's life in't. Come, an you get it, you shall   200
get it by running. Sa, sa, sa, sa!
[*Exit running followed by Attendants.*]
Gentleman: A sight most pitiful in the meanest wretch,
Past speaking of in a king! Thou hast one daughter
Who redeems nature from the general curse
Which twain have brought her to.   205
Edgar: Hail, gentle sir.
Gentleman: Sir, speed you. What's your will?

207 *toward?:* about to take place, in preparation
208 *Most sure and vulgar:* most certain, and a matter of common knowledge
209 *Which can distinguish sound:* who can hear at all

211-212 *and on speedy foot:* moving swiftly; *The main ... thought:* The main body of troops is expected to be in view within the hour.

213-214 *Though that ... on:* Though Cordelia is here for a special reason (to seek her father), her troops have moved ahead.

215 *take my breath from me:* choose when to make me die
216 *worser spirit:* the evil side of my nature

217 *father:* This word would not reveal Edgar's identity to Gloucester, since it was used as a term of respect by younger to older men.
219 *made tame:* resigned
220-221 *Who, by ... pity:* who, through the instruction provided by heartfelt sorrow, am easily moved to pity. More simply, Edgar says: Since I have experienced deep sorrow, I can readily feel pity for others.
222 *biding:* shelter, lodging
223 *bounty and the benison:* reward and the blessing
224 *To boot, and boot:* in the highest degree; *A proclaimed prize:* a criminal with a reward on his head; *Most happy:* This is a happy opportunity for me!
225 *framed:* created

227 *thyself remember:* Pray for your sins; *the sword is out:* Oswald draws his sword as he speaks.

228 *friendly:* because it offers the death Gloucester wants

230 *published:* proclaimed
231-232 *Lest that ... thee:* lest his ill-luck become yours

233 *Chill:* I'll. Edgar adopts conventional rustic stage dialect, much like that of rural Somerset; *zir:* sir; *'casion:* occasion, reason

Edgar: Do you hear aught, sir, of a battle toward?
Gentleman: Most sure and vulgar. Every one hears that
   Which can distinguish sound.
Edgar: But, by your favour,
   How near's the other army?   210
Gentleman: Near and on speedy foot. The main descry
   Stands on the hourly thought.
Edgar: I thank you, sir. That's
     all.
Gentleman: Though that the Queen on special cause is here,
   Her army is moved on.
Edgar: I thank you, sir.
                             [Exit Gentleman.]
Gloucester: You ever-gentle gods, take my breath from me;   215
   Let not my worser spirit tempt me again
   To die before you please!
Edgar: Well pray you, father.
Gloucester: Now, good sir, what are you?
Edgar: A most poor man, made tame to fortune's blows,
   Who, by the art of known and feeling sorrows,   220
   Am pregnant to good pity. Give me your hand;
   I'll lead you to some biding.
Gloucester: Hearty thanks.
   The bounty and the benison of heaven
   To boot, and boot!
   [Enter Oswald the Steward.]
Oswald: A proclaimed prize! Most happy!
   That eyeless head of thine was first framed flesh   225
   To raise my fortunes. Thou old unhappy traitor,
   Briefly thyself remember: the sword is out
   That must destroy thee.
Gloucester: Now let thy friendly hand
   Put strength enough to't.   *[Edgar interposes.]*
Oswald: Wherefore, bold peasant,
   Darest thou support a published traitor? Hence!   230
   Lest that th' infection of his fortune take
   Like hold on thee. Let go his arm.
Edgar: Chill not let go, zir, without vurther 'casion.
Oswald: Let go, slave, or thou diest!

235   *go your gait:* Go your way; *volk:* folk, people
235-236   *An chud ... vortnight:* If I could have been frightened out of
               my life by bold words, I should have been dead a couple of
               weeks ago. (Edgar accuses Oswald of mere braggery, not
               real courage.)
238-240   *Keep out ... you:* Stand back, I warn you, or I shall try to
               find out whether your head or my club (ballow) is the hard-
               er. I'll be plain with you.
241   *dunghill:* born on a dunghill; low-born
242-243   *Chill pick ... foins:* I'll knock your teeth out, sir. Come at me.
               I don't care about your sword thrusts (foins).
244   *Villain:* serf (in contrast to Edgar's use of "villain," line 249)

248   *Upon the English party:* on the side of the English

249   *serviceable villain:* evil fellow ready to be used
250   *duteous:* obedient

254   *May be my friends:* may be able to help me
255   *deathsman:* executioner
256   *Leave:* by your leave; *wax:* with which the letter was sealed;
               manners, blame us not: The normal respect with which we
               view the letters of others should not count here.
257-258   *To know ... lawful:* To know what our enemies are thinking,
               we would tear their hearts from their bodies. To rip open
               their letters is more justifiable.
259   *reciprocal vows:* See Act 4, Scene 2, lines 21-24.
260-261   *to cut him off:* to murder Albany; *If your will want not:* if you
               are not lacking in desire
261   *time and place:* i.e., for his murder
262   *nothing done:* There is nothing to be done.
266   *would:* would like to: *servant:* lover
267   *O indistinguished ... will:* O, the limitless scope of a
               woman's lust.
269-270   *Here ... unsanctified:* Edgar says he will bury Oswald, but
               the precise meaning is unclear; *sands:* Gloucester believes
               they are on the beach; perhaps Edgar is speaking for his
               father's benefit; *rake up:* cover up, bury; *post unsanctified:*
               unholy messenger

Edgar: Good gentleman, go your gait, and let poor yolk   235
    pass. An chud ha' bin zwagger'd out of my life, 'twould
    not ha' bin zo long as 'tis by a vortnight. Nay, come
    not near the old man. Keep out, che vor' ye, or Ise
    try whither your costard or my ballow be the harder.
    Chill be plain with you.   240
Oswald: Out, dunghill!
Edgar: Chill pick your teeth, zir. Come! No matter vor your
    foins.   [*They fight and Oswald falls.*]
Oswald: Slave, thou hast slain me. Villain, take my purse.
    If ever thou wilt thrive, bury my body,   245
    And give the letters which thou find'st about me
    To Edmund Earl of Gloucester. Seek him out
    Upon the English party. O, untimely death! Death!
                              [*He dies.*]
Edgar: I know thee well. A serviceable villain,
    As duteous to the vices of thy mistress   250
    As badness would desire.
Gloucester: What, is he dead?
Edgar: Sit you down, father; rest you.
    Let's see these packets; the letters that he speaks of
    May be my friends. He's dead; I am only sorry
    He had no other deathsman. Let us see.   255
    Leave, gentle wax; and manners, blame us not:
    To know our enemies' minds, we rip their hearts;
    Their papers is more lawful.   [*Reads the letter.*]
    "Let our reciprocal vows be remembered. You have
    many opportunities to cut him off. If your will want   260
    not, time and place will be fruitfully offered. There
    is nothing done if he return the conqueror. Then am
    I the prisoner, and his bed my jail; from the loathed
    warmth whereof deliver me, and supply the place for
    your labour.   265
    Your (wife, so I would say) affectionate servant,"
                              GONERIL.
    O indistinguished space of woman's will!
    A plot upon her virtuous husband's life,
    And the exchange my brother! Here in the sands
    Thee I'll rake up, the post unsanctified   270

271   *murderous lechers:* lustful and murderous persons (Goneril
           and Edmund); *in the mature time:* when the proper moment
           arrives
272-273   *ungracious paper:* evil letter; *strike the ... Duke:* show to the
           Duke of Albany, whose death is plotted
275   *vile sense:* vile, because his senses make him fully aware of
           his losses and sorrows but do not give him the relief of
           insanity
276   *ingenious:* conscious
277   *distract:* mad
278-280   *So should ... themselves:* If I were mad (like Lear), my
           thoughts and griefs would be separated, and my sorrows
           would be lost amid mad illusions (wrong imaginations).
282   *bestow you with:* leave you in the care of; *friend:* How
           Edgar managed to get in touch with a friend is anybody's
           guess.

Of murderous lechers; and in the mature time
With this ungracious paper strike the sight
Of the death-practised Duke. From him 'tis well
That of thy death and business I can tell.
Gloucester: The King is mad. How stiff is my vile sense,   275
That I stand up, and have ingenious feeling
Of my huge sorrows! Better I were distract.
So should my thoughts be severed from my griefs,
And woes by wrong imaginations lose
The knowledge of themselves.   [*A drum afar off.*]
Edgar: Give me your hand.   280
Far off methinks I hear the beaten drum.
Come, father, I'll bestow you with a friend.   [*Exeunt.*]

Act 4, Scene 6: Activities

1. The segment of this scene in which Gloucester tries to jump off the cliff has often been criticized as being so contrived to be unbelievable. In groups, decide how you might stage this segment so that it can be believed by an audience. Assume that you have nothing to work with but a bare stage. Present your ideas to classmates.

   If you were to film the segment for a movie, how would you depict Gloucester's fall?

2. A symbol is usually defined as something that stands for or represents something else. A friend of yours has just seen a production of *King Lear* for the first time and has no prior knowledge of the play. Your friend senses there is something symbolic in the suicide sequence in this scene. How do you explain it to him or her? Share your understanding with others.

3. Many people regard the coming together of Lear and Gloucester in this scene as representational, standing for many things other than two old men meeting by chance. Discuss with classmates what their meeting may represent in light of your understanding of the play to this point. Write your own interpretation of the meeting in a brief essay.

4. Lear's speeches in this scene appear initially to make no sense at all. Upon careful examination, however, it becomes clear that there are threads tying them together. In groups, sort out what Lear is recalling. What do his recollections reveal about him that we did not know previously? How do you think an audience seeing the play for the first time would respond to these speeches? How much sense do you think they would make of them?

   In modern fiction, the technique Shakespeare uses in Lear's speeches is referred to as "stream of consciousness" – a narrative in which a character recounts different experiences, responses, and ideas in a continuous flow. Assume that Gloucester, on hearing Lear's voice, also goes mad. Write a speech for him employing the stream-of-consciousness technique, drawing on events from Gloucester's past.

5. Some productions of *King Lear* use this scene to emphasize the idea that the world is essentially evil and that all good is eventually crushed out of it. In your group, discuss to what extent you believe this to be the theme of this scene.

6. In this scene, Lear continues to rail bitterly against women. What kind of woman do you think his wife might have been? Do you think she may have been partly responsible for the way Lear's daughters turned out? Write the dialogue that could result from a conversation you have with Lear's wife in which you ask her what it was like to have been married to Lear. Be sure to include questions on the way each of them treated their children.

7. After Oswald is killed, his personal video diary is discovered. Use the information contained in it as part of an inquest into his death to determine whether he was truly an evil man or one simply used by others. In your written report, reveal as much information as you can about him and draw specific conclusions about his motivations, based on your evidence.

8. In lines 107-131, Lear gives a scathing assessment of women. While his reasons for doing so may be understandable, you have decided to object to this portrayal as unfair and unjust. What arguments do you use? Write your response as a speech about male perceptions of females, and in it, use some of Lear's images as your points of reference.

For the next scene ...

What do you know about parent-child bonding? Describe an experience you had in which you became aware of a special bond that was developing between a parent and child.

Act 4, Scene 7

In this scene ...

In the French camp, Cordelia thanks Kent for his loyalty to her father. She invites him to remove his disguise but he tells her that he still requires it. We learn that Cordelia has finally rescued her father and that he has been attended to by a doctor.

Lear has been sleeping for some time, and still asleep, he is brought to Cordelia. She wakes him and asks him for his blessing and, now that his mind is calmed, Lear begs her forgiveness. As they leave together, we hear that the enemy is approaching and that a bloody battle is about to ensue.

The scene closes with news of Cornwall's death and of Edgar's leading his troops. Kent observes that the outcome of this battle will determine whether or not he has reached his objectives.

3   *measure:* attempt
4   *To be acknowledged:* to be recognized (for one's work)
5   *All my ... truth:* Everything I have reported (about Lear) conforms to the simple truth.
6   *Nor more nor clipped:* no more, no less; *so:* as I say; *suited:* dressed
7   *These weeds ... worser hours:* These clothes are reminders of the worst hours.
8   *I prithee:* I beg you.
9   *Yet to ... intent:* If I am to reveal myself now, I shall not be able to carry out my intentions.
10   *boon:* request
11   *meet:* suitable

15   *breach in his abused nature:* damage in his disturbed mind
16-17 *Th' untuned ... father:* Tune the untuned and discordant senses of this father who has been made mad (also made into a child) by the savagery of his children. The image is based upon the tuning of a stringed musical instrument.
18   *That we may:* may we
19   *Be governed by:* act according to
20   *I' the sway of:* according to

Scene 7

A tent in the French camp.
Enter Cordelia, Kent, Doctor,
and Gentleman.

Cordelia: O thou good Kent, how shall I live and work
  To match thy goodness? My life will be too short
  And every measure fail me.
Kent: To be acknowledged, madam, is o'erpaid.
  All my reports go with the modest truth;   5
  Nor more nor clipped, but so.
Cordelia: Be better suited:
  These weeds are memories of those worser hours:
  I prithee put them off.
Kent: Pardon, dear madam.
  Yet to be known shortens my made intent.
  My boon I make it that you know me not   10
  Till time and I think meet.
Cordelia: Then be it so, my good lord. [*To the Doctor.*] How
  does the King?
Doctor: Madam, sleeps still.
Cordelia: O you kind gods,
  Cure this great breach in his abused nature!   15
  Th' untuned and jarring senses, O, wind up
  Of this child-changed father!
Doctor: So please your Majesty
  That we may wake the King? He hath slept long.
Cordelia: Be governed by your knowledge, and proceed
  I' the sway of your own will. Is he arrayed?   20
  [*Enter Lear in a chair carried by Servants.*]
Gentleman: Ay, madam. In the heaviness of sleep.
  We put fresh garments on him.

23	*Be by:* Be nearby, remain close at hand.
24	*I doubt ... temperance:* I have no doubt that his sanity will have returned; I am certain he will be calm.
26-27	*restoration hang ... lips:* May my kiss serve as medicine to restore you to your former state.
29	*in thy reverence:* to you, to whom all showed reverence
30	*Had you not been:* even if you had not been; *these white flakes:* these strands of white hair
31	*Had challenged:* would have called for; *of:* from
33	*dread-bolted:* with its dreadful thunderbolts
35	*perdu:* lost one
36	*this thin helm?:* this head, with scanty hair
38	*Against:* near; *fain:* glad
39	*To hovel thee:* to take shelter; *rogues:* vagabonds, tramps
40	*short and musty:* broken and damp
41	*at once:* at a single moment
42	*concluded all:* come to an end
43	*fittest:* most fitting, most suitable, best
47	*that:* so that
50	*far wide:* far wide of the mark, far away from sanity
51	*scarce:* scarcely
53	*mightily abused:* greatly deceived, greatly deluded
54	*thus:* in my present state
56-57	*Would ... condition:* I wish I could be confident about my state of being.

Doctor: Be by, good madam, when we do awake him.
   I doubt not of his temperance.
Cordelia: Very well.   [*Music.*]
Doctor: Please you draw near. Louder the music there!   25
Cordelia: O my dear father, restoration hang
   Thy medicine on my lips, and let this kiss
   Repair those violent harms that my two sisters
   Have in thy reverence made!
Kent: Kind and dear princess!
Cordelia: Had you not been their father, these white flakes   30
   Had challenged pity of them. Was this a face
   To be opposed against the warring winds?
   To stand against the deep dread-bolted thunder?
   In the most terrible and nimble stroke
   Of quick, cross lightning? to watch—poor perdu!—   35
   With this thin helm? Mine enemy's dog,
   Though he had bit me, should have stood that night
   Against my fire; and wast thou fain, poor father,
   To hovel thee with swine and rogues forlorn,
   In short and musty straw? Alack, alack!   40
   'Tis wonder that thy life and wits at once
   Had not concluded all.—He wakes; speak to him.
Doctor: Madam, do you; 'tis fittest.
Cordelia: How does my royal lord? How fares your Majesty?
Lear: You do me wrong to take me out o' the grave.   45
   Thou art a soul in bliss; but I am bound
   Upon a wheel of fire, that mine own tears
   Do scald like molten lead.
Cordelia: Sir, do you know me?
Lear: You are a spirit, I know. Where did you die?
Cordelia: Still, still, far wide!   50
Doctor: He's scarce awake. Let him alone awhile.
Lear: Where have I been? Where am I? Fair daylight?
   I am mightily abused. I should e'en die with pity,
   To see another thus. I know not what to say.
   I will not swear these are my hands. Let's see: 55
   I feel this pin prick. Would I were assured
   Of my condition!
Cordelia: O, look upon me, sir,

58	*benediction:* blessing
60	*fond:* senile, foolish
61	*Fourscore:* eighty years
62	*deal plainly:* speak bluntly
64	*this man:* likely Kent
65	*mainly:* entirely
66	*skill:* sense
77	*abuse:* deceive
78	*rage:* frenzy, madness
79-80	*and yet ... lost:* and yet it is dangerous to make him try to fill in the gap in the time that he does not recollect
81	*Desire him:* ask him
82	*Till further settling:* till his mind settles still further
84	*bear with:* be sympathetic towards, be understanding towards
85	*Holds it true:* Is it confirmed as truth?
88	*conductor:* leader

And hold your hands in benediction o'er me.
No, sir, you must not kneel.
Lear: Pray, do not mock me.
  I am a very foolish fond old man,   60
  Fourscore and upward, not an hour more nor less;
  And, to deal plainly,
  I fear I am not in my perfect mind.
  Methinks I should know you, and know this man;
  Yet I am doubtful; for I am mainly ignorant   65
  What place this is; and all the skill I have
  Remembers not these garments; nor I know not
  Where I did lodge last night. Do not laugh at me;
  For (as I am a man) I think this lady
  To be my child Cordelia.
Cordelia: And so I am, I am.   70
Lear: Be your tears wet? Yes, faith. I pray weep not.
  If you have poison for me, I will drink it.
  I know you do not love me, for your sisters
  Have, as I do remember, done me wrong:
  You have some cause, they have not.
Cordelia: No cause, no cause.   75
Lear: Am I in France?
Kent: In your own kingdom, sir.
Lear: Do not abuse me.
Doctor: Be comforted, good madam. The great rage
  You see is killed in him; and yet it is danger
  To make him even o'er the time he has lost.   80
  Desire him to go in. Trouble him no more
  Till further settling.
Cordelia: Will't please your Highness walk?
Lear: You must bear
    with me.
  Pray you now, forget and forgive. I am old and foolish.
    [*Exeunt Lear, Cordelia, Doctor, and Attendants.*]
Gentleman: Holds it true, sir, that the Duke of Cornwall   85
    was so slain?
Kent: Most certain, sir.
Gentleman: Who is conductor of his people?
Kent: As 'tis said, the bastard son of Gloucester.

92   *changeable:* unreliable
93   *powers:* military forces; *apace:* speedily
94   *The arbitrement ... bloody:* The deciding encounter, or
      battle, is likely to be a bloody one.
96   *My point and period:* the end of my life ("point" and
      "period" are synonyms); *wrought:* worked out, i.e.,
      my destiny will be completely worked out
97   *Or ... or:* either ... or

Gentleman: They say Edgar, his banished son, is with the   90
    Earl of Kent in Germany.
Kent: Report is changeable. 'Tis time to look about; the
    powers of the kingdom approach apace.
Gentleman: The arbitrement is like to be bloody.
    Fare you well, sir.   [*Exit.*]   95
Kent: My point and period will be throughly wrought.
    Or well or ill, as this day's battle's fought.   [*Exit.*]

Act 4, Scene 7: Activities

1. a) Children sometimes suffer greatly at the hands of their parents, as Cordelia has done. Some people find that the reconciliation between Lear and Cordelia is unrealistic because no child so wronged could be so all-forgiving. Create a conversation that you might have with Cordelia if you had a chance to talk to her at this moment. How do you think she would respond to you?

   In your journal, record what advice you might give to parents and children who have differences.

   b) What might Shakespeare argue in defense of his characterization of Cordelia? Consider exchanges that Lear and Cordelia had previously. Is there any similarity between the exchange in this scene and previous ones? Explain your response.

2. Some directors feel that this scene is too long and slows down the action of the play. As a director, how might you shorten it and still retain its essence? Present your shortened version to classmates.

3. Some directors claim that this scene serves no dramatic purpose and is simply intended to play on the emotions of the audience. How would you respond to this criticism? Write an article for a theatre review magazine in which you argue your case.

4. As Cordelia, you know that your father is dying. You have decided to prepare his obituary. When a person of high importance dies, the obituary usually appears on the front page of the newspaper. Keep this convention in mind, and make certain that you include all the positive contributions Lear has made during his lifetime without exaggerating the truth.

5. Some readers and audiences believe that part of the blame for what happens in the play belongs to Cordelia. She knew what her father was like and should never have confronted him as she did in Act 1. These people may think that, in this scene, she is simply attempting to ease

her own guilty conscience. How would you respond to this observation? Prepare your argument and defend your position against others in the class who hold opposing points of view.

Act 4: Consider the Whole Act

1. As Lear's lawyer before he divided his kingdom, how would you have worded the contract between Lear and his daughters? In Lear's defence, and considering what has happened, whom would you sue and on what grounds?

2. As a strategic consultant accompanying the French army, you have observed Lear's actions in this scene and have decided that he is just play-acting in order to get attention and sympathy. Write the report that you would send to Cordelia, justifying your theory.

3. As a doctor, reflect on Lear's actions in this scene. Decide what his actions suggest about his state of mind. How would you classify what is wrong with him? Write a report on his condition in which you label the disease and make recommendations for treatment.

4. Frequently, our perceptions trick us into believing illusions. As Gloucester, recount what is going through your mind as you prepare to jump off the cliffs at Dover. In your own opinion, can the mind create its own reality? How does your opinion affect your response to events in this act?

5. You are a resident of Lear's kingdom and have observed that the weather has been terrible for some time. You know that the king has abdicated. What connections do you make between the weather and political events? Create a conversation in which you communicate your beliefs to someone you know well. What do you tell him or her? What evidence do you use? What is this person's reaction?

6. We have all met someone whom we believe is just too good to be true. As a television journalist, you have interviewed Cordelia in this act and have decided that she is not all she appears to be. On your program, called "Expose," reveal what you have discovered.

7. You are an Elizabethan and have just seen the first performance of this play. You are particularly puzzled by some of the things that have gone on in this act. In talking to a prospective theatre-goer, you mention these things. What things do you tell him or her?

8. You are a spy or intelligence agent working for Cornwall and Albany. You have infiltrated the French forces in France. What have you learned about their plans, motivations, and specific goals? What do you discover is Cordelia's role and interests in all of this? Create a means of communicating your findings to the two Dukes so that the information would be meaningless to anyone who intercepted it. Share your message with the class to see how much of it they can decipher. Finally, read your message to them so they can understand what you really did discover. Remember to use as much information from the play as you can. You may wish to undertake this activity with your group.

9. There are, undoubtedly, important issues in the play that you have focussed on. Make a list of these issues, call it "The Top Ten" and convene a panel to discuss as many of these as you can in twenty minutes. In your journal, record your thoughts about the whole process: what was resolved, what wasn't, and are panel discussions really helpful or effective?

For the next scene ...

Describe a time when you created an elaborate plan to advance yourself at the expense of someone else, only to have the plan backfire. What actually happened? How did you feel when you were finally exposed? Would you ever do something similar again?

Act 5, Scene 1

In this scene ...

Edmund and Regan are in command of an army to repel the French invading force. They are joined by Albany and Goneril leading their own army. Albany states that his main intention is to drive the French out of Britain, rather than to assist Lear. In the meantime, Regan is preoccupied with trying to keep Goneril and Edmund apart, while Goneril is so jealous of her sister that she would rather lose the battle than give Edmund up to Regan.

Edgar, now disguised in the uniform of a knight, draws Albany aside briefly and gives him the letter he took from Oswald. Edgar offers to prove the truth of the letter in personal combat: he is proposing to challenge Edmund to a duel to the death, according to the rules of proper knightly combat.

When Edmund is left alone on stage, he reveals that, no matter which sister he marries, his aim is to destroy Albany, Lear, and Cordelia leaving himself the undisputed ruler.

1   *Know of:* ask; *purpose:* plan or decision; *hold:* remains the same
2   *since he ... aught:* more recently he has been warned by anything or any chance
4   *self-reproving:* i.e., keeps changing his mind

5   *miscarried:* came to grief
6   *doubted:* feared

7   *intend upon:* intend to grant

9   *honoured:* honourable
10   *brother's:* brother-in-law, Albany's
11   *forfended place?:* forbidden place. Regan asks if Edmund has committed adultery with Goneril; *abuses:* does you wrong
12-13   *doubtful:* fearful; *conjunct and bosomed:* joined in the most intimate way; *as far ... hers:* in the fullest possible way

15   *familiar:* intimate; *Fear:* distrust

19   *loosen:* separate
20   *well bemet:* a greeting. We are fortunate in meeting you.

22   *rigour of our state:* oppression of our rule
23   *cry out:* protest; *honest:* honourable

Act 5, Scene 1

The British camp near Dover.
Enter, with Drum and Colours,
Edmund, Regan, Gentlemen,
and Soldiers.

Edmund: Know of the Duke if his last purpose hold,
  Or whether since he is advised by aught
  To change the course. He's full of alteration
  And self-reproving. Bring his constant pleasure.
                         [*Exit an Officer.*]
Regan: Our sister's man is certainly miscarried.   5
Edmund: 'Tis to be doubted, madam.
Regan: Now, sweet lord,
  You know the goodness I intend upon you.
  Tell me, but truly, but then speak the truth,
  Do you not love my sister?
Edmund: In honoured love.
Regan: But have you never found my brother's way   10
  To the forfended place?
Edmund: That thought abuses you.
Regan: I am doubtful that you have been conjunct
  And bosomed with her, as far as we call hers.
Edmund: No, by mine honour, madam.
Regan: I never shall endure her. Dear my lord,   15
  Be not familiar with her.
Edmund: Fear me not.
  She and the Duke her husband!
  [*Enter, with Drum and Colours, Albany, Goneril, Soldiers.*]
Goneril: [*Aside.*] I had rather lose the battle than that sister
  Should loosen him and me.
Albany: Our very loving sister, well bemet.   20
  Sir, this I hear: the King is come to his daughter,
  With others whom the rigour of our state
  Forced to cry out. Where I could not be honest,

24-27   *For this ... oppose:* This business (of Cordelia's returning to her father) concerns us, not because it assists Lear and some others who oppose us, but because the King of France is invading our territory; *heavy:* serious

28   *Why is this reasoned?:* How do you arrive at that conclusion?

30   *these domestic and particular broils:* these family and personal quarrels

32   *ancient:* those with experience
33   *presently:* immediately

36   *convenient:* fitting
37   *riddle:* hidden reason

39   *overtake you:* catch up to you (spoken to Goneril, Regan, and Edmund)

41   *ope:* open

44   *champion:* a knight who is willing to undergo trial of combat with another knight, in place of a pitched battle between two armies; *prove:* by the trial of single combat
45   *avouched:* claimed, asserted, maintained; *If you miscarry:* if you should have an accident (i.e., are defeated and killed)
47   *machination:* plotting to take your life; *Fortune love you:* Good luck!
49   *When time shall serve:* when it is the right time; *herald:* official appointed to announce and organize knightly challenges and the order of combat
51   *o'erlook:* look over

52   *draw up your powers:* Deploy your forces.
53   *Here:* Edmund holds up a paper; *guess:* estimate
54   *By diligent discovery:* by careful observation

I never yet was valiant. For this business,
It touches us as France invades our land,   25
Not bolds the King, with others, whom, I fear,
Most just and heavy causes make oppose.
Edmund: Sir, you speak nobly.
Regan: Why is this reasoned?
Goneril: Combine together 'gainst the enemy;
For these domestic and particular broils   30
Are not the question here.
Albany: Let's then determine
With th' ancient of war on our proceeding.
Edmund: I shall attend you presently at your tent.
Regan: Sister, you'll go with us?
Goneril: No.   35
Regan: 'Tis most convenient; pray go with us.
Goneril: [*Aside.*] O, ho, I know the riddle.—I will go.
          [*As they are going out, enter Edgar disguised.*]
Edgar: If e'er your Grace had speech with man so poor,
Hear me one word.
Albany: I'll overtake you.
          [*Exeunt all but Albany and Edgar.*]
Speak.   40
Edgar: Before you fight the battle, ope this letter.
If you have victory, let the trumpet sound
For him that brought it. Wretched though I seem,
I can produce a champion that will prove
What is avouched there. If you miscarry,   45
Your business of the world hath so an end,
And machination ceases. Fortune love you!
Albany: Stay till I have read the letter.
Edgar: I was forbid it.
When time shall serve, let but the herald cry,
And I'll appear again.   50
Albany: Why, fare thee well. I will o'erlook thy paper.
                      [*Exit Edgar.*]
[*Enter Edmund.*]
Edmund: The enemy's in view; draw up your powers.
Here is the guess of their true strength and forces
By diligent discovery; but your haste
Is now urged on you.

55   *We will greet the time:* We will face the crisis promptly.

57-58   *jealous:* suspicious; *as the ... adder:* just as those who are bitten by a snake are suspicious of it

62   *carry out my side:* successfully complete my plans

64   *countenance:* authority

66   *taking off:* murder

69-70   *my state ... debate:* My future demands that I act rather than think about these issues, weighing their pros and cons.

Albany: We will greet the time.   [*Exit.*]   55
Edmund: To both these sisters have I sworn my love;
    Each jealous of the other, as the stung
    Are of the adder. Which of them shall I take?
    Both? One? Or neither? Neither can be enjoyed
    If both remain alive. To take the widow   60
    Exasperates, makes mad her sister Goneril;
    And hardly shall I carry out my side,
    Her husband being alive. Now then, we'll use
    His countenance for the battle, which being done,
    Let her who would be rid of him devise   65
    His speedy taking off. As for the mercy
    Which he intends to Lear and to Cordelia,
    The battle done, and they within our power,
    Shall never see his pardon; for my state
    Stands on me to defend, not to debate.   [*Exit.*]   70

Act 5, Scene 1: Activities

1. Edmund could easily be a character in a modern television soap opera with his essential traits of greed, desire for power, and driving sexuality. Goneril likewise, as a seductress with nothing but adultery and property on her mind, could fit into a soap opera cast of characters. As one of the writers for the soap opera starring Edmund and Goneril, create an outline of an episode for the two characters.

   Share your ideas in a group. Each group might present its story idea to a panel of judges.

   Develop and present the winning story entry to an audience.

2. As Albany, explain why you do not immediately read the letter Edgar has given you. How do you respond to the contents of the letter once you do read it? Write a short explanation of your behaviour and responses. Share your ideas with classmates.

3. Paraphrase Edmund's speech in lines 56–70. What are your feelings towards him when you read this soliloquy? Do you identify with any of the sentiments? Write a response to him and share it with others.

4. Write five questions you would like to ask one of Albany, Edmund, or Regan. Have one member of your group ask the questions and another, in the role of the character you are questioning, respond. Decide what additional information you have learned about the chosen character as a result of being able to interview him or her. Remember, the information must fit logically into the framework of the play and be consistent with the character.

5. What is the riddle that Goneril refers to in line 37, and what do you think it means in terms of the relationship between the sisters? If Goneril were to meet Oswald after she exits, record what she would likely say to him.

For the next scene ...

Imagine you were about to go into a risk-taking situation, such as driving in a bad snowstorm, writing an important exam, or fighting in physical warfare. What might you think about just before you entered the situation?

Act 5, Scene 2

In this scene ...

Cordelia's army is on its way to confront the English forces. Edgar leaves Gloucester out of harm's way, but returns to report that the French have been defeated and both Lear and Cordelia have been captured. Gloucester must run for his life.

Stage Direction – *Alarum:* alarm, a call on trumpets accompanied by drums, signifying that troops must press forward to the attack. Presumably, the actors form a processional that crosses the stage.

2   *host:* shelter

5   *Away:* Leave this place.
6   *ta'en:* taken prisoner, captured

8   *rot:* die
9   *in ill thoughts:* in a despairing mood

11   *Ripeness:* readiness (for death)

Scene 2

A field between the two camps.

*Alarum within. Enter, with
Drum and Colours, Lear, Cordelia,
and the Powers of France over the
stage, and exeunt.
Enter Edgar and Gloucester.*

Edgar: Here, father, take the shadow of this tree
  For your good host. Pray that the right may thrive.
  If ever I return to you again,
  I'll bring you comfort.
Gloucester: Grace go with you, sir!

                                   [*Exit Edgar.*]

  [*Alarum and retreat within. Enter Edgar.*]

Edgar: Away, old man! Give me thy hand! Away!   5
  King Lear hath lost, he and his daughter ta'en.
  Give me thy hand! Come on!
Gloucester: No further, sir. A man may rot even here.
Edgar: What, in ill thoughts again? Men must endure
  Their going hence, even as their coming hither;   10
  Ripeness is all. Come on.
Gloucester: And that's true too.   [*Exeunt.*]

Act 5, Scene 2: Activities

This is the shortest scene in the play. As a director, decide if you are justified in combining this scene with Act 5, Scene 1 or Act 5, Scene 3. Discuss your decision with a partner. What would you lose or gain by taking the course of action you have decided?

For the next scene ...

Stories don't always end in the way we want; however,
if you could end this story the way you wanted, how
would you end it?

Act 5, Scene 3

In this scene ...

Lear and Cordelia have been captured. They are brought before Edmund who sends them to prison under the charge of a captain with secret instructions to kill them both. Lear and Cordelia are reconciled. Lear is completely happy in the reunion and seems oblivious to everything else.

Albany appears with Goneril and Regan. He takes command, declaring Edmund a traitor. Regan claims power for Edmund, asserting that he is Cornwall's successor; Goneril, too, defends Edmund but argues that he has no need of Regan's protection. It becomes clear that Regan is, in fact, in no position to protect Edmund since she has been poisoned by Goneril. Albany challenges Edmund to defend his name in a duel, either against Albany himself or against any other knight who chooses to come forward.

In response to a herald's call for challengers, Edgar enters. Because he is wearing full armour, his identity is hidden. Edmund agrees to fight his unknown challenger and is mortally wounded. As Edmund lies dying, Albany confronts Goneril with her letter to her lover. Horrified by the turn of events, she rushes away.

Edgar reveals his identity and tells the court of Gloucester's death and Kent's loyalty to Lear. On the point of death, Edmund shows signs of remorse. A gentleman enters, bringing the news that Regan has died from her sister's poison and Goneril has stabbed herself.

As the bodies of the sisters are brought in, Kent arrives and reminds Albany of the prisoners, Lear and Cordelia. Edmund confesses the plot against them, but his confession comes too late. Lear arrives with Cordelia's body in his arms. Broken-hearted, Lear then dies.

The action draws to a close as Albany invites Edgar and Kent to rule the kingdom. Kent indicates that he also is dying and will not live to rule. Edgar ends the play with his contemplation that those who have lived longest have endured the most and that his generation "shall never see so much, nor live so long."

1-3   *Good guard ... them:* Guard them strictly until the desires of those in command, who will pass judgement upon them, are known.

4   *with best meaning ... worst:* with best intention have suffered the worst outcome

6   *else outfrown false fortune's frown:* otherwise overlook misfortune; i.e., fortune cannot cast me down

13   *gilded butterflies:* perhaps a reference to courtiers; *rogues:* vagabonds (the opposite of courtiers)

16-17   *And take ... spies:* and pretend that we can solve all the mysteries of nature as if God had given us special powers of observation; *wear out:* outlast

18   *pacts and sects:* in groups and parties; i.e., parties at court

19   *That ebb ... moon:* that change monthly

20   *sacrifices:* renunciation of the world; also the sacrifice Cordelia has made

22   *brand:* flame

23   *fire us hence like foxes:* part us as hunters part (or drive) foxes from their burrows with fire

24   *goodyears:* a strange word that has inspired much speculation. Lear means that some misfortune – probably disease or pestilence –will overtake those who try to hurt him and Cordelia again; *fell:* skin

Scene 3

The British camp, near Dover.
Enter, in conquest, with Drum
and Colours, Edmund; Lear
and Cordelia as prisoners;
Soldiers, Captain.

Edmund: Some officers take them away. Good guard
  Until their greater pleasures first be known
  That are to censure them.
Cordelia: We are not the first
  Who with best meaning have incurred the worst.
  For thee, oppressed king, I am cast down;   5
  Myself could else outfrown false Fortune's frown.
  Shall we not see these daughters and these sisters?
Lear: No, no, no, no! Come, let's away to prison.
  We two alone will sing like birds i' the cage.
  When thou dost ask me blessing, I'll kneel down   10
  And ask of thee forgiveness. So we'll live,
  And pray, and sing, and tell old tales, and laugh
  At gilded butterflies, and hear poor rogues
  Talk of court news; and we'll talk with them too,
  Who loses and who wins; who's in, who's out;   15
  And take upon's the mystery of things,
  As if we were God's spies; and we'll wear out,
  In a walled prison, packs and sects of great ones
  That ebb and flow by the moon.
Edmund: Take them away.
Lear: Upon such sacrifices, my Cordelia,   20
  The gods themselves throw incense. Have I caught thee?
  He that parts us shall bring a brand from heaven
  And fire us hence like foxes. Wipe thine eyes.
  The goodyears shall devour 'em, flesh and fell,

27	*hark:* Listen, pay attention
28	*note:* death warrant

31-32	*that men ... is:* that men must act as the circumstances dictate; i.e., that they must act cruelly in time of war
33	*sword:* soldier active in war; *employment:* assignment
34	*bear question:* permit discussion

36	*About it:* Go to it, then! *write happy:* regard yourself as happy, i.e., consider yourself fortunate because I shall reward you; *th':* thou
37	*Mark:* note, observe
38	*set it down:* planned it (in the warrant he has given)
39	*I cannot ... oats:* I'm not a horse – a beast of burden – but a man.
41	*valiant strain:* courageous lineage or descent

43	*opposites:* opponents, enemies
44	*I do ... you:* I ask you to turn them over to me
45	*merits:* what they deserve

48	*retention:* detention, imprisonment; *guard:* where he can be kept and properly guarded
49-52	*Whose age ... them:* whose age and whose royal rank attract the sympathy of the people and turn the conscripted forces, which we command, against us
53	*My reason all the same:* for the same reason
54	*at further space:* at a later time
55-56	*session:* trial; *At this ... bleed:* In this battle barely over, we are in no condition to judge this matter calmly.
57-58	*And the ... sharpness:* The best causes may be poorly judged by those who have been poorly affected by them, and whose emotions have not yet cooled.
59-60	*The question ... place:* Lear and Cordelia would not get a fair trial under the circumstances. Edmund is speaking hypocritically; *fitter:* more suitable

Ere they shall make us weep! We'll see 'em starved first.   25
Come.   [*Exeunt Lear and Cordelia, guarded.*]
Edmund: Come hither, Captain; hark.
   Take thou this note. [*Gives a paper.*] Go follow them to
      prison.
   One step I have advanced thee; if thou dost
   As this instructs thee, thou dost make thy way   30
   To noble fortunes. Know thou this, that men
   Are as the time is; to be tender-minded
   Does not become a sword. Thy great employment
   Will not bear question; either say thou'lt do't,
   Or thrive by other means.
Captain: I'll do't, my lord.   35
Edmund: About it! And write happy when th' hast done.
   Mark—I say, instantly; and carry it so
   As I have set it down.
Captain: I cannot draw a cart, nor eat dried oats;
   If it be man's work, I'll do't.   [*Exit.*] 40
   [*Flourish. Enter Albany, Goneril, Regan, Soldiers.*]
Albany: Sir, you have showed today your valiant strain,
   And fortune led you well. You have the captives
   Who were the opposites of this day's strife;
   I do require them of you, so to use them
   As we shall find their merits and our safety   45
   May equally determine.
Edmund: Sir, I thought it fit
   To send the old and miserable King
   To some retention and appointed guard;
   Whose age had charms in it, whose title more,
   To pluck the common bosom on his side   50
   And turn our impressed lances in our eyes
   Which do command them. With him I sent the Queen,
   My reason all the same; and they are ready
   Tomorrow, or at further space, t' appear
   Where you shall hold your session. At this time   55
   We sweat and bleed: the friend hath lost his friend,
   And the best quarrels, in the heat, are cursed
   By those that feel their sharpness.
   The question of Cordelia and her father
   Requires a fitter place.

61   *subject:* subordinate
62   *brother:* equal; *That's as ... him:* That is the manner in which
        we wish to regard him (i.e., as an equal).

65-67   *Bore the ... brother:* acted as my deputy, and his present
        rank of general justifies his being considered your equal

67   *hot:* fast
68   *grace:* merit; *exalt himself:* become more powerful
69   *in your addition:* the titles and offices you have given him

70   *invested:* granted; *compeers:* equals
71   *That ... you:* That would be fully accomplished if he should
        marry you.
72   *Jesters do oft prove prophets:* Many a true word is spoken
        in jest; *Holla, holla:* Hello, hello!
73   *asquint:* literally cross-eyed, i.e., with a prejudiced eye or
        distorted vision
75   *From a full-flowing stomach:* with a flood of anger
76   *patrimony:* inheritance from my father
77   *the walls are thine:* You have gained victory by overcoming
        the outer defences.

80   *The let-alone ... will:* The prevention is not within your
        power.
81   *Half-blooded fellow:* bastard
82   *prove:* by trial of combat
84   *On capital treason:* on the charge of high treason; *attaint:*
        condemnation (for treason) involving death and the forfeit of
        wealth and honour
85   *This gilded serpent:* Goneril: beautiful, but venomous;
        sister: sister-in-law, i.e., Regan
87   *sub-contracted:* already betrothed, bound by a contract
88   *contradict your banes:* protest against the announcement of
        your marriage to him; *banes:* banns, the proclamations
        made in church to announce a forthcoming marriage.
        The announcements are made to provide an opportunity
        for anyone to give valid reasons against performing the
        marriage within the church.
89   *make your loves to me:* love suits or pledges of love
90   *bespoke:* promised, engaged, spoken for; *interlude:* little
        play, comedy

Albany: Sir, by your patience,   60
    I hold you but a subject of this war,
    Not as a brother.
Regan: That's as we list to grace him.
    Methinks our pleasure might have been demanded
    Ere you had spoke so far. He led our powers,
    Bore the commission of my place and person,   65
    The which immediacy may well stand up
    And call itself your brother.
Goneril: Not so hot!
    In his own grace he doth exalt himself
    More than in your addition.
Regan: In my rights
    By me invested, he compeers the best.   70
Goneril: That were the most if he should husband you.
Regan: Jesters do oft prove prophets.
Goneril: Holla, holla!
    That eye that told you so looked but asquint.
Regan: Lady, I am not well; else I should answer
    From a full-flowing stomach. General,   75
    Take thou my soldiers, prisoners, patrimony;
    Dispose of them, of me; the walls are thine.
    Witness the world that I create thee here
    My lord and master.
Goneril: Mean you to enjoy him?
Albany: The let-alone lies not in your good will.   80
Edmund: Nor in thine, lord.
Albany: Half-blooded fellow, yes.
Regan: [*To Edmund.*] Let the drum strike, and prove my
     title thine.
Albany: Stay yet; hear reason. Edmund, I arrest thee
    On capital treason; and, in thine attaint,
    This gilded serpent. [*Points to Goneril.*] For your claim,
     fair sister,   85
    I bar it in the interest of my wife.
    'Tis she is sub-contracted to this lord,
    And I, her husband, contradict your banes.
    If you will marry, make your loves to me;
    My lady is bespoke.
Goneril: An interlude!   90

91   *armed:* in full armour. Edmund has just come from battle;
Let the trumpet sound: See Act 5, Scene 1, line 42.
92   *prove:* See line 82.
93   *heinous:* villainous, monstrous
94   *pledge:* to do battle; *make it on thy heart:* I'll prove the truth
of my allegation by trying to take your life.
95   *Ere I taste bread:* before I eat again; *thou art:* that you are

96   *Sick, O, sick:* I am very sick.
97   *medicine:* poison. Goneril has poisoned her sister.
98   *exchange:* signifying that Edmund has accepted the
challenge
99   *he lies:* This was by convention a direct challenge to mortal
combat. It was called the "lie direct."
101   *On him ... not:* on anybody at all

103   *A herald ... herald:* They call for an official to organize their
duel and make the necessary announcements.
104   *thy single virtue:* your unaided courage
105   *levied:* recruited
106   *Took:* taken

111   *of quality or degree:* of rank and social standing
112   *lists:* list of names, catalogue of soldiers
113-114   *manifold traitor:* a traitor without equal, has all the attributes
of a traitor

Stage Direction – *Enter Edgar, armed:* Edgar wears full armour. His
face is concealed by a closed helmet; *a Trumpet before him:* a trum-
peter ahead of him. Trumpets were part of the formal procedure of
duels among knights.
118   *purposes:* intentions
120   *quality?:* rank

Albany: Thou art armed, Gloucester. Let the trumpet sound.
  If none appear to prove upon thy person
  Thy heinous, manifest, and many treasons,
  There is my pledge! [*Throws down a glove.*] I'll make it
    on thy heart,
  Ere I taste bread, thou art in nothing less   95
  Than I have here proclaimed thee.
Regan: Sick, O, sick!
Goneril: [*Aside.*] If not, I'll ne'er trust medicine.
Edmund: There's my exchange. [*Throws down a glove.*] What
    in the world he is
  That names me traitor, villain-like he lies.
  Call by thy trumpet. He that dares approach,   100
  On him, on you, who not? I will maintain
  My truth and honour firmly.
Albany: A herald, ho!
Edmund: A herald, ho, a herald!
Albany: Trust to thy single virtue; for thy soldiers,
  All levied in my name, have in my name   105
  Took their discharge.
Regan: My sickness grows upon me.
Albany: She is not well. Convey her to my tent.
                    [*Exit Regan, led.*]
  [*Enter a Herald.*]
  Come hither, herald. Let the trumpet sound,
  And read out this.
Captain: Sound, trumpet!   [*A trumpet sounds.*] 110
Herald: [*Reads.*] "If any man of quality or degree within
    the lists of the army will maintain upon Edmund,
    supposed Earl of Gloucester, that he is a manifold
    traitor, let him appear by the third sound of the
    trumpet. He is bold in his defense."   [*First trumpet.*] 115
Herald: Again!   [*Second trumpet.*]
Herald: Again!   [*Third trumpet.*]
              [*Trumpet answers within.*]
  [*Enter Edgar, armed, a Trumpet before him.*]
Albany: Ask him his purposes, why he appears
  Upon this call o' the trumpet.
Herald: What are you?
  Your name, your quality? And why you answer   120

122	*By treason's ... canker-bit:* by the canker-worm (caterpillar), treason
124	*cope:* meet, encounter
127	*That:* so that
128	*arm:* weapon and insignia embossed on a knight's shield; *mine:* Edgar stretches out his right hand, having drawn his sword.
129-130	*Behold, it ... profession:* It is the privilege of my knighthood to draw my sword. I do this to challenge a traitor and it is my privilege as a knight to have my challenge answered.
131	*Maugre:* in spite of; *place:* high command; *eminence:* status
132	*victor sword:* victory in the recent battle; *fire-new fortune:* completely new (recently forged) wealth and power
136	*extremest upward:* topmost part
137	*descent:* lowest part of the body
138	*toad-spotted:* covered with the poisonous marks of treason as a toad is covered with warts; *Say:* if you say
139	*spirits:* courage; *bent:* directed
141	*liest:* See line 99; *name:* Edmund would not be obliged under the rules of combat to accept the challenge of one who was not a gentleman.
143	*say:* indication, proof
144	*safe and nicely:* cautiously, with precise, legal justification; *delay:* postpone
145	*spurn:* cast aside, ignore
147	*the hell-hated lie:* the lie (of high treason), hated even in hell, or hated as hell is hated
148	*Which:* the treason; *for they ... bruise:* since as yet they do not harm you (since the accusations which I give back to you merely bounce off you)
149-150	*This sword ... ever:* This sword of mine will return (them) with more force upon your head, where they will remain for-ever.
151	*Save:* spare his life, do not kill him; *practice:* trickery

This present summons?

Edgar: Know my name is lost;
By treason's tooth bare-gnawn and canker-bit.
Yet am I noble as the adversary
I come to cope.

Albany: Which is that adversary?

Edgar: What's he that speaks for Edmund Earl of
   Gloucester?   125

Edmund: Himself. What sayest thou to him?

Edgar: Draw thy
   sword,
That, if my speech offend a noble heart,
Thy arm may do thee justice. Here is mine.
Behold, it is the privilege of mine honours,
My oath, and my profession. I protest,   130
Maugre thy strength, place, youth, and eminence,
Despite thy victor sword and fire-new fortune,
Thy valour and thy heart, thou art a traitor,
False to thy gods, thy brother, and thy father;
Conspirant 'gainst this high illustrious prince;   135
And from th' extremest upward of thy head
To the descent and dust beneath thy foot,
A most toad-spotted traitor. Say thou "no,"
This sword, this arm, and my best spirits are bent
To prove upon thy heart, whereto I speak,   140
Thou liest.

Edmund: In wisdom I should ask thy name;
But since thy outside looks so fair and warlike,
And that thy tongue some say of breeding breathes,
What safe and nicely I might well delay
By rule of knighthood, I disdain and spurn;   145
Back do I toss those treasons to thy head,
With the hell-hated lie o'erwhelm thy heart,
Which, for they yet glance by and scarcely bruise,
This sword of mine shall give them instant way
Where they shall rest for ever. Trumpets, speak!   150
                    [*Alarums. Fight. Edmund falls.*]

Albany: Save him, save him!

Goneril: This is mere practice,
   Gloucester.

152-153   *By the ... opposite:* See line 141; *opposite:* opponent

154   *cozened and beguiled:* deceived and fooled

155   *Hold, sir:* Just a moment; wait a minute

158-159   *Say if I do:* You say, if you like, whether I know the letter or not; *the laws ... for't?:* The laws are mine to make, not yours (since I am the ruling sovereign). Who can bring me to trial? As sovereign, I am above the law.

160   *this paper?:* the letter

161   *desperate:* distraught, not in her right mind; *govern:* control, restrain

164-165   *But what ... me?:* But who are you that has won this victory over me?

166   *charity:* forgiveness
167   *blood:* lineage, nobility
168   *more:* more noble in blood since Edmund, being illegitimate, is only half-noble
170   *The gods are just:* because they hate sin and wickedness; *pleasant:* pleasure-giving
172-173   *The dark ... eyes:* the secret and sinful place where Edmund was conceived. Edgar suggests that the dark sin of adultery has earned Gloucester darkness (blindness). In other words, one is suitably punished for one's sins.
174   *The wheel ... circle:* The Wheel of Fortune has made a complete revolution. Edmund began at the bottom, rose to the top, and now finds himself at the bottom again, as the goddess Fortune sat by and turned the wheel to which all mortals were said to cling. See Act 2, Scene 2, line 169.
175   *gait:* manner of walking, movement, posture; *prophesy:* suggest
178   *thee:* Edgar
181   *By nursing them:* by caring for them; *List:* listen to

By the law of arms thou wast not bound to answer
An unknown opposite. Thou art not vanquished,
But cozened and beguiled.
Albany: Shut your mouth, dame,
    Or with this paper shall I stop it. [*Shows her her letter to
        Edmund.*]—[*To Edmund.*] Hold, sir.   155
    [*To Goneril.*] Thou worse than any name, read thine own
        evil.
    No tearing, lady! I perceive you know it.
Goneril: Say if I do—the laws are mine, not thine.
    Who can arraign me for't?
Albany: Most monstrous! O!
    Knowest thou this paper?
Goneril: Ask me not what I know.   160
                                                [*Exit.*]
Albany: Go after her. She's desperate; govern her.
                                [*Exit an Officer.*]
Edmund: What you have charged me with, that have I done,
    And more, much more. The time will bring it out.
    'Tis past, and so am I. But what art thou
    That hast this fortune on me? If thou'rt noble,   165
    I do forgive thee.
Edgar: Let's exchange charity.
    I am no less in blood than thou art, Edmund;
    If more, the more th' hast wronged me.
    My name is Edgar and thy father's son.
    The gods are just, and of our pleasant vices   170
    Make instruments to plague us.
    The dark and vicious place where thee he got
    Cost him his eyes.
Edmund: Th' hast spoken right; 'tis true.
    The wheel is come full circle; I am here.
Albany: Methought thy very gait did prophesy   175
    A royal nobleness. I must embrace thee.
    Let sorrow split my heart if ever I
    Did hate thee, or thy father!
Edgar: Worthy prince, I know't.
Albany: Where have you hid yourself?
    How have you known the miseries of your father?   180
Edgar: By nursing them, my lord. List a brief tale;

183-187 *The bloody ... rags:* The necessity of escaping the death
         warrant that came near to claiming me taught me to dress
         in a madman's rags; *O, our ... once:* Life is so sweet that we
         choose to suffer death every hour rather than die at once
         and have it over!
187   *semblance:* dress, appearance
188   *habit:* clothing
189   *rings:* eye sockets
190   *precious stones:* eyes

193   *past:* ago
194   *success:* victory over Edmund

196   *pilgrimage:* the path I took (after being declared an outlaw);
         flawed: broken
197   *conflict:* the conflicting emotions of sadness at the suffering
         he had inflicted upon Edgar and the joy of knowing him to
         be a loving, faithful son
198-199 *'Twixt two ... smilingly:* Gloucester has died from excessive
         emotion. Grief broke his heart and the sudden surge of
         happiness was too much for him.

203   *dissolve:* melt into tears

204-207 *This would ... extremity:* To describe even one more sorrow
         in detail would be to go beyond any limit (to go too far).

208   *big in clamour:* loud in my grief
209   *estate:* condition
210   *abhorred:* detestable
211   *endured:* suffered

213   *As:* as if; *him:* himself

215   *recounting:* telling
216-217 *puissant:* overwhelming, powerful, mighty; *strings of ...
         crack:* threads of life which kept him alive, began to break.
         Kent has had a heart attack and is near to death.
217   *Twice then the trumpets sounded:* signalling the battle
218   *tranced:* in a trance, unconscious

And when 'tis told, O that my heart would burst!
The bloody proclamation to escape
That followed me so near (O, our lives' sweetness!
That we the pain of death would hourly die   185
Rather than die at once!) taught me to shift
Into a madman's rags, t' assume a semblance
That very dogs disdained; and in this habit
Met I my father with his bleeding rings,
Their precious stones new lost; became his guide,   190
Led him, begged for him, saved him from despair;
Never (O fault!) revealed myself unto him
Until some half hour past, when I was armed;
Not sure, though hoping of this good success,
I asked his blessing, and from first to last   195
Told him my pilgrimage. But his flawed heart
(Alack, too weak the conflict to support!)
'Twixt two extremes of passion, joy and grief,
Burst smilingly.
Edmund: This speech of yours hath moved me,
And shall perchance do good; but speak you on;   200
You look as you had something more to say.
Albany: If there be more, more woeful, hold it in;
For I am almost ready to dissolve,
Hearing of this.
Edgar: This would have seemed a period
To such as love not sorrow; but another,   205
To amplify too much, would make much more,
And top extremity.
Whilst I was big in clamour, came there a man,
Who, having seen me in my worst estate,
Shunned my abhorred society; but then, finding   210
Who 'twas that so endured, with his strong arms
He fastened on my neck, and bellowed out
As he'd burst heaven; threw him on my father;
Told the most piteous tale of Lear and him
That ever ear received; which in recounting   215
His grief grew puissant, and the strings of life
Began to crack. Twice then the trumpets sounded,
And there I left him tranced.
Albany: But who was this?

220-221   *enemy king:* hostile king, the king who declared him an enemy; *service improper for a slave:* the lowest and most menial duties, those necessary to care for an old and help-less man

Stage Direction – *Gentleman:* member of the court circle, fit company for a king

223   *smokes:* steams
224   *came even from:* just came from

228   *contracted:* engaged to be married; betrothed
229   *marry:* unite, are united

230   *be they alive or dead:* whether they are alive or dead

232   *Touches us not with pity:* does not cause us to feel pity; *is this he?:* Is it you, Kent?
233   *compliment:* ceremony
234   *very manners:* ordinary politeness
235   *aye:* forever

236   *Great thing of us forgot:* I forgot about this; *of us:* by us

238   *object:* spectacle, sight

239   *Yet Edmund was beloved:* Two women died for his love: a triumph of sorts.

245-246   *for my writ ... the life of:* I have given orders to take the life of; *writ:* written order

Edgar: Kent, sir, the banished Kent; who in disguise
  Followed his enemy king and did him service   220
  Improper for a slave.
  [*Enter a Gentleman with a bloody knife.*]
Gentleman: Help, help! O, help!
Edgar: What kind of help?
Albany: Speak,
  man.
Edgar: What means this bloody knife?
Gentleman: 'Tis hot, it smokes.
  It came even from the heart of—O, she's dead!
Albany: Who dead? Speak, man.   225
Gentleman: Your lady, sir, your lady! And her sister
  By her is poisoned; she hath confessed it.
Edmund: I was contracted to them both. All three
  Now marry in an instant.
Edgar: Here comes Kent.
  [*Enter Kent.*]
Albany: Produce the bodies, be they alive or dead.   230
                      [*Exit Gentleman.*]
  This judgement of the heavens, that makes us tremble,
  Touches us not with pity. [*To Kent.*] O, is this he?
  The time will not allow the compliment
  Which very manners urges.
Kent: I am come
  To bid my king and master aye good night.   235
  Is he not here?
Albany: Great thing of us forgot!
  Speak, Edmund, where's the King? And where's Cordelia?
  [*The bodies of Goneril and Regan are brought in.*]
  Seest thou this object, Kent?
Kent: Alack, why thus?
Edmund: Yet Edmund was beloved.
  The one the other poisoned for my sake,   240
  And after slew herself.
Albany: Even so. Cover their faces.
Edmund: I pant for life. Some good I mean to do,
  Despite of mine own nature. Quickly send
  (Be brief in't) to the castle; for my writ   245
  Is on the life of Lear and on Cordelia.

248	*office?:* duty, assignment
249	*token of reprieve:* sign of pardon
251	*for thy life:* as if your life depended on it
255	*fordid:* destroyed, killed
256	*hence:* away from this place
257	*men of stones:* men incapable of feeling, like statues
258	*eyes:* for seeing and for weeping
259	*vault:* wide arch of heaven, sky
261	*a looking glass:* a mirror
262	*stone:* the mirror (of crystal or polished stone)
263	*the promised end?:* the Last Judgment, the end of the world. Is it to this that all things lead?
264	*Or image of that horror?:* or the exact likeness of that day; *Fall and cease:* Let the heavens fall and let there be an end to everything.
268	*Prithee away:* Lear does not at first recognize Kent.

Nay, send in time.

Albany: Run, run, O, run!

Edgar: To who, my lord? Who has the office? Send
   Thy token of reprieve.

Edmund: Well thought on. Take my sword;   250
   Give it the Captain.

Edgar: Haste thee for thy life.

                              [*Exit an Officer.*]

Edmund: He hath commission from thy wife and me
   To hang Cordelia in the prison and
   To lay the blame upon her own despair
   That she fordid herself.   255

Albany: The gods defend her! Bear him hence awhile.

                   [*Edmund is borne off*]

[*Enter Lear, with the dead Cordelia in his arms, Captain
   and others following.*]

Lear: Howl, howl, howl! O, you are men of stones.
   Had I your tongues and eyes, I'd use them so
   That heaven's vault should crack. She's gone for ever!
   I know when one is dead, and when one lives.   260
   She's dead as earth. Lend me a looking glass.
   If that her breath will mist or stain the stone,
   Why, then she lives.

Kent: Is this the promised end?

Edgar: Or image of that horror?

Albany: Fall and cease!

Lear: This feather stirs; she lives! If it be so,   265
   It is a chance which does redeem all sorrows
   That ever I have felt.

Kent: O my good master!

Lear: Prithee away!

Edgar: 'Tis noble Kent, your friend.

Lear: A plague upon you, murderers, traitors all!
   I might have saved her; now she's gone for ever!   270
   Cordelia, Cordelia! Stay a little. Ha!
   What is't thou sayest? Her voice was ever soft,
   Gentle, and low—an excellent thing in woman.
   I killed the slave that was a-hanging thee.

Captain: 'Tis true, my lords, he did.

Lear: Did I not, fellow?   275

276	*biting falchion:* sharp sword, light sword with point bent slightly inwards
278	*crosses:* troubles; *spoil me:* weaken me as a swordsman
279	*I'll tell you straight:* I'll recognize you in a moment.
280-281	*If fortune … behold:* If fortune boasts of two people she most loved or most hated, then Lear is the most unfortunate (hated) of all.
282	*This is a dull sight:* I can't see clearly; or, this is a sad spectacle.
283	*Caius?:* apparently the name used by Kent when he was disguised
285	*strike:* as in "a blow"
287	*I'll see that straight:* I'll understand that in a moment.
288	*from your … decay:* from the beginning of your change in fortunes and their decline
291	*fordone:* destroyed
292	*desperately:* in a state of despair
294	*bootless:* useless
295	*a trifle:* of no importance here, where the tragedy of Lear and Cordelia is greater
297	*decay:* the tragic decline of Lear
298-300	*applied:* used, employed; *For us … power:* Albany is ruler because Cornwall, Goneril, and Regan are dead. However, he resigns his office for the short time that Lear has to live so that Lear may die as king; *you to your rights:* The words "We will restore" are understood before "you."
301	*With boot, and such addition:* with such additional titles and rights; *honours:* brave deeds
305	*fool:* Cordelia. "Fool" was a term of endearment. Some scholars believe that, since the Fool made Lear face absolute truthfulness, and since Cordelia also stood for utter truthfulness, the two have become as one in Lear's mind.

I have seen the day, with my good biting falchion
I would have made 'em skip. I am old now,
And these same crosses spoil me. Who are you?
Mine eyes are not o' the best, I'll tell you straight.
Kent: If fortune brag of two she loved and hated,   280
  One of them we behold.
Lear: This is a dull sight. Are you not Kent?
Kent: The same;
  Your servant Kent. Where is your servant Caius?
Lear: He's a good fellow, I can tell you that.
  He'll strike, and quickly too. He's dead and rotten.   285
Kent: No, my good lord; I am the very man—
Lear: I'll see that straight.
Kent: That from your first of difference and decay
  Have followed your sad steps.
Lear: You are welcome hither.
Kent: Nor no man else! All's cheerless, dark, and deadly.   290
  Your eldest daughters have fordone themselves,
  And desperately are dead.
Lear: Ay, so I think.
Albany: He knows not what he says; and vain is it
  That we present us to him.
Edgar: Very bootless.
  [*Enter a Captain.*]
Captain: Edmund is dead, my lord.
Albany: That's but a trifle here.   295
  You lords and noble friends, know our intent.
  What comfort to this great decay may come
  Shall be applied. For us, we will resign,
  During the life of this old Majesty,
  To him our absolute power; [*To Edgar and Kent.*] you
    to your rights;   300
  With boot, and such addition as your honours
  Have more than merited. All friends shall taste
  The wages of their virtue, and all foes
  The cup of their deservings.—O, see, see!
Lear: And my poor fool is hanged! No, no, no life!   305
  Why should a dog, a horse, a rat, have life,
  And thou no breath at all? Thou'lt come no more,
  Never, never, never, never, never!

309   *Pray you ... sir:* Lear feels the suffocation preceding his death, but thinks that his clothing restricts his breathing.

310   *Do you ... lips:* Some scholars suggest that Lear dies of joy, believing Cordelia to be alive. Lear is trying to believe that the terrible finality of Cordelia's death is impossible.

312   *Break, heart; I prithee break:* Kent may be speaking of his own heart, but more probably he is beginning a prayer, continued in his next speech for mercy on Lear; *prithee:* I pray, I beg you.

313   *ghost:* departing spirit

314   *rack:* instrument of torture that stretched a victim's joints until dislocation took place

315   *longer:* both for a longer time and with his body stretched further by the rack (an instrument of torture that stretches a person's body)

317   *usurped:* wrongly held possession of, lived beyond his rightful span of life

320   *gored:* wounded, war-ravaged; *sustain:* maintain, support

321-322   *I have ... no:* Kent evidently feels that after Lear's death little is left in life, and that he must prepare for his own death; *calls me:* to follow him (Lear) into the darkness

323   *weight:* sorrow

323-326   *The weight ... long:* In some versions of the play, these lines are given to Albany. Some critics believe it is right for the older man to speak the epilogue; others believe that the reference to "we that are young" indicates the lines were meant to be spoken by Edgar.

325   *oldest:* Lear and Gloucester

Pray you undo this button. Thank you, sir.
Do you see this? Look on her! Look! Her lips!   310
Look there, look there!   [*He dies.*]
Edgar: He faints! My lord, my lord!
Kent: Break, heart; I prithee break!
Edgar: Look up, my lord.
Kent: Vex not his ghost. O, let him pass! He hates him
    That would upon the rack of this tough world
    Stretch him out longer.
Edgar: He is gone indeed.   315
Kent: The wonder is, he hath endured so long.
    He but usurped his life.
Albany: Bear them from hence. Our present business
    Is general woe. [*To Kent and Edgar.*] Friends of my soul,
      you twain
    Rule in this realm, and the gored state sustain.   320
Kent: I have a journey, sir, shortly to go.
    My master calls me; I must not say no.
Edgar: The weight of this sad time we must obey,
    Speak what we feel, not what we ought to say.
    The oldest hath borne most; we that are young   325
    Shall never see so much, nor live so long.
                  [*Exeunt with a dead march.*]

Act 5, Scene 3: Activities

1. Reread the lines Lear speaks when he enters with Cordelia's body (lines 257–263). In groups, discuss to what extent you believe these lines to be a commentary on the action of the play as a whole. Remember to consider Lear's comments at various places in the play. As an observer of a performance of the play for the first time, write a letter to a friend, or a note in your journal, recording your reactions to these lines.

2. Lear's final speech (lines 305–311) frequently puzzles directors because it is not clear whether Lear dies happily or in misery. In groups, discuss how you would interpret the speech in light of what has happened in the play. Prepare a careful reading of it and present it to a partner or to the class. You have succeeded when your audience clearly recognizes your intent.

3. Do you think it is necessary for both Lear and Cordelia to die? In groups, discuss what alternative endings might be possible and how they might affect the outcome of the play. Share your ideas with the members of other groups.

4. Throughout most of the play, Edmund seems to know exactly what he wants and how to get it. It is only in this final scene that he seems willing to accept a different kind of responsibility. What do you think causes this change in Edmund? Make a note of your ideas and share them with a partner or members of your group.

5. An epitaph is an inscription on a tombstone that usually tells something about the personality of the deceased. In groups, select one character from the following list and write an epitaph for him or her: Edmund, Kent, King Lear, Cordelia, Goneril, or Regan. You may wish to research several epitaphs before you begin this activity. Share your epitaphs with the class. If you wish, you can draw and label your monument for display.

6. Imagine you are Edgar about to take over as the ruler of England. In your notes or your journal make a list of the things you feel must be done in order to restore peace and stability to the land, as well as to gain the support of the people. Share your list with others in your group.

7. Some critics argue that Goneril and Regan are not characters at all, but symbols of evil daughters as depicted in many folk tales. Is this a valid assessment, or do you find yourself identifying with these characters as actual people with a plan? Use your group discussion as the starting point for a 500 word essay on the subject. If you believe the two sisters to be authentic characters, what is your analysis of each of them?

8. Edgar's final speech, lines 323-326, seems somewhat enigmatic, like a riddle. What do you think he means? Write your explanation and share it with the rest of the class. In your opinion, is this a fitting way to end the play?

9. As Edgar, you have decided to write epitaphs for all the characters who died at the end of the play. Knowing all of them as you do, what will you write for each without being too harsh?

Consider the Whole Play

1. There are many puzzling moments, incredible moments, and unexpected moments in this play. In a group, find the location in the play of as many of these as you can recall. In each case, discuss the extent to which you can or cannot accept them and explain why.

2. The words "nature," "nothing," and "fool" are constantly repeated in *King Lear*. In your group, select one of these words and trace where and how it is used throughout the play. What do you think the repetition of the word you have selected adds to the play? Present your findings to the class.

3. *King Lear* raises many general questions of a philosophical nature. Some of these questions are, "Why do bad things happen to good people?", "Are human beings governed by fate?", and "Are some people naturally evil?" In your group, brainstorm and make a list of as many of these general, philosophical questions as you can. Select one that seems particularly interesting, and as a group, explore all its possibilities. Before deciding on an answer, be sure to consider all possible objections, using *King Lear* as a resource, and reply carefully to those questions you have raised.

4. With your group, select one scene or a segment of a scene in the play and convey dramatically the important information it contains. You might do this in one of the following ways:

   - by telling the story in the role from one character's point of view;

   - by using movement only;

   - by creating a story theatre, using narration, dialogue, and movement;

   - by creating an improvisation;

   - by rewriting it and presenting it as reader's theatre (see Act 1, Scene 3, Activities, page 46.)

5. With the entire class, simulate a courtroom trial using lawyers for the defence and the prosecution, a judge, a

jury, a court clerk, and witnesses. Try King Lear for tearing apart his kingdom and causing the death of his daughter.

In order to keep your trial orderly and meaningful, keep the following guidelines in mind:

- The court clerk is the person who makes all announcements and swears in all witnesses.
- The accused is presumed innocent until proven guilty.
- The prosecution must establish guilt beyond any shadow of doubt.
- The jury acts on the facts presented, and members of the jury can ask for clarification on points at any time during the trial.
- The judge sustains or overrules objections from the prosecuting and defence attorneys and generally keeps order in the proceedings.
- The judge determines the sentence after the jury has reached a verdict.

6. Retell the story of *King Lear* through five tableaux – one from each act. Imagine that these tableaux are to be used as actual illustrations for the text. Explain why you have made the selections that you have and why you think they are significant to an understanding of the play.

7. With your group, choose one character in the play who you all agree would make an interesting subject for a case study. Have each person assume a different relationship to that character, such as a father, brother, sister, social worker, psychiatrist, or doctor. Have each of these people prepare and present an individual report on the character. As a group, create a single case study that takes these differing perspectives into account.

8. Select a character from the play and assume that he or she had been given one last opportunity to comment on his or her life. In your journal, record your character's recollection of events. Remember that, with the pressure of events, the character's memory may hide, distort, or embellish the reality of what actually happened. You may wish to share the recollection with other members of your group.

9. In groups, plan a video that conveys your feelings about King Lear in the last scene of the play. You may decide to shoot one complete sequence of the scene, or several brief segments from different places in the scene.

Before you shoot, decide how you wish to portray King Lear:

- What qualities do you wish to highlight?
- What mood do you wish to establish?
- How do you want your audience to respond?

Remember to prepare a video script describing the kind of camera shot you want to use for each frame of your segment. Make sure that your beginning and ending have dramatic impact.

Share your video with your classmates to see how they respond.

10. John Keats recorded his response to *King Lear* in the following sonnet:

On Sitting Down to Read *King Lear* Once Again

O golden-tongued Romance with serene lute!
    Fair pluméd Siren! Queen of far away!
    Leave melodizing on this wintry day,
Shut up thine olden pages, and be mute:
Adieu! for once again the fierce dispute   5
    Betwixt damnation and impassioned clay
    Must I burn through; once more humbly assay
The bitter-sweet of this Shakespearean fruit.
Chief Poet! and ye clouds of Albion,
    Begetters of our deep eternal theme,   10
When through the old oak forest I am gone,
    Let me not wander in a barren dream,
But when I am consuméd in the fire,
Give me new Phoenix wings to fly at my desire.

John Keats (1818)

Keats interprets the essence of *King Lear* to be a "fierce dispute/Betwixt damnation and impassioned clay" that he, as a reader, must "burn through." Do you think that King Lear, either consciously or unconsciously, chose to "wander in a barren dream"? Write a response to Keats in a poem in which you support his point of view, disagree with him, or hold an entirely different perspective.

11. As a class, create an overview graph for the play. To do this, write all the characters' names down the left side of a large sheet of paper. List the numbers of each act and its scenes across the top of the page. Now form five groups. Each group should concentrate on only one act. Your task is to check off the scenes where each character appears on stage. When all the groups are finished, you will have a master graph. From your graph, determine:

   • who is on stage the most;

   • who is on stage the least;

   • who appears in every act;

   • who is off stage more than on;

   • if there is a balance of any sort.

12. Students often complain that literature is often too morbid and tragic. Nineteenth-century directors must have felt that way also because they frequently altered the ending of *King Lear* to make Lear and Cordelia live happily ever after. If you could speak to one of these directors, how would you respond to such a practice? Write your response as a letter, a journal entry, or a magazine article for a drama publication.

13. Often, the body language we all use when we speak conveys as much as what we say. In fact, many of us exhibit a habitual or defining gesture. With a group, select the characters from the play who you think would have pronounced gestures. Select three of these characters and pair each one in a conversation with a character. Present a brief interchange between one pair of characters, emphasizing the body language and gestures of the chosen character. Rehearse the scene several times, emphasizing words to complement the

body language and gesture. Perform the conversation for classmates.

In a group, note the effect that body language, gesture, and word emphasis can have on the presentation of a character.

14. In his final speech, King Lear makes the comment, "And my poor fool is hanged!" (line 305). Many people interpret this to mean that the dying king links Cordelia and the Fool together because he has always regarded them both in the same way. What do you think? What ultimately happened to the Fool? Express your own convictions in a journal entry. Then discuss your thoughts with your group.

15. With a group, read the illustrated children's book *Moss Gown* by William H. Hooks (Clarion Books, New York, 1987). What, if any, features of this story are similar to events in *King Lear*?

On your own, draft a children's story or legend that you might create from any aspect of *King Lear*. You may prefer to create a group story. Illustrate it and present it to an elementary school class. After your presentation, decide what alterations you might make to your story if you were to present it to another group of young children.

16. This play is filled with memorable lines. Create your own list of quotes that stick in your head. You might put them in order in terms of theme, commonality, or emotions. When you have completed your list, hold a quiz show with your class to see how much they actually know about the events of the play. (You will need to create a few clues for each quotation to help the contestants.)

17. An elegy is a melancholy poem intended as a lament for the dead. Write your version of an elegy for King Lear. You might wish to refer to several elegiac poems before you attempt one of your own. Some suggestions are *An Old Woman's Lamentations* by J.M. Synge, *Anthem for Doomed Youth* by Wilfred Owen, *I Think Continually* by Stephen Spender, *Tears, Idle Tears* by Alfred Lord Tennyson, and *She Dwelt Among the Untrodden Ways* by William Wordsworth.

18. Design a T-shirt based on a significant quotation from *King Lear* using original artwork to highlight the quotation. You might work with your group to come up with some powerful quotations, which you can share with the class. Your final product can be a group effort based on one of these quotations.

19. You are delivering an address to a group of business people on how to move up the corporate ladder. You have decided to use *King Lear* as the basis of your speech because it contains characters who make mistakes that end up being very costly. Your point is to indicate the necessity of avoiding these pitfalls. What situations from the play are you going to use as your examples, and how are you going to make them appeal to business people? Write your speech; you may wish to try it out on the class for their response.

20. With your group, write a fifteen-minute version of *King Lear*. How do you effectively reduce each act to three minutes using only the actual words from each act? Present one or two of your scenes for the class to determine your success.